Democracy in Suburbia

Democracy in Suburbia

J. Eric Oliver

PRINCETON UNIVERSITY PRESS

PRINCETON AND OXFORD

Library of Congress Cataloging-in-Publication Data

Oliver, J. Eric, 1966–
    Democracy in suburbia / J. Eric Oliver.
      p. cm.
    Includes bibliographical references and index.
    ISBN 0-691-08879-9 — ISBN 0-691-08880-2 (pbk.)
    1. Local government—United States. 2. Political participation—United States.
3. Suburbs—United States. 4. Suburban life—United States. 5. Segregation—
United States. 6. Social stratification—United States. I. Title.
JS391.O44 2001
320.8′5′0973—dc21   2001016370

British Library Cataloging-in-Publication Data is available

To my father,
Richard Oliver,
who quietly made it all possible

Contents

Maps and Figures

Tables

Acknowledgments

IT IS FITTING that a book about social contexts is itself such a product of its various environments. This book owes much to the talents, interest, and support of the people and institutions that I was fortunate to be associated with over the past five years. Foremost credit goes to the members of the Political Science Department and the Survey Research Center at the University of California, Berkeley. My deepest debts are to Raymond Wolfinger who, as chair of my dissertation, spent countless hours commenting on the hundreds of pages and ideas that were an earlier version of this work. The stamp of his patient and careful guidance is everywhere in this book. I am equally grateful to Henry Brady for his boundless enthusiasm, support, and intellectual contributions during this project's inception. Laura Stoker and Claude Fischer also provided invaluable suggestions and ideas about how to study suburban civic behavior. A special acknowledgment also goes to Henry Brady who, with Sidney Verba, Kay Schlozman, Nancy Burns, and Glen Beamer, graciously made the Citizen Participation Data available for my research. Without their generosity, this project simply would not have happened. Many others at Berkeley also gave key assistance, including Arthur Burris, Kateri Carmola, Jack Citrin, Ilona Einkowski, Fredric Gey, Fern Glover, Judy Gruber, Ben Highton, Marcus Kurtz, Samantha Luks, Eric Patashnick, Nelson Polsby, Cara Wong, and Terri Wright.

Since leaving Berkeley, I have enjoyed help from many quarters. At Princeton, Doug Arnold, Larry Bartels, Dan Carpenter, Mike Danielson, Jim Doig, Mark Fischle, Fred Greenstein, Jennifer Hochschild, Jeff Lewis, Karen Stenner, and Tom Romer all provided important suggestions, and I owe particular thanks to Tali Mendelberg for her generous collegiality. I am grateful to Princeton University for providing a leave of absence to write the book and to the Health Policy Scholars Program of the Robert Wood Johnson Foundation for funding my sabbatical. Even more valuable than the financial support has been the intellectual stimulation from the community of RWJ scholars, particularly at Yale, which includes Rogan Kersh, Taeku Lee, Ted Marmor, Gary McKissick, Mark Schlesinger, and Mark Suchman. At Yale, Janelle Wong also offered much help in the final stages of writing and Doug Rae assisted me with the maps. Early versions of various chapters were also improved by the comments of John Brehm, Robert Huckfeldt, Jane Junn, Jan Leighley, and Mark Schneider. Chuck Myers and Lauren Lepow at Princeton University Press were fantastic editors.

Finally, a project like this cannot be accomplished without a huge amount of moral support. Many people who provided intellectual feedback were equally generous in this regard. Thanks go to them and to Adam Beyda, Lloyd Chinn, Renee and Craig Dalton, Marianne Evans, Sky Frautschi, Richard and Linda Oliver, Derek and Judy Van Hoorn, Bill Veiga, and all my other friends and family who are always ready to lend a hand, shoulder, or ear.

Democracy in Suburbia

CHAPTER ONE

The Rise of a Suburban *Demos*

SPRING VALLEY, TEXAS, is a small suburb west of Houston. Like its neighbors Bunker Hill and Hunter's Point, Spring Valley is not particularly well named: it sits on a pancake-flat prairie, has no identifiable water sources, endures a swamplike climate, and, being a few miles from downtown, is more "urban" than a good portion of Houston proper. As a town, Spring Valley does not have much of a municipal identity. It has no main street, no parks, no monuments, no library; for much of its history, it ran city business out of a nondescript office next to a convenience store. Socially, it is very homogeneous, composed mostly of three-bedroom homes on half-acre lots inhabited by white, middle-class families. With its homeowning population largely supportive of its restrictive zoning codes, few issues ever cause controversy. Spring Valley is a very quiet place where residents mostly keep to themselves. In the past few decades, Spring Valley has also become the typical American town.

Over the past half century, a tremendous change has occurred in the types of places Americans call home. In 1950, most Americans resided in either large cities or small, rural towns. Today, most Americans live somewhere in between; places outside of big cities but still within greater metropolitan areas—places like Spring Valley, places commonly known as suburbs. These suburbs are dissimilar to both their urban and their rural counterparts. Unlike older, central cities, they are often very singular in their social composition and land use—many contain nothing but homes, nothing but white people, or nothing but the affluent. Unlike rural towns, suburban places are highly interconnected with and dependent on a larger metropolis. Whereas people in rural towns typically worked and shopped in the same place, suburbanites often pursue each activity in other locales. Suburbanization has been one of the biggest changes in American society over the past fifty years. It has affected the ways Americans relate to their families, friends, and neighbors, understand local government, and experience community.

Yet, despite the enormity of this suburban transformation, its implications for American democracy are largely unknown. While the social consequences of suburbanization, such as racial segregation and urban sprawl, are well documented, the effects of America's suburban expansion on its basic mechanisms of democratic government are not understood. Take, for example, civic participation. Recent trends suggest a possible negative relationship between suburbanization and political and civic engagement. Over the past four decades, as Americans have been moving to suburbs, they have also become less likely to vote, less attached to political parties, and less trusting of their political institutions.[1] Many scholars believe that the past decades have brought not just the erosion of America's civil society but a disturbing loss of community and fellowship among citizens. From Robert Putnam's requiem for bowling leagues to Alan Ehrenhalt's lamentations for the "lost city," from Ray Suarez's remembrances of communities long gone to Thomas Geoghegan's elegy for a public citizenship, a chorus of scholars and journalists have recently pronounced civil society and community in America to be in ill-health.[2]

In these criticisms, suburbs like Spring Valley have been fingered as likely suspects. Whether it is the shape of their houses, the design of their neighborhoods, or their absence of public spaces, suburbs are routinely accused of stifling the social interaction, sense of membership, and democratic engagement that once existed in America's cities and towns.[3] Along with this loss of community, suburbanites allegedly have lost the capacities and incentives to be involved in public affairs. In other words, Americans do not vote, do not trust their government, or do not join the PTA partly because the physical design and social composition of suburbs are keeping them isolated and preoccupied with private concerns. In his exhaustive analysis of the decline of civic engagement in America over the past thirty years, Robert Putnam estimates that suburbanization and sprawl are accountable for about 10 percent of the problem.[4] "The suburb," as architects Andres Duany and Elizabeth Plater-Zyberk argue, "is the last word in privatization and spells the end of authentic civic life."[5]

Like most assertions about the suburbs, however, such claims are without any empirical basis. We have no real evidence on whether suburbanites are less civically engaged than nonsuburbanites or what impact, if any, suburban social environments are having on America's democratic processes. Suburbs like Spring Valley may now be the typical American town, but we have little understanding of how they affect Americans' commitment to their communities or their ability to govern themselves. This absence of knowledge comes largely from three sources.

---

[1] Orren 1997, Putnam 1995, Teixeiria 1992.

[2] In the past five years, several books and articles have emerged on the decline or loss of community in the United States, including Ehrenhalt 1995, Geoghegan 1998, Suarez 1999, Putnam 1995, Eberly 1994, Wuthnow 1998.

[3] Criticisms of suburbs have come mostly from architectural circles. See, for example, Langdon 1994, Katz 1994, Calthorpe 1993, Kunstler 1993, Duany and Plater-Zyberk 1991. Kenneth Jackson's masterful history of suburbanization, *Crabgrass Frontier* (1985), is also quite negative in its conclusions about suburban civic life.

[4] Putnam 2000, p. 283.

[5] As quoted in Schneider 1992.

First, most of us are unclear about what exactly a "suburb" is. Most places that are within a metropolitan area but not part of the central city are counted as suburbs, yet this usage is confusing because it equates places that are quite different in form and composition—for example, wealthy Beverly Hills, eclectic Santa Monica, residential Walnut, and impoverished Compton are all one kind of place (suburb), as distinguished from Los Angeles (city). Given the wide diversity of places that are within metropolitan areas but outside of central cities, such crude taxonomies do more to obfuscate than to clarify the real picture of suburban life. Architectural commentaries are not very useful either. Suburban civic malaise is often attributed to the absence of public spaces, the predominance of single-family homes with garage facades, and the prevalence of private yards; yet none of these studies enumerate how many suburbs actually have these characteristics or whether such traits are unique to suburban areas.[6] Indeed, large portions of Los Angeles, Houston, and Orlando have these "suburban" traits, while many suburbs—like Cranbury, New Jersey, or Petaluma, California—more closely resemble traditional small towns. The concept of the suburb has become saddled with so many stereotypes and misconceptions that most people have little understanding of what really distinguishes America's cities and suburbs from each other.[7]

Second, critics of suburbs have been equally vague about how suburban environments may distort the process of democracy. Most studies of local politics in America are of large cities, with scholars wrangling over whether cities are dominated by a governing elite or subject to more pluralistic political pressures.[8] Little research on local politics, however, has focused on suburbs. Meanwhile, other critics who bemoan the loss of "community" or "civil society" rarely specify what these terms mean or why they are important for democratic organization.[9] A protean term like "civil society" can include activities as diverse as gathering informally with neighbors and going to the gym,[10] and it is not clear that all such activities are either essential or beneficial for democratic governance. As was demonstrated in Weimar Germany, a strong civil society is no guarantee of stable democratic institutions or peaceful coexistence among the

[6] Langdon 1994, Katz 1994, Calthorpe 1993, Kunstler 1993, and Jackson 1985.
[7] These vague definitions are further complicated by critics who falsely equate suburban living with suburban lifestyles. Suburbs are often criticized for the amount of time their residents spend commuting or the prevalence of television consumption (Langdon 1994), factors that have more to do with individual lifestyle choices (or necessities) than with distinct environmental characteristics.
[8] For an excellent summary of this debate, see Judge, Stoker, and Wolman 1995.
[9] Kunstler 1993, Schneider 1992, Duany and Plater-Zyberk 1991, Rowe 1997, and Jackson 1985.
[10] Hall 1995.

citizenry.[11] In their preoccupation with vague notions of community, most criticisms of suburbs have largely ignored other essential questions of democratic governance. For instance, do suburbs limit or enhance the ways that citizens can govern themselves? Does suburbanization create any biases in the democratic process? If citizens in suburbs are less civically engaged, does this necessarily undermine their ability to govern themselves? Most critiques of suburbs and community do not address these questions.

Third, after decades of research, no conclusive evidence exists on whether or not suburban environments actually do shape individual civic or political behavior. Most assertions about suburban civic life are based on either pure speculation or case studies of individual places done in the 1950s and 1960s.[12] Interestingly, these early works mostly portrayed suburbs as "hotbeds of participation," with the typical suburbanite frantically running from one type of civic activity to another. Some even described suburbs as embodying the democratic ideal. Although these studies provide interesting descriptions of particular communities, they do not reveal whether any differences that may exist between suburban and nonsuburban residents are systematic. In other words, it is impossible from a study of one suburban community to determine whether the activity level in that place is universal to suburbs or something specific to that locale. To draw conclusions about suburbs as a whole, the researcher must examine a wide range of places to see whether consistent differences arise. Unfortunately, the few studies that employ such data (i.e., cross-sectional surveys of large populations) use only crude city/suburb dichotomies or sample from only a few cities.[13] Not surprisingly, these studies have found few effects of suburban contexts on civic behavior, leading some to question whether suburbs have any consequence for American democratic life.[14]

In short, America may be a nation of suburbs and its citizens may be disengaged from civic affairs, but we still have no idea whether these phenomena are related or what their larger democratic consequences may be. Yet scores of academics, journalists, and public commentators continue to assert that Americans have lost a sense of community and civic responsibility, and that suburbs are, somehow, to blame. Are sub-

---

[11] Berman 1997.

[12] For example, in the 1950s and 1960s, a number of sociologists conducted in-depth ethnographic studies of new suburbs, including David Reisman's *The Lonely Crowd* (1953), Seeley, Sim, and Loosley's *Crestwood Heights* (1956), William Whyte's *Organization Man* (1956), and Herbert Gans's *The Levittowners* (1967) (see also Popenoe 1985, Baldassare 1992, Baumgartner 1988, Berger 1960, Martin 1956).

[13] Wirt et al. 1972, Fischer and Jackson 1976.

[14] Wirt et al. 1972.

urbs really affecting the ways Americans interact with their communities? If so, is this a cause for alarm? Or are suburbs simply the unfortunate victims of an intellectual and cultural bias? This book seeks to answer these questions.

GENERAL ARGUMENT OF THE BOOK

In the pages to follow, I will argue that suburbanization is undermining the optimal functioning of America's local democratic institutions. Local government is important primarily because it provides an accessible and small-scale arena for the resolution of social and economic conflict. According to what I term the *authentic governance principle*, America's municipalities and other local institutions, as instruments of state governments, should function so as to bring together most people within a geographic vicinity to collectively solve problems related to their area. Local political institutions, as democracies, should be organized so as to directly articulate, or maximize the representation of parties to, conflicts within a particular region. Local governments best perform these functions by maximizing citizen input on salient issues for *all* residents of a community.

At first glance, suburbs hold great promise for meeting the standards of the authentic governance principle. One of the primary by-products of suburbanization is the movement of Americans living in large metropolitan areas into smaller municipal jurisdictions. Today, more urbanized Americans are governed by smaller municipalities than ever before. These smaller local governments allow citizens to come together in more intimate and immediate settings to resolve their political differences. As I show in chapter 2, residents of smaller places are more engaged in community affairs and active in civic life. Learning the practices of compromise, consensus, and organization building among their neighbors, citizens become better skilled in the difficult art of self-governance. Through the growth of these smaller polities, suburbanization promises the cultivation of a richer democratic practice.

Yet the potential benefits of "small-town" government are lost in the economic and racial segregation that suburbs promote. According to an authentic governance principle, municipalities need to adequately encompass the social cleavages and disagreements that occur among people within a particular area. Suburbs often distort this conflict mandate by dividing citizens along class and racial lines. Many suburban governments are constituted solely by people of one class, one race, or one type of land tenure. When municipal borders separate citizens in such ways, social conflicts that once existed among citizens are transformed into conflicts between local governments. This transformation of conflict, as I show in chapters 3 through 6, deters citizen involvement in local civic life.

To elucidate the consequence of this citizen demobilization, I offer a second new concept, *civic capacity*. The term refers to the extent to which a community's members are engaged in both political and civic activities. In many ways it is akin to the concept of social capital that has recently been popularized by James Coleman and Robert Putnam. Social capital refers to the social connections between individuals that "facilitate action."[15] Like notions of human or physical capital, social capital is a resource individuals utilize to achieve their goals. In Putnam's now famous argument, individuals gain social capital primarily by participating in voluntary organizations, an activity that builds networks and norms of reciprocity and trust and leads to greater health, happiness, and well-functioning societies.[16] But where social capital is primarily a measure at the individual level, civic capacity refers to communities. Individuals may hold stocks of social capital; communities have civic capacity. Moreover, where Putnam's understanding of social capital is based primarily in voluntary, nongovernmental action (indeed, political participation is an outgrowth of social capital), civic capacity is not so constrained. It refers to *all* types of civic and political activities, be they softball leagues or political campaigns.

Civic capacity is crucial for sustaining the well-being of America's democracy. In the United States, we ask a lot of our local governments. They must adjudicate between different interests, aggregate information from their constituents, and perform a multitude of functions with little control over productive resources. To meet their social needs and facilitate the process of self-rule, American localities traditionally have relied on the voluntary activities of their residents. In other words, localities have relied upon their civic capacity to maintain the functioning and promote the well-being of society. Just as an economy profits from its unpaid working sector, such as housekeeping and child rearing, so a polity benefits from its unpaid civic sector. Localities with greater civic capacity have more human resources available to identify and prioritize social problems, lobby for governmental solutions, and find alternatives where public resources are unavailable. Democracies with low civic capacity have fewer resources to solve social problems and are more likely to be subject to greater tensions, through riots, corruption, or civil disorder. Democracies with greater civic capacity not only will be more responsive to social problems but will have more citizens offering extrainstitutional solutions, thus providing greater social stability.

[15] Coleman 1990, p. 304.
[16] See Putnam 1993 and 2000.

Suburbanization, by segregating the population and suppressing citizen involvement in community affairs, is depriving many localities and metropolitan areas of their civic capacity and thus their ability to solve many contemporary social problems. Extreme concentrations of urban poverty, high degrees of racial segregation, and the rampant sprawl of unplanned growth are all predicaments of metropolitan life, the geographic community in which most Americans live. These social ills continue to defy solution partly because of the political divisions between cities and suburbs. At the institutional level, suburban political fragmentation puts local governments in competition with each other and inhibits intermunicipal cooperation.[17] And, as I will show in my empirical analysis, suburban segregation demobilizes citizens and deprives metropolitan areas of valuable human resources to address these problems. By encouraging certain residents to "tune out" local politics or to see themselves as different from the greater metropolis, suburban institutions are depriving the metropolitan community of vital civic capacity. Consequently, social problems that require institutional cooperation and active citizen involvement are going unaddressed. Unplanned growth and sprawl and severe economic and racial segregation contribute to high levels of traffic congestion, pollution, and periodic social unrest. These social ills have cost lives, billions of dollars in property damage, and unquantifiable losses in America's quality of life. If such problems are to be solved, the civic capacity of localities must be increased.

How can this be done? Just as the problems of suburban democracy are institutional in origin, so must be their solutions. By institutional change, I do not mean necessarily the form of local government; as I show in chapter 7, replacing council-manager with mayor-council governments or other such reforms will not enhance the civic capacity of a municipality. Rather, the institutional change must be with the way that municipal borders are drawn and land-use decisions are made. The social and economic segregation causing suburban civic withdrawal is the consequence of municipalities' having inordinate power to determine who lives within their borders. If local democracy is to be reinvigorated, the current structure of municipal government needs to be reconfigured. Previous research in both large cities and rural areas demonstrates that when local institutions bring together a variety of perspectives, political solutions that consider all citizen viewpoints can be found.[18] This logic needs to be applied to suburbs. Municipalities must be small enough to generate community among residents but socially and economically representative of the greater metropolitan area, so that citizens do not distance

---

[17] See Frug 1999, Lewis 1994, Weiher 1991.
[18] Berry, Portney, and Thomson 1993, Couto 1999.

their immediate community from that of their greater surroundings. This could serve to make institutions more cooperative and could reintegrate citizens into the public realm. Local institutions need to function as arenas that bring together the diverse elements and interests of the metropolis, not ones that keep them apart. In chapter 8, I will comment more on how this can be done. Let me now offer some clarification of the central ideas of this study.

Defining a Suburb

Ask most people to describe a suburb, and they will probably conjure images of ranch homes, tree-lined streets, and quiet neighborhoods. It is a picture of residential repose and domestic peace, minivans and soccer moms, and daily commutes and weekend barbecues. The reality of suburbanization is, of course, more complex. Suburbanization actually has been a number of different processes of development that have been occurring for over 150 years. Some suburbs started primarily as residential, middle-class communities; others began life as industrial enclaves situated around large employers; and others still were once rural hamlets that are now transformed by shopping malls and housing developments. Some older suburbs have retained their segregated and residential character, while other suburbs have morphed into large commercial or industrial districts. The vast expansion of suburban areas since 1950 has created an enormous variety of places that exist outside of urban areas. Social analysts have coined a host of terms—such as inner-ring and outer-ring suburb, ex-urb, post-suburb, trans-burb, and edge city—in an effort to capture this diversity. The range of places that now fall under the suburban moniker creates a big dilemma for anyone trying to determine what a suburb exactly is.

According to the categorization scheme provided by the U.S. Census Bureau, a suburb could be considered any part of a "metropolitan area" that is not in the central city. A metropolitan area is a major population center composed of a central city of at least 50,000 people and the surrounding county or counties that are densely populated and economically interconnected with the central city. In 1990, as illustrated by map 1.1, there were 329 different metropolitan areas ranging in size from the 18 million people in the greater New York area to 56,735 people in Enid, Oklahoma. These large metropolitan areas contain an enormous variety of cities, towns, townships, villages, and other municipalities, designated by the census as "places." All places that are not central cities within metropolitan areas typically get counted as suburbs.

The census scheme, however, does not offer much assistance for distinguishing suburbs from either central cities or each other. Take the exam-

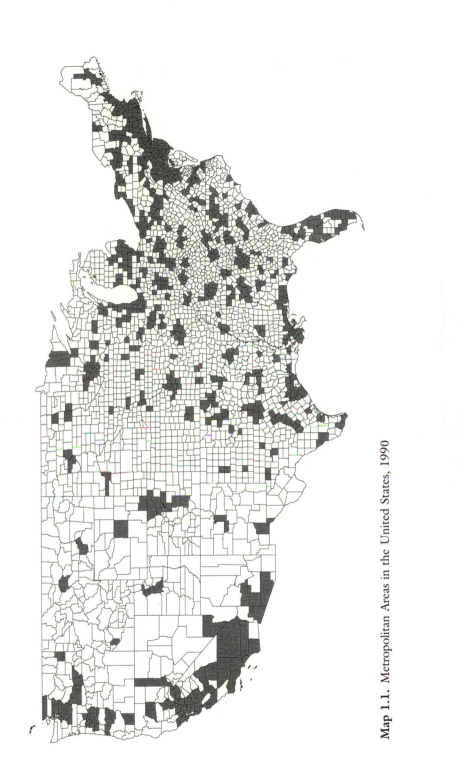

Map 1.1. Metropolitan Areas in the United States, 1990

ple of New Jersey, a state composed almost entirely of "suburbs." The U.S. Census Bureau has classified the entire state as part of a metropolitan area, yet New Jersey has few dominant cities. Newark is overshadowed by New York City, while Trenton and Camden are eclipsed by nearby Philadelphia. The remainder of New Jersey's municipalities and townships, while meeting the census definition of suburbs, are hardly uniform: Elizabeth and Hoboken are gritty and industrial, Montclair is middle-class and racially diverse; Short Hills is affluent and residential; Princeton has office parks, a university, and shopping malls; Cranbury and Hopewell still retain the flavor of small, rural towns. If all these places are considered suburbs, then how do we distinguish them, not only from cities like Philadelphia and New York, but from each other as well? Aside from their smaller size, middle-class Montclair, affluent Short Hills, and rural Hopewell have little in common that distinguishes them from gritty Elizabeth or academic Princeton.

The observations of architectural commentators are not very useful either. Many critics of suburbs focus on certain environmental characteristics, like uniform single-family homes widely spaced with fenced, private yards; solely residential communities composed of nothing but mass-produced tract homes; or residential developments oriented primarily around maximizing privacy and ease of automotive transportation. Indeed, an entire architectural design movement has arisen in response to the isolating and privatizing characteristics of America's suburbs. "New urbanist" communities such as Seaside, Florida, or Laguna West, California, seek to integrate housing, workplaces, and shopping in new patterns to restore public spaces and rebuild the community that is putatively absent in so many contemporary suburbs.[19]

Yet not all suburbs share these isolating characteristics—many, like Petaluma, California, or Concord, Massachusetts, were quintessential small, rural towns that were swallowed up by expanding nearby metropolitan areas. Many older suburbs, like New Rochelle, New York, are celebrated for their pro-civic orientation. And not all large cities have neighborhoods that promote social interaction. Significant parts of Houston, Phoenix, and Jacksonville are composed of residential neighborhoods with single homes, large yards, and high fences. While many of these commentators' assertions about the alienation and privatization of suburban designs are provocative and important to consider, most architectural criticisms are simply too vague and unspecified to meaningfully designate places in the contemporary metropolis.

Clearly, a new way of classifying metropolitan places is needed. Toward this end I start with the following deductions. When we address the dem-

---

[19] Katz 1994.

ocratic implications of suburbanization, the most important factor to consider is the distinct political identity of the suburb. Suburbanization is, as Michael Danielson argues, primarily "a political phenomenon."[20] At the most basic level, municipal boundaries are what separate central cities from suburbs and suburbs from one another. Spring Valley, Texas, is physically contiguous with neighboring Houston but is a separate social and political community by virtue of its municipal government. Municipal boundaries, by dividing the metropolitan population into distinct political entities, also create communities with particular interests, interests that often compete with those of other municipalities.[21] With particular zoning laws and municipal ordinances, suburban governments thus shape the social composition of the community. Town government is also the most primary unit of American democracy: it defines political membership, the agenda of local politics, and the ways people interact. Municipal policies determine who lives in a community, what activities take place, what public issues its residents face, and even what types of public space it contains. When we think of suburbs in terms of their political institutions, all incorporated places within metropolitan areas, from the smallest hamlet to the largest city, can be considered as similar units of analysis. Despite their many differences, giant Houston and tiny Spring Valley are fundamentally comparable as units of democracy. *For this study, I will not be comparing suburbs to central cities or analyzing just suburban places; rather, I will be examining all municipalities within a metropolitan area (central cities, suburbs, edge cities, etc.) and counting them as comparable measurement units.*

But if all municipalities within a metropolitan area are equivalently similar as units of analysis, then what are the most appropriate characteristics by which these places can be distinguished from one another? This query has no easy answer. In today's diverse metropolis, municipalities can be distinguished by hundreds of traits ranging from their sewage facilities to their street widths. Unfortunately, previous research on America's cities is not very useful in providing a definitive list. Classic theories of urban sociology from Louis Wirth differentiated large cities from rural areas by their size, density, and social heterogeneity.[22] Although large central cities resemble each other in these ways, not all suburbs are uniformly small, sparse, and homogeneous. Nor are the observations of contemporary critics useful, because many civically offending traits, such as the absence of public spaces or the presence of privatizing architectural forms, are so

---

[20] Danielson 1976, p. 17.
[21] For details of how metropolitan political fragmentation shapes intermunicipal competition, see Danielson 1976, Schneider 1987.
[22] Wirth 1969 [1939].

difficult to specify. For example, are streets public spaces? If so, then would not wider streets, an often criticized characteristic of the modern suburb, be counted as more public space? Are the negative effects of private yards more important than the positive effects of front porches? Even if one could answer these questions, it is not clear how they would translate into easily quantifiable measures.

To properly distinguish among municipalities in the contemporary metropolis, we need to look beyond simple city/suburb dichotomies and find indicators that are easily measured. In the recent historical development of American metropolitan areas, there are six dominant trends in place differentiation.[23] As America suburbanized over the past fifty years, its cities and towns have become increasingly distinguishable by these six characteristics:

1. *Population size*. The most distinguishing aspect of suburbanization has been the migration of the metropolitan population away from large central cities to smaller and medium-size places. Whereas in 1950 most urbanized Americans lived in large cities of over 100,000 in population, today most people live in smaller places. This diminution in the size of the typical metropolitan place is the very essence of suburbanization. In their most rudimentary form, suburbs represent the fragmentation of metropolitan areas into smaller political units. However, not all suburbs are identically small. Some hold only a few hundred residents, while others, like Garland, Texas, or Livonia, Michigan, contain over 100,000 people. Population size thus distinguishes *all* places in the contemporary metropolis.

2. *Economic composition*. With the political fragmentation of the metropolis, American cities have become increasingly distinguished by their affluence and economic composition. Until recently, most American cities contained a wide assortment of social classes and were within a relatively narrow economic range of each other. With suburbanization, however, America's cities have become highly stratified by their affluence. Some communities are desperately poor, with a median household income below $20,000 a year; others are quite affluent, with median household incomes well over $150,000 a year. In this stratification, these places have become distinguishable not just by their wealth but by their economic homogeneity. Many places, like Short Hills, New Jersey, are inhabited almost solely by wealthy people, while older, industrial towns, like Camden, New Jersey, are populated largely by the poor. Affluence thus differentiates not just America's citizens but its cities as well.

3. *Racial composition*. Although America's cities have always held ethnic neighborhoods, most larger municipalities were still ethnically and

---

[23] For discussions on methods of classifying cities, see Alford 1972 and Berry 1972.

racially mixed places. As with affluence, suburbanization has taken the racial divisions that once separated neighborhoods within cities and institutionalized them with municipal boundaries. Today, most African Americans and Latinos living in metropolitan areas are concentrated in a few neighborhoods of central cities or a handful of "minority suburbs," while most whites live in predominantly white suburbs. These racial divisions do not simply mirror economic status. In many metropolitan areas there exist both poor white suburbs, such as Merrionette Park, Illinois, and middle-class suburbs with significant minority populations like Cheverly, Maryland. Race itself has become a distinguishing characteristic of the American city.

4. *Land use*. For most of its history, America's cities had a combination of residential, industrial, and commercial areas. Because of limited transportation resources most people needed to be close to their work, and most people traveled to downtown areas for shopping and entertainment. But with suburbanization and the expansion of the highway system, the accessibility of transportation made possible by the automobile has also served to differentiate places by their land use. In today's metropolis, places are now composed solely of homes (Spring Valley, Texas), or businesses (Industry, California), or are even noted for their shopping malls (King of Prussia, Pennsylvania). Although a large portion of suburbs are residentially predominant, not all are bedroom communities. Many still retain a mixture of commercial and residential sites. In today's polymorphous metropolis, land use distinguishes suburbs both from central cities and from other suburbs.

5. *City age*. The rapid expansion of suburban areas in the past thirty years has made city age an important characteristic for distinguishing American cities. Much of this expansion has been part of a larger regional migration to new metropolitan areas in the Sun Belt such as Jacksonville, Houston, Phoenix, and Atlanta. In many of these places, new communities with over 20,000 residents have sprung up within a couple of years. Meanwhile, many older cities and suburbs in the Northeast and Midwest have either ceased growing or lost population. In the ever expanding American metropolis, age has become an increasingly prominent community trait.

6. *Political institutions*. It is impossible to understand suburbs without looking at their political characteristics. Suburbs are the consequence of political boundaries, and their distinct social composition is the result of municipal practices in zoning ordinances, development, taxation, and land use. But beyond this, suburbs often have distinctive types of electoral systems and institutions of government that can influence citizen activity. Many suburbs have "reform-style" political institutions (e.g., council-manager governments with at-large representative districts and

nonpartisan elections), while larger and older cities often elect mayors and council members from specific districts. But while reform governments are more prominent outside of central cities, not all central cities have prereform-style governments, particularly in the Sun Belt and western states. And, as the Republican political machine in Nassau County, New York, demonstrates, not all suburbs are without partisan-style political structures. As with social characteristics, municipal institutions distinguish all cities and suburbs from each other.

Taken together, these six characteristics best distinguish the variety of places that constitute the American metropolis. And while some of these traits are mildly correlated with each other, each represents a distinct dimension of America's recent suburbanization. To gauge the civic consequences of suburbanization, we must consider the effect of each of these traits separately. To understand the democratic consequences of suburbanization, we cannot simply compare places as either city or suburb; rather, we must estimate how a community's size, affluence, racial composition, and the like, distinctly affect the process of self-governance. Once each of these characteristics is examined separately, then we can evaluate them in concert to understand the effects of suburbanization. In other words, in that suburbanization has led to the increasing polarization of America's municipalities along these dimensions, we can understand the cumulative civic consequences of suburban growth by comparing how each of these traits shapes civic involvement. Just as a physician determines the health of an individual by examining a variety of factors—such as temperature, heart rate, and cholesterol level—in concert, so too must we seek to understand democracy in suburbia by examining each of the relevant factors individually and then making a cumulative assessment.

Of course, by focusing on municipalities as the unit of analysis, we lose the ability to examine other contextual areas. In particular, we will not be able to ascertain the civic effects of neighborhoods or architectural design. This is an important drawback. After all, as a whole, New York City can be an anonymous and isolating place, but many of its residents find their neighborhoods quite friendly, personable, and interconnected. The same holds for most suburban places. Indeed, many critics of suburbs focus less attention on suburbs as a whole than on particular characteristics that are common to suburban neighborhoods, such as missing sidewalks or gated streets. Relying on municipalities as units of analysis, we relinquish the ability to know whether these aspects of urban and suburban environments shape civic life. The municipal focus also means that we cannot ascertain the effect of living in the unincorporated outskirts of a metropolis. For many suburbanites, local government is that of a county or a series of special districts. It is unclear how these political arrangements are civically different from an incorporated area. But to examine both neighborhoods and unincorporated places raises a host of measurement and methodological problems like the ones mentioned above. Moreover, local government law rarely gives any rights or powers to neighborhoods.[24] Important as they may be for feelings of community, neighborhoods are much less important as arenas for social and political organization. Consequently, in the trade-off between what is clearly identifiable and measurable and what is not, I have chosen to concentrate on the former.

CITIZEN PARTICIPATION AND LOCAL DEMOCRACY IN AMERICA

Local government is the foundation of American democracy. It is the most visible and immediate unit of government—locally based services such as education, roads, police, and water are the functions of government that have the most impact on citizens' daily lives. It is the most accessible arena of government—whereas the voices of citizens in a nation of 280 million are necessarily faint, in a city of a few thousand they are loud and clear. It is also a vital component of public policy—since the 1960s, many federal programs, ranging from urban redevelopment empowerment zones to the rehabilitation of hazardous waste sites, have been assigned statutory mandates requiring local citizen participation in policy formulation. Similarly, with the devolution of responsibility for the control and administration of other policies, such as TANF (Temporary Assistance for Needy Families)—formerly AFDC (Aid to Families with Dependent Children)—health care, and environmental regulation, local governments have become essential instruments in the maintenance of social welfare. Local government is also the proving ground of a democratic citizenry. Through participating on local boards, joining with neighbors for community actions, or working in city elections, citizens acquire crucial skills and become familiar with the public realm. In short, municipalities are where most citizens are both learning and exercising the arts of self-governance.

Yet despite their significance, our understanding of how well localities function as democracies is incomplete, particularly in an era of suburbanization. Most studies of local democratic government have revolved around a long and exhaustive debate about community power and "who governs" America's cities. Since the 1950s, political scientists and sociologists have factionalized: some view local communities as controlled by a "power elite" of social and economic luminaries, while others view government decisions as subject to pluralistic competition between groups

[24] Frug 1999.

that have varying influence in different policy arenas.[25] Later scholars have tried to reconcile these perspectives by focusing on the land-oriented nature of local politics and the advantages that small groups of economically powerful interests hold for constructing governing "regimes," particularly when they center on the imperatives of economic growth and development.[26]

Although this debate illuminates much of the logic behind policy making in large cities, it is not particularly useful for exploring the democratic implications of suburbanization. Theorists of community power focus mostly on larger cities. Their analyses typically presume plurality of interests within a community and then work to determine how well those interests are represented within the policy-making process. Yet such explanations are of questionable validity for suburbs, a great many of which are very singular in their social composition or quite limited in their land use. In a community that is composed only of the affluent or homeowners, many presumptions about pluralistic competition between interest groups or the machinations of growth regimes are no longer germane. Few theories of local government consider how systematic differences in the social composition of American localities affect the dynamics of democratic government. In other words, even though American cities are becoming increasingly differentiated by their size, affluence, and racial composition, most existing frameworks for evaluating local democracy cannot explain how this differentiation affects citizens' ability to represent their interests and make their political institutions responsive to their concerns.

An alternative perspective on local politics that takes social segregation into account comes from economics. According to "public choice" theorists, intermunicipal competition in a politically fragmented metropolitan area has changed the nature of traditional democratic organization, with market-driven efficiencies replacing traditional mechanisms of democratic decision making.[27] Under this framework, local leaders in politically frag-

[25] According to "elite" theorists such as Hunter (1953) and Mills (1956), American cities were effectively governed by a small clique of powerful social and business luminaries. These characterizations of "who governs" American cities were contradicted by "pluralist" studies from Dahl (1961), Polsby (1963), and Wolfinger (1974), who viewed power in urban areas as decentralized and varying according to issue areas.

[26] Clarence Stone (1989) has advocated a regime model of urban politics, arguing that cities which accomplish large public works often do so by creating successful governing coalitions among elected officials, large business interests, and leaders of powerful interest groups. Paul Peterson's landmark work (1981) noted how city leaders are constrained by the competition for ratables and are forced to pursue policies that promote economic development. Logan and Molotch (1989) extend this argument by noting how varying groups in a city, such as unions, newspapers, and universities, often join with business interests to create "growth machines" that put pressure on elected leaders to pursue pro-growth policies.

[27] The seminal public choice work comes from Tiebout (1956), who characterized local

mented metropolitan areas compete for ratables (i.e., those who pay more in taxes than they require in services) and development. Consequently, leaders are under great pressure to tailor services to particular constituencies at a minimum cost. Citizens, in this view, are transformed into consumers, basically shopping among various suburbs for the optimal balance between taxes and services offered. If citizens do not like policies, they can simply "vote with their feet" and move elsewhere. This marketlike competition between suburbs will create more homogeneous polities where citizen interests are easily represented and services delivered with greater efficiency.

But while appealing in its logic and simplicity, the public choice perspective is not very good at explaining the dynamics of democratic politics. To begin with, most economic models are based on very heroic assumptions about citizen/consumer information and behavior. Little evidence exists that citizens are aware of most services offered by their city and neighboring cities, or that they actually calculate these as the primary determinants of their residential choice.[28] People may choose to live in a place because it has good schools or less crime, but they are also constrained by many other factors, such as the housing market, proximity to employment, and such personal desires as proximity to family. Moreover, from the perspective of democratic government, the public choice model is inherently biased. The ends of democracy can be achieved through intermunicipal competition only if all citizens have equal resources. In other words, democratic citizens can be consumers only if they all have equal amounts of "shopping" power. Yet not all citizens are equally mobile—affluent people enjoy a much higher degree of residential choice than poor folks and are more desirable as taxable ratables. Consequently, in the municipal market, the affluent have disproportionate power as citizens to dictate public policy. This violates the fundamental principles of democratic politics, which presumes equality among all citizens in representing their preferences. While useful for explaining some of the pressures faced by local leaders and the logic of policy outcomes, the public choice model is not well suited for evaluating the democratic implications of suburbanization.

The inadequacies of existing theories thus require that we step back and reconsider the determinants of local democracy. The United States, like all democracies, faces a continual struggle between the prerequisites of popular rule and the practices of actual governance. Most people understand the term "democracy" in relation to its Greek origins: democ-

governments as similar to business firms seeking to optimize the ratio of service costs to revenue (i.e., taxes). Similar perspectives have been advocated by Ostrom, Bish, and Ostrom (1988) and Parks and Oakerson (1989).
[28] Schneider 1989.

racy is literally the sovereignty or rule (*kratos*) of the people (*demos*). Yet built into this deceptively simple concept are numerous difficult and intractable issues concerning who the *demos* are, how exactly they are to rule, over what they rule, and to what ends. For instance, are the *demos* simply a numeric majority or all the citizenry? In a world of diverse and particularized interests, how can a democracy reconcile the demands of minorities holding intense preferences on a few issues and a majority harboring diffuse and limited preferences on all issues? How can a democracy protect the rights of numeric minorities yet still respect the demands of the sovereign majority?

Of course, answering all these questions is not only beyond the scope of this book but would simply reproduce a vast literature within democratic theory that is better explicated elsewhere.[29] Therefore, for the purposes of this study, I adopt the simple proposition that a true democracy depends upon all citizens' being able to express their preferences with equal measure. As Robert Dahl would argue, the conundrums of democracy noted above are most effectively resolved not from policies or procedures based on the desires of the majority but from the consent of the largest number of citizens.[30] The best corrective for the dynamic tensions inherent in democratic government is maximizing the input of the citizenry. In James Madison's design, by extending the sphere of representation (i.e., increasing the amount of citizen input), democracies can counteract the harmful tendencies of political factions.[31] Minority interests can best protect their rights and the majority can best express its preferences when citizens are actively and continually making their wishes known. In other words, democratic government may be rule of the people in principle, but in order for the people to rule in practice, they must regularly articulate their preferences to others and their political institutions.

Therefore, the first step in evaluating the democratic consequences of suburbanization is to examine how citizens articulate and represent their interests to their local governing institutions and fellow citizens. Of course, examining citizen participation alone will not provide a complete description of whether or how suburban governments are performing as democracies. We must consider other factors, such as the structure of local institutions and the fiscal limitations of the localities, when evaluating local political outcomes. Furthermore, as I will discuss in chapter 8, low levels of citizen participation do not necessarily indicate that all citizen preferences are going unmet. Nevertheless, citizen participation is influential in shaping government policy: citizens who make their prefer-

---

[29] For a full description of the problems of democracy, see Held 1987, Dahl 1998.
[30] Dahl 1998, p. 46.
[31] Hamilton, Madison, and Jay 1982 [1789]; see numbers 10 and 51.

ences known are more likely than citizens who are silent to get those preferences represented.[32] Participation may not be the only determinant of democratic governance and is not always the most important one; it is, however, the most essential one. Without some level of effective citizen participation in the governing processes, democracy cannot exist. Therefore, by focusing on civic participation, we can evaluate the ways in which suburban citizens are representing their own interests to local governments.

For this study, I focus on the five important types of local civic activity:

1. *Voting.* Arguably, voting is the most important civic act within any democratic system. It is the most common form of participation, the easiest way that citizens can voice their preferences, and possibly the best means for gauging the overall sentiments of a polity. Voting is also the key mechanism for controlling political leaders, with the reelection mandate ensuring some responsiveness to citizen concerns. Thus the simplest and crudest way of gauging a polity's democratic performance is to see whether or not its citizens are voting.

2. *Contacting officials.* Although voting may be a crucial mechanism by which citizens control their political leaders, it is a rather blunt instrument for expressing their preferences. Outside of referenda and ballot initiatives, voters rarely determine specific policies and are usually just electing representatives, often with unclear mandates. Nor is it clear that places with low voter turnout, such as the United States or Switzerland, are any less democratic than places where everyone votes. Thus other forms of participation are important to consider. One effective way that citizens express their preferences is through directly contacting local officials. By writing letters, making phone calls, and even scheduling meetings, citizens articulate their particular concerns to greater effect. While contacting may be less common and more difficult than voting, it can convey the intensity and strength of preferences. Elected officials who face reelection and are interested in gauging the sentiments of their constituencies in the absence of information thus pay particular attention to these calls. The extent to which citizen are able to contact their officials is, therefore, some indicator of the polity's responsiveness.

3. *Attending community board meetings.* In the devolution of policy implementation from the federal to local governments, community board meetings have become an ever more important mechanism of gathering citizen input and ensuring institutional accountability. From school districts to planning commissions, from city councils to mosquito abatement zones, board meetings are vital elements in the administration of local services. In many ways, these meetings are a good venue for citizens

---

[32] See Verba, Schlozman, and Brady 1995.

to voice their opinions, as most meetings are specifically designed to be receptacles for community opinion. Participation in these meetings therefore is also an indicator of how well citizens control the affairs of their community. Governments with higher meeting attendance are, in theory, places that are also hearing more citizen input on the direction of local policy.

4. *Participating in voluntary organizations.* In recent years, scholars have begun to focus on the importance and role of associational activity or "civil society" for democratic government. According to many thinkers, the political norms and networks of reciprocity that citizens develop in voluntary organizations are vital for maintaining the health of democracy.[33] By associating with neighbors and taking part in organizations, people come to know the issues that shape their lives, acquire techniques for acting collectively, and adopt norms of consensus and compromise necessary for democratic governance. Voluntary public, associational activities are a crucial component of democratic life. In places with a richer associational life, citizens will be able to link more easily with their neighbors, will be informed about local issues, and will express their opinions to local institutions.

5. *Working informally with neighbors.* Other important civic components of local democracy involve less formalized patterns of association among citizens. Many critics believe that as a by-product of suburbanization the sense of "community" that once existed in America's cities and rural towns has been supplanted by an individualistic and private-regarding orientation. Although the term "community" is somewhat vague, a theme common in these criticisms is that suburbanites are somehow less committed to the localities and less interactive with their neighbors. Such alienation is potentially threatening to a democracy, where citizen preferences are best expressed in concert and where social problems require voluntary collective action. The degree to which citizens work with their neighbors demonstrates their experience of community and their ability to congregate with fellow citizens of their localities.

Taken together, these five civic activities represent a broad cross section of citizen activities that are essential for democratic governance. Of course, one may wonder whether such a list is too broad to permit any generalizations about the civic consequences of suburbanization. Why would a suburban environment affect voting rates in the same way it influences attendance at PTA meetings? Although the five activities may not all be affected by the suburban environment in quite the same way, we must consider a large set of behaviors when considering the civic implications of suburbanization. Like the proverbial blind men trying to

[33] Putnam 1995, Rosenblum 1998, Skocpol and Fiorina 1999.

describe an elephant, if we focus on any one civic activity, as each blind man senses only one of the elephant's body parts, we may wrongly characterize public, associational activity as a whole: a person may belong to the local Moose Lodge but otherwise be discouraged from local civic activity; a mother may never vote but be quite active in working with neighbors on the PTA; an elderly man may always vote but feel unable to express his more specific preferences to elected officials. Using any single act as a measure, we may misrepresent the whole of suburban civic life.

Conversely, some may wonder about other important civic activities not listed here. For example, churches are important centers for local civic life, serving as places for recruitment and dissemination of local information. Similarly, campaign work, protesting, and contributing to organizations are also ways that citizens express their opinions. All of these behaviors are important to local democracy, but they are not necessarily well suited for this study. Church activity is notoriously difficult to measure: survey respondents often misreport their activity; church involvement is not easily quantified, as church attendance may measure feelings of religious intensity rather than the amount of social contact.[34] Campaign work and protesting are among the least common forms of participation, with fewer than 5 percent of the population taking part in either activity, particularly at the local level.[35] Given the low rates of activity, it will be hard to find significant differences across different types of places. Similarly, political contributions are largely related to individual-level income, mostly national in direction, and not necessarily a good indicator of local civic involvement. Therefore, for this study, I have limited the analysis to those activities which best represent the interactions among citizens, their political institutions, and their communities.

These activities also provide a rough sketch of the social patterns of residents and how they interact with each other to organize their society. In other words, taken together, these behaviors outline the contours of this slippery and problematic term—"community." Although defining a protean concept like community is beyond the scope of this book, these types of political interaction, particularly the less formal types of political behavior, such as attending organizational meetings or working with neighbors, illustrate the ways that people do interact with their neighbors. Insofar as community is constituted by the interaction of a set of members, comparing civic behaviors across metropolitan social contexts allows us to evaluate how suburbanization has shaped patterns of community in the contemporary United States.

[34] For a full discussion, see Wald, Kellstedt, and Leege 1993.
[35] Verba, Schlozman, and Brady 1995, p. 89.

SOCIAL CONTEXTS AND CIVIC PARTICIPATION

Having come to an understanding of how to define suburbs and an appreciation for the need to study local civic participation, we must next determine how the two are related. In other words, how does the size, affluence, or land use of a place shape the way its inhabitants participate in the five civic activities listed above? This question is important to answer. Suburbs may be distinguished by their affluence and residents of nonaffluent places may vote less, but without any theory linking the affluence of a place to its residents' voting behavior, any correlation between the two may be spurious.

Unfortunately, previous research is not very helpful in this regard. Most scholars who have studied social environments generally ignore civic participation.[36] For instance, Louis Wirth, the father of modern urban sociology, speculated about the social and psychological effects of urban environments but was generally unconcerned with questions of civil society or local political involvement. The best he could offer was the idea that alienated urbanites compensated for their loneliness by joining clubs and organizations, an assertion that has never been substantiated.[37]

Similarly, political theorists who have considered the civic implications of social environments, such as Rousseau, Montesquieu, and Dahl, often arrive at contradictory speculations because they do not first postulate why citizens actually participate in civic life. For example, in their book *Size and Democracy*, Dahl and Tufte reason, "[S]maller democracies provide more opportunity for citizens to participate . . . but, larger democracies provide citizens opportunities to participate in decisions . . . to control the most important aspects of their situation."[38] But in making their claims, Dahl and Tufte *assume* that smaller places provide more opportunities for participation and that these increased opportunities stimulate citizen involvement. Such assumptions, however, are neither based on any general theory of civic involvement nor empirically tested. We do not know whether a city's size really changes opportunities for participation, whether opportunities really do influence involvement, or what other characteristics might affect the relationship between a city's size and its residents' levels of civic involvement.

Contemporary empirical research on how and why citizens participate is not very helpful either for explaining the impact of social environments,

---

[36] For example, the founders of urban sociology (Simmel 1969 [1905], Tonnies 1988, Weber 1986 [1898], Wirth 1969 [1939]), generally did not concern themselves with political participation. Their speculations about the effects of urban environments were largely limited to social behaviors.

[37] See Wirth 1969 [1939].

[38] Dahl and Tufte 1973, p. 18.

because most studies typically view citizens in isolation. Over the past fifty years, political scientists have explained why citizens participate with a host of theories that range from early learned behaviors and unconscious needs, to analyses of individual class position and interests, to "rational choice" models that treat citizens as sequestered utility maximizers participating only when the benefits of their actions outweigh their costs.[39] None of these theories really factor environmental effects into their explanations. With the notable exception of voter turnout, most *theories* of civic participation do not take the social or political environment of the respondent into account.[40] Citizens are characterized as atomistic creatures making political choices and decisions largely in a social and institutional vacuum. Despite the near axiom that human behavior is the function of both individual and environmental characteristics, most past research on social contexts and political participation has focused on one to the exclusion of the other.

To understand how suburban environments may shape civic life, we need to start with some basic deductions and form some new hypotheses. The first question we will want to ask is whether civic acts themselves differ across various places. In other words, is casting a ballot, writing a letter to an elected official, or meeting with neighbors a different experience in Boston from what it is Bellevue or Baton Rouge? For the most part, the answer seems to be no. While state laws and local procedures may change the ease of voter registration or allow people to vote by mail, the act of voting itself is probably impervious to the affluence or racial composition of a locality. Similarly, a place's size or land use may affect how difficult it is to meet with neighbors or contact an official, but the act of meeting or contacting is ostensibly the same no matter where one lives.[41] In terms of practice, civic activity is roughly the same in Houston as it is in Hoboken.

Therefore, if social contexts are shaping individual civic behavior, they must be doing so indirectly by influencing the *determinants* of participa-

[39] For the classic proponents of the psychological dispositions, see Campbell et al. 1960. Class-based arguments are evident in Verba and Nie 1972 and Piven and Cloward 1989. Classic rational choice arguments are made in Downs 1957 and Olson 1965.

[40] Theories of voting that have taken context into account are Wolfinger and Rosenstone 1980 and Rosenstone and Hansen 1994, with the former looking at registration laws and the latter looking at mobilization environments. In terms of general participation, Huckfeldt (1984) and Leighley (1990) have examined the effects of social environments, although neither has developed a full theory of local contexts. Books and Prysby (1991) did try to construct a model of local contextual effects, although they did not base this on theories of why citizens participate.

[41] The one notable exception to this would be in electoral registration and voting, where large differences exist across states in time, eligibility, the ability to vote by mail or vote early, and the like.

tion. Put differently, a place's racial composition does not make the act of voting any different, but it does change the *other* factors that influence whether one is likely to vote. What are these other determinants of participation? Here, the voluminous literature within political science offers a wide selection of choices ranging from the incentives to participation to the costs.[42] In the most recent and comprehensive study of political participation in the United States, Sidney Verba, Kay Schlozman, and Henry Brady offer what they call the "civic voluntarism" model.[43] According to this framework, the major influences on civic participation can be roughly grouped into three categories: skills and resources, interest, and mobilization. People are more likely to participate if they have knowledge of politics or financial means, if they are more psychologically engaged by politics or concerned with political local events, or if they are recruited by others to take part. Verba, Schlozman, and Brady conclude that many individual-level influences identified by other researchers, such as education or age, ultimately can be subsumed under one of these three characteristics. In other words, education is important for political participation because it stimulates political interest, age provides citizens with greater skills and knowledge, and so forth. Thus, according to the civic voluntarism model, if we want to understand why citizens may or may not participate, we need to first determine why they are more interested in public affairs, how they acquire civic skills and resources, or why they are more likely to be mobilized for political action.

When we reflect on the civic voluntarism model (or any other model of civic participation, for that matter), the social and political characteristics of metropolitan places come into consideration. Although this was not explored in the original formulation of the civic voluntarism model, political interest, mobilization, and resources are all affected by a person's social surroundings and can vary in *systematic* ways. Take, for example, why people are interested in local affairs. One reason usually overlooked by political scientists is the simple fact that politics is a lot more exciting in some places than in others. In cities like New York or Philadelphia, a range of political issues and visible, colorful political candidates enliven local political contests; in many small towns, local politics barely penetrates the public consciousness. Of course, not all small towns are boring—some places have vicious fights between local figures that are the topic of endless town gossip. Nevertheless, political scientists have long asserted that politics is more interesting where there are bigger stakes in question or where larger social cleavages are dividing the community.

---

[42] For examples, see Olson 1965, Rosenstone and Hansen 1994, Teixeira 1992, Verba and Nie 1972, Wilson 1972, Wolfinger and Rosenstone 1980.
[43] Verba, Schlozman, and Brady 1995.

The same could be said of political mobilization. In some places, people are more familiar with their neighbors or host more local events; in other places, people hardly know their fellow townsfolk. Where such people are socially familiar, neighbors are more likely to talk about politics and recruit others for local activities.[44] Even the impact of individual resources on participation is relative to context—where participation is more difficult, the relevance of individual knowledge and skills grows.[45]

Continuing with the civic voluntarism model, we can identify the linkages between suburbanization and civic participation. I believe that the civic effects of suburban places originate in their local political institutions. Partly this comes from their form of government. Partly this comes from zoning ordinances, taxes, annexation, and other policies that then define the social composition of a community, such as its population size, economic composition, land use, the age of its building structures, and, to a limited extent, its racial composition. These social characteristics, in turn, shape the local political agenda, the social relations between neighbors, and emotional ties of residents to their community. Places that are racially and economically homogeneous are less likely to have political controversies but may have stronger ties between neighbors. Such factors then influence the determinants of civic participation. For instance, as outlined in the civic voluntarism model, local political issues shape interest politics; familiarity between neighbors alters patterns of mobilization and the value of resources. These determinants, in turn, shape the actual civic behaviors, ranging from the informal meeting of neighborhood groups to attending board meetings to voting in local elections. Of course, this causal influence is not entirely a one-way street. Through political action, citizens can change the character of local political institutions and practices. For example, a local organization can galvanize the citizenry to change municipal zoning practices, which then may influence the social composition of a place, and so on. Nevertheless, for the purposes of this book, I will focus primarily on the ways that the social composition of suburbs influences the primary determinants of local civic action.

DATA AND MEASURES

The final challenge in examining the democratic consequences of suburbanization is to test the relationships listed above with actual data. In many ways, this presents the biggest challenge to the research. Most existing studies of cities and suburbs are inadequate because they focus only

---

[44] Huckfeldt and Sprague 1995.
[45] Wolfinger and Rosenstone 1980.

on one particular community.[46] While this approach can highlight specific details of policy making within a community, it is inadequate for drawing systematic conclusions across a wide range of places such as suburbs. Indeed, this is a problem with most people's opinions about suburbs: most people have an experience or an opinion about civic life in suburbia, but few know whether their view is shared by others. In order to develop sound empirical conclusions about suburban civic life, we need to sample from a wide number of people across a wide number of places.

Unfortunately, most existing data are not appropriate in the study of suburbs. Most data are either solely on the aggregate level (e.g., county-level demographic statistics or voting patterns) or the individual level (e.g., surveys of individual respondents). This greatly limits whatever conclusions can be drawn about the effects of one level on the other.[47] For example, if we make generalizations about suburban behavior by comparing aggregate voting rates in suburbs and cities, we have few ways of knowing what effects are related to the social characteristics of place and what are related to the characteristics of the individual inhabitants. Turnout in local elections may be higher in a suburb like Spring Valley than in nearby Houston, but with only aggregated data it is impossible to know why: is this because Spring Valley's more affluent and educated citizens are just more likely to vote than Houstonians, or is there something specific about living in Spring Valley that makes people more civically oriented? On the other hand, if we look only at individual-level data as in most surveys, we have no way of gauging the effects of the social context. To appropriately measure contemporary metropolitan social contexts, we need data that measure individual traits and behavior, contain information on the context, and sample from a wide variety of places.

The bulk of my arguments come from a unique series of datasets that merge individual-level survey data with aggregate census data. Most of the individual-level data come from the 1990 Citizen Participation Study (CPS), currently the most comprehensive source of information on the participatory activities of the American public.[48] The Citizen Participation Study is a large-scale, two-stage survey of a random sample of Americans conducted in 1989 and 1990. In the first stage, 15,053 Americans were interviewed by telephone about their voluntary and political activities and demographic characteristics. In the second stage, longer, in-person interviews were conducted with 2,517 of the original 15,053 respondents, with more detailed questions regarding their social and political activities. To measure the social context, I extracted information on both city- and

---

[46] For examples, see Hunter 1953, Dahl 1961, Polsby 1963, Stone 1989.
[47] See Achen and Shively 1993.
[48] Verba et al. 1995.

metropolitan-level social characteristics from the 1990 Census (Census of Population and Housing 1990) for all of the respondents in these studies whose city of residence could be identified. For the CPS, this provided information on 1,633 different places for the screener data and 822 different places in the follow-up study. Together these data constitute what I will refer to throughout this study as the Citizen Participation/Census (CPC) dataset. I have also supplemented the CPC with data from the 1996 American National Elections Studies (NES). The NES, conducted before and after every congressional election by the survey research center at the University of Michigan, is the preeminent source of data on American political attitudes. It offers a wide range of questions on citizen attitudes toward political institutions, assessments of political efficacy, feelings of trust, and policy opinions. Once again, where each respondent's place of residence could be identified, place-level census information was appended. Combined, these data represent a truly unique opportunity for discerning the effects of suburban environments.

These data are unique because they allow us to overcome the major difficulty in estimating the effects of metropolitan contexts—isolating their effects per se. For example, if we were to compare the simple rates of voter turnout between small and large cities, we would not be able to know which effects are due to a city's size and which are due to the characteristics of the individuals who live in such places. Multilevel data allow for the contextual effects of social environments on individual behavior to be differentiated from the individual-level characteristics of the residents. In other words, these data will allow us to estimate how much variation in people's behavior is attributable to their social surroundings as opposed to their own education, age, income, and the like. Drawing from a national sample, these data also allow for sampling from a wide variety of places. And, using so large a survey as the CPS, most of the analyses are based on a large number of individual cases.

Of course, distinguishing these effects also depends upon using statistical techniques that allow the distinct effects of the social context to be isolated while taking into account other characteristics of both the city and its inhabitants. To meet these ends, I rely on a multivariate regression analysis, which allows for the effects of a particular variable, such as a place's size, to be estimated while taking into account the effects of other variables, such as an individual survey respondent's education, age, race, or length of residence.[49] All of the individual-level traits that would be

---

[49] For discussion of OLS and logistic regression procedures, see Hanushek and Jackson 1977 and Aldrich and Nelson 1984. The contextual variables come from separate estimates of city populations from the 1990 Census, and thus problems of intercorrelation between the individual- and city-level variables should be minimal. Even though many of the con-

associated with the city-level characteristics can be controlled with the regression techniques, and the distinct effects of the contextual variables can be isolated. The regression analyses include all of the major individual demographic characteristics associated with civic participation: education, income, age, sex, race, length of residence, and homeownership.[50]

Many contextual models employing aggregated data are subject to intense selection biases that can produce artificial contextual effects.[51] By using measures of a social context that are aggregations of the individual-level characteristics of its members, the contextual variable may be incorporating individual processes that relate to the particular behavior that is being analyzed. For example, people in large cities may be less likely to belong to organizations, not because city size discourages their participation, but because they are the types of people not likely to join associations because of some individual-level characteristic. These techniques are limited by the data available, and there may be other individual-level characteristics associated with living in an affluent or all-white suburb that these measures do not take into account. We must be wary of inadvertently capturing unmodeled effects with the contextual data, but, in general, this should not pose a problem. Controlling for the above individual demographic traits is sufficient to eliminate most of the "noise" that the city-level variables might be picking up. Places where self-selection is more problematic will be discussed in greater detail in the chapters to follow.

Finally, the multivariate analyses allow for the several dimensions of metropolitan places to be considered simultaneously. As I noted above, the diversity of suburban places requires examining several aspects of their social composition (i.e., size, affluence, racial composition, etc.) separately. Yet it is also important to consider how each of these factors operates in the context of the others. The multivariate equations allow for the effects of each dimension to be considered while holding the others constant. In other words, when estimating the effects of city size, the multivariate equations also control for the affluence and racial composition of a community. Similarly, when exploring the impact of residential predominance, we will see that most of the effects of living in a "bedroom suburb" disappear once their economic and racial composition is taken into account. Using these techniques, we can then determine

---

textual measures are aggregate variables and thus subject to measurement bias, the correlation in measurement error between levels should not be problematic (Bryk and Raudenbush 1992).

[50] For an authoritative analysis of how these factors shape civic participation, see Verba, Schlozman, and Brady 1995 and Wolfinger and Rosenstone 1980.

[51] Achen and Shively 1993.

which aspects of this complex and multidimensional process of suburbanization are shaping American civic life.

OUTLINE OF THE BOOK

With these concepts in hand, we are now ready to explore the civic implications of suburbanization. The book's central chapters examine how each of the six major characteristics that distinguish places is shaping civic behavior. Chapter 2 explores population size. Residents of smaller municipalities are more active in local politics, more interested in local affairs, and generally more engaged by the democratic process, irrespective of the size of the surrounding metropolis. The remainder of the chapter explores why municipal boundaries are important in an age of metropolitan sprawl, how place size differently affects various demographic groups (particularly men and women), and what civic potential municipal fragmentation holds for metropolitan areas.

Chapter 3 examines the municipal segregation of Americans according to income. The first part of the chapter explores how suburbanization has contributed to municipal economic differentiation. Economic composition not only separates rich suburbs from poor cities but also distinguishes suburbs from one another—most middle-income suburbs have a wide range of income groups, while rich and poor suburbs are more economically homogeneous. Such economic segregation bridles civic vitality. People in economically homogeneous places are less interested in politics and are less active. The remainder of the chapter outlines how this civic withdrawal reflects the changing role of local democratic institutions in segregated suburbs. Democratic government is supposed to provide a place where diverse social groups come together and peacefully resolve their differences. But when social classes are divided by municipal borders and people cease to participate in politics, local governments lose their republican character. Most important, economic segregation limits the range of interests that can get represented.

Chapter 4 is about the civic paradoxes of racial segregation. With suburbanization, an overwhelming number of suburban municipalities have become predominantly white, while most larger cities are racially heterogeneous. This racial bifurcation has mixed implications for democracy in suburbia. For more social or symbolic types of civic behavior, such as voting and organizational participation, racial homogeneity is a stimulant for activity—both whites and blacks who live among more of their own race are more likely to take part in these activities. For more instrumental types of civic action, however, racial segregation deters citizen involvement. People of all races in predominantly white communities are much less likely to work with neighbors, contact officials, or lobby community boards, largely because such places face few of the problems of more urbanized and racially integrated communities. By separating racial groups along municipal boundaries, suburbanization stifles debate around racial issues, effectively demobilizing citizens from public life.

In Chapter 5, I explore the impact of residential land use. Land use is central to local politics, dictating the agenda of public debate, the direction of public resources, and the character of governing regimes. One of the key characteristics of suburbanization has been the creation of cities made up of nothing but homes. In these "bedroom suburbs," zoning codes bar most nonresidential development and restrict the range of local political conflict. Since people in bedroom suburbs must go to other places to work, shop, and even play, they spend less time in their home communities and are less socially connected to their neighbors. Contrary to the stereotype of the alienated suburbanite, the data show that people in "residentially predominant" places are no more disengaged, apathetic, and removed from politics than people in cities with mixed land uses, once the racial and economic composition of the bedroom suburb is taken into account. In other words, at first glance people in bedroom suburbs are less civically involved, but this is only because of the affluence and racial segregation of their communities. Although land use may be an important determinant of policy making in city halls, it is not a crucial factor in shaping the civic actions of the mass public.

Metropolitan expansion has also increased the differentiation of places by their building age. In the past thirty years, "Snow Belt" places like Cleveland and Buffalo have lost population, while "Sun Belt" places like Atlanta, Dallas, and Phoenix have doubled in size. Some researchers have observed high levels of civic activity in new places. New suburbanites are often portrayed as pioneers, making a fresh start and collectively engaged in community building. Other critics, however, believe that the design and architectural forms of many new places stifle spontaneous social contact, or that they lack the history and civic traditions needed to sustain an active community. Chapter 6 tests these arguments and explores the impact of place age on civic participation. People in newer places are generally no less politically active, except in the Sun Belt. Residents of young Sun Belt communities are the least civically engaged of any Americans. Further analysis reveals that these patterns are not the product of reform-style governments in the Sun Belt. The chapter then examines the distinctiveness of southern suburbanization and why the population expansion of the Sun Belt discourages political and civic activism.

Chapter 7 focuses on the role of institutional arrangements for shaping civic participation. Past research finds that residents of cities with reform-style governments (council-manager or commission governments and representatives elected at large) are more likely to vote than people in cities with mayor-council governments and representatives elected in smaller districts.[52] None of this research has examined, however, the impact of such arrangements on other types of participation. In general, I find few effects of institutions on any civic acts outside of voting. The form of institutions seems less important for local civic engagement than the political agenda that is determined by their social composition.

In chapter 8, the conclusion, I draw the findings of the previous chapters together to make some generalizations about the civic consequences of suburbanization. By creating smaller political communities within larger metropolitan sprawls, suburbanization offers great promise for nurturing America's civic health. But political fragmentation also encourages higher levels of social segregation, which, in turn, weakens civic capacity. I then speculate on what the ideal contemporary municipality might be. I argue that smaller yet more heterogeneous places, like New Rochelle, New York, should have higher participation rates than their more homogeneous counterparts. The most civically active municipalities are ones that combine the intimacy of a small town and the social diversity of a large city. Civic capacity is maximized when municipalities provide accessible venues for citizens to resolve their most important differences.

The rest of chapter 8 examines why suburban civic withdrawal should be a concern, and proposes alternatives for renewing civic life in suburbia. With suburbanization, local government becomes a mechanism of exclusion rather than a forum for public debate. Struggles over land use and public resources become contests between institutions rather than among citizens, thus undermining an important need for intermunicipal cooperation. As the federal government assigns more responsibility to localities, the solution to many urban problems, such as sprawl and poverty, depends upon active citizens and municipal cohesion. If suburbanization prevents this civic engagement and sets municipalities against each other, the ability to solve these problems is undercut.

Reversing this suburban civic malaise depends upon changing local political institutions. A little-known but important fact is that municipal government is the creature of state government. States, therefore, must bear the responsibility for reworking local institutional arrangements when their municipalities foster dysfunctional civic behavior and inhibit solutions to problems such as poverty and sprawl. While the political constituency for any such changes will be hard to find, policy advocates need to consider alternative ways of governing local areas. In this spirit I return to suggestions made by Woodrow Wilson and Robert Dahl that metropolitan areas should be governed by federations of smaller places. Metropolitan areas do constitute authentic political communities and de-

---

[52] Alford and Lee 1968, Karnig and Walter 1983.

serve to be governed as such. Indeed, the most pressing problems facing our communities, such as racial segregation, concentrations of poverty, and sprawl, are really problems of the metropolis. Creating metropolitan-level governments, as in Portland or Minneapolis, provides citizens with institutions that reflect their urbanized environment. A political system that integrates municipalities into larger metropolitan governments will produce a meaningful context for citizen activity and encourage a renewal of community and local democratic life in America.

CHAPTER TWO

All Cities Great and Small

IF AN ASTRONAUT were to look at the southwest shore of Lake Michigan from space, she could easily get the impression that she was looking at one unified, massive community. Spreading outward from the towering skyscrapers of downtown is an uninterrupted expanse of apartment buildings, homes, warehouses, office parks, and shopping centers extending for miles along Lake Michigan and westward into Illinois. Outside of the downtown, large office buildings and factory spaces periodically surface amid the thick expanse of development as thousands of cars crowd multilane highways that crisscross the whole area. From above, Chicago seems like one giant insect colony, all interdependent and interconnected.

The seamlessness of this development belies, however, a fragmented political reality. As illustrated in map 2.1, the greater Chicago Metropolitan Area, like most urbanized regions in the United States, is divided into hundreds of separate and independent political communities. Chicago itself, with over 2.7 million residents, is a colossal city, yet it holds only roughly a third of the region's 8 million residents. The lion's share of the population is spread across more than 284 surrounding municipalities and the remaining unincorporated areas of the eleven constituent counties of the Chicago metropolis. A few, like Aurora (pop. 103,543), are large places in their own right, but most of the communities, such as Bedford Park, Indian Creek, and Kinsman, contain under 25,000 residents, and many are closer in size to small towns. Chicago, far from being a single, unified community, is really a patchwork of adjacent and autonomous polities of all shapes and sizes.

This political fragmentation between elephantine Chicago and its lilliputian suburbs is a good starting point in our exploration of suburban democratic life. Philosophers since the time of Aristotle have puzzled over the optimal size for a democracy. According to most, cities as big as Chicago usually prevent citizens from actively determining many important aspects of their lives in common. When democracies become too large, citizens putatively lose the capacity to directly control their political institutions and be truly self-governing. However, if a democracy is too small, it may not be able to tackle meaningful political issues or solve many social problems. A town like Bedford Park could never build Chicago's ballparks or convention centers and would be hard-pressed to finance a public hospital or transportation system. The ideal-size polity, the

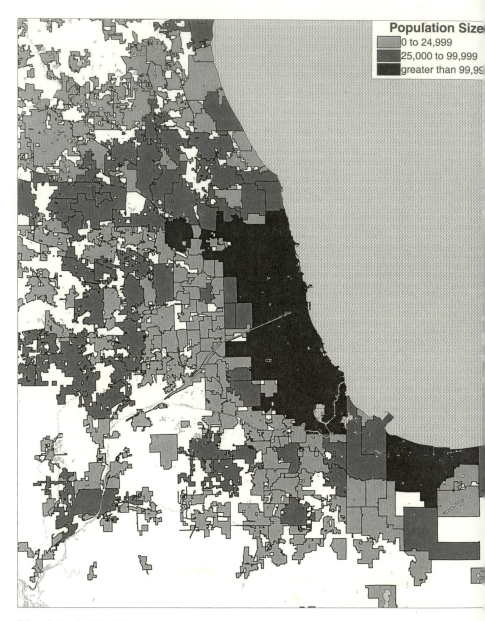

Map 2.1. Political Fragmentation in the Chicago Area

philosophers have reasoned, should be large enough to achieve collective goals but small enough that political involvement is not simply a routinized act. What is this size? Aristotle calculated it to be the number of citizens that could be gathered within shouting distance of each other; Montesquieu, the eighteenth-century French philosopher, believed democracies operated best with 20,000 citizens; Robert Dahl, the preeminent democratic theorist of *our* time, believes that the ideal solution is to reconfigure large, metropolitan areas as federations of municipalities, each with a population between 50,000 and 200,000 in size.[1]

Interestingly, current population trends are making Dahl's vision an American reality. Until quite recently, the United States was sharply bifurcated between very large and very small places. For example, at the beginning of the twentieth century, over 60 percent of Americans lived either on farms or in small towns, and as late as 1950, 40 percent still lived in rural places. Those who were not isolated in rural areas were mostly crowded into large cities. The demands of industrial production and limited transportation technologies promoted the growth of large and densely populated cities like Buffalo, Cleveland, Pittsburgh, and Trenton. This trend continued throughout the first half of the twentieth century: whereas only one in five Americans lived in a large city (over 100,000 in population) in 1900, by 1950, one in three did. At midcentury, most Americans experienced community as either a large city or an isolated rural town.

Since that time, however, the sharp distinction between city and country has blurred. On the one hand, America has become more urbanized. Between 1950 and 2000, the rural portion of the American population declined from 40 to 23 percent. Over three out of four Americans now live in a census-designated metropolitan area—regions composed of densely populated counties surrounding a city of least 50,000 people. On the other hand, proportionately fewer Americans are residing in large cities. Since 1950, the share of Americans in large cities (over 100,000 in size) has shrunk to under 25 percent. More and more Americans now live in small to medium-size municipalities or "places" within large, densely populated metropolitan areas.

This simultaneous congregation into large, metropolitan areas and fragmentation into distinct, smaller municipalities is the essence of suburbanization. The most basic definition of a suburb is that part of a metropolis not within the *political boundaries* of the central city. As is evident in the map of Chicago, suburbanization is fundamentally the political fragmentation of metropolitan populations into smaller, separate towns. Most suburban residents, although surrounded on all sides by a metro-

[1] See Dahl 1967, Dahl and Tufte 1973.

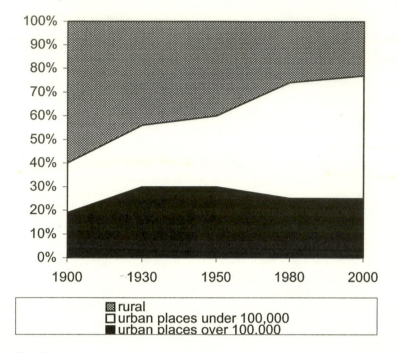

Fig. 2.1. American Urban and Rural Population by City Size, 1900–2000 (sources: U.S. Bureau of the Census, *Statistical Abstract 1995, Historical Statistics Colonial Times to 1957*)

politan area, live under a set of political rules and practices distinct from their neighbors. Chicagoans, Aurorans, and Bedford Parkers are part of the same urbanized community, but each has a different experience of local politics. This pattern of municipal political fragmentation across a densely populated urban territory is evident in almost every major metropolitan area.[2] From a population standpoint, Robert Dahl's vision seems to be unfolding. More and more Americans are living in small to medium-size cities within larger metropolitan areas.

Yet the civic consequences of this suburban political fragmentation are unclear. From an empirical standpoint, we still lack any decisive evidence on whether or how a community's size influences its residents' civic behaviors, and previous investigations have arrived at strikingly different conclusions. On one side, the migration to smaller, suburban places has

---

[2] Some commentators, most notably David Rusk (1993), have seized on this type of political fragmentation as a central element fostering urban decay. According to Rusk, central cities that are more "elastic" (i.e., that have the ability to annex the surrounding urbanized territory) are less segregated and do fiscally better than their inelastic neighbors. In this framework, political fragmentation is the most important characteristic of a metropolis.

coincided with a well-documented decline in voting and organizational membership. This coincidence suggests that people in smaller suburbs are less civically active than people in larger cities, a finding supported by some research.[3] Yet several other studies find that residents of smaller places are *more* likely to participate in local affairs.[4] Unfortunately, none of these studies are very definitive: either they fail to consider the larger metropolitan area, they compare only "urban" and "rural" places, or they base their conclusions on a small number of cases.[5]

Speculating about the civic effects of population size is also made more complicated because of new challenges for defining community in a suburban context. Until recently, it was easier to make conjectures about a community's size because most population settlements were isolated from each other by mountains, wilderness, or undeveloped land. Today, however, most suburban cities are parts of contiguous urban areas. For instance, the only way a person driving away from Chicago can tell whether she is in Evanston, Kenosha, or Schaumberg is by the color of the street signs.

Such continuous urban sprawl calls our traditional notions of community into question. If we think of community as defined primarily by local political entities, then suburbanization is the proliferation of smaller places. In other words, if municipal boundaries are important for defining community, then suburbanization is a return to small-town life. But if community means the congregation of people in geographic proximity, then community is the metropolis, as most people in urbanized areas work, shop, recreate, and even socialize in other towns. In an era of metropolitan sprawl, uninterrupted land development, and interdependent local economies, we may wonder whether the municipal boundary is still meaningful as a demarcation of community. This situation creates many perplexing questions. Is the most important community we live in our municipality or our metropolis? Does the ideal city of 50,000 residents have a richer civic life if it is isolated on a Kansas plain rather than embedded in metropolitan Chicago? This chapter explores these questions and the civic impact of city size in the contemporary metropolis.

How Size Might Harm Civic Association

There are few experiences of a large urban population more visceral than Penn Station in New York City at rush hour. Board a train in New Jersey or Long Island, and you will see a handful of people. If it's your home-

[3] Fischer 1976.
[4] Kasarda and Janowitz 1974, Nie, Powell, and Prewitt 1969, Verba and Nie 1972.
[5] Such works also fail to consider the individual-level differences of residents in big and small places, compare only "urban" and "rural" places, or draw conclusions from a small number of cases.

town, there might be an acquaintance with whom to share the ride in. People make eye contact with each other and are generally friendly. By the time you leave the train at Penn Station, the intimate and cordial experience has turned into something profoundly different. To get from the train platforms to the Seventh Avenue exit, you must brave with salmonlike fortitude thousands of harried commuters rushing forth in a torrential flood of humanity. The experience is jarring, not simply because you must dodge and jostle with so many people, but because you must dodge and jostle with so many *strangers*. In many ways, Penn Station at rush hour is an intense slice of the urban experience, for what is urban living but close contact with large numbers of unfamiliar people?

This was a central question for many of the first scholars who examined urban living. Early sociologists like Max Weber, Ferdinand Tonnies, and Louis Wirth speculated that the social environments of big cities had profoundly alienating effects on human social interaction.[6] For the better part of their history, humans have gathered mostly in small settlements of fewer than eighty people. These small communities created highly overlapping social relations. People knew their neighbors over generations, residents had emotional ties to each other, and social norms were rigidly enforced through highly interconnected social networks. In short, rural, small-town life was an experience of intense familiarity and interdependence among community members. With the emergence of large cities in the industrial era, the associational life of people dramatically changed. The size, density, and social heterogeneity of larger cities radically altered rural patterns of social interaction. Because people in large cities are surrounded by so many strangers, the early sociologists reasoned, they must retreat into more private-regarding orientations. Unlike the familiarity of small towns, social relations in large cities were seen as more superficial, rational, or mercenary. Later scholars have tried to verify the existence of urban alienation with a variety of perspectives. Whether through experiments with overcrowded rats or comparative studies of helping behavior, many researchers have concluded that living in larger, more crowded settings makes people more individualistic, predatory, and cut off from a greater community.[7]

This characterization of urban living has profound consequences for our inquiry into suburban civic life. As I noted in chapter 1, social contexts influence civic interaction primarily by changing people's psychological interest in their communities, their patterns of social interaction, or the importance of their own individual resources and skills. According to these early characterizations of urban life, larger populations close off

[6] See Weber 1986 [1898], Tonnies 1988 [1898], Wirth 1969 [1939].
[7] Freedman 1975, Levine, Martinez, and Brase 1994.

these pathways to civic engagement. If these early theories about urbanism are correct, living around more people may depress civic activity in all three ways.

First, large places dampen citizens' psychological connections to their community and their interest in local political life. According to many researchers, the psychological consequences of urban residence are profound. Surrounded by more strangers and greater social uncertainty, big-city residents are more likely to be solitary, to seek psychic refuge in their primary social relations, to shy away from spontaneous social contact, and to feel content as bystanders to public activities.[8] Such behavior is not conducive to active citizen participation. If the size and scope of a community is so large that residents feel little efficacy in the realm of local affairs or little identification with their neighbors, they are less likely to involve themselves in local activities. With so little citizen interest, civic participation in big cities will diminish.

Second, people in smaller communities are likely to have what sociologists call geographically proximate social networks. In other words, people in smaller towns are likely to know their neighbors or run into acquaintances in public places, while residents of larger cities tend to be less familiar with people they live near, are less likely to have friends in common, and are less likely to see familiar faces on their streets. This fact is a simple function of community size. To meet every resident of Chicago (assuming a minute per person and sleepless nights) would take over five years; in a town like Bedford Park, it could be done in less than a day. With so many strangers in such a small place, social relations between neighbors in larger places are less likely to be geographically proximate. This social dislocation has profound consequences for civic life because friends and neighbors are important conduits for community involvement.

Finally, civic participation may be more difficult in larger cities, thus discouraging citizen action. Larger cities require more complex bureaucracies, their city offices and citizens are spatially farther apart, and their elected officials represent more people. This may make relatively simple acts, such as attending organizational meetings or political functions, more time-consuming or costly. For instance, if, by living in a big city, I have to drive across a city, fight traffic, search and pay for parking, and find where to go, I'm probably less likely to attend a city council meeting. Or, given the range of alternative activities that larger communities provide, the opportunity costs of sitting in on the council meeting may be quite high. Civic activity may be more attractive in a small place with few theaters, restaurants, or museums, because there is nothing else to

---

[8] Finifter 1970, Latane and Darley 1970, Reisman 1953, Verba and Nie 1972.

do. In short, the hassles and many distractions of big-city living may reduce the incentives of people to get involved with their community.

How Size Might Enhance Civic Association

This negative characterization of civic life in larger communities, however, is not shared by all. Many contemporary studies have challenged these traditional views of urban living and even suggest that larger cities are beneficial for civic activity. Perhaps the most persuasive critic is sociologist Claude Fischer. After twenty-five years of research, Fischer has provided convincing evidence that big-city residents do not suffer any distinct psychological consequences from living in an urban environment.[9] People in suburbs or on farms do not have personalities that are any different from those of dwellers in large cities, nor are they any more lonely or profoundly alienated. Fischer believes that this is because larger urban areas typically spawn a wide variety of subcultures. While people in bigger cities may not be as affectively close to their neighbors, that does not mean they are without social connections. They can and do form intense bonds based on shared interests or identities. For example, in a city like Boston, on any given night one can attend meetings of the Fenway Action Coalition, the Insight Meditation Society, the New England Science Fiction Association, or the Boston Mycological Club. With so many people in one geographic area, large communities provide a critical mass allowing such distinct subcultures to form, subcultures that then draw people into associational life. Indeed, people have opportunities to find others who share their idiosyncratic and distinct passions, thus forming more intense social bonds.

Outside of providing more subcultures, larger populations may stimulate citizen activity in other ways. As Robert Dahl has noted, the greatest advantage of larger democracies is that they are able to accomplish a larger and more meaningful array of public projects and, therefore, have a more interesting political life.[10] Compare, for example, the political issues facing New York City and New Paltz, New York. New York City has a budget of $34 billion a year. It provides for mass transit, hospitals, social services, parks, stadiums, convention centers, and scores of other public services. The city manages over 600,000 units of public housing—which house more people than all but the fourteen largest American cities! New Paltz, in contrast, has a city budget of $5 million and is concerned mostly with basic municipal services such as police, fire, sewage, water, and road-

[9] See Fischer 1982, 1996.
[10] Dahl 1967.

ways. For any large-scale public services, it is heavily dependent upon the state or federal government.

According to Dahl, the larger public endeavors of big cities create more compelling issues that ignite citizen interest, foster political coalitions, and stimulate more citizen activity. For instance, New York City has scores of public interest groups that revolve around its services, ranging from the Straphangers, a commuter advocacy group, to the Green Guerillas, an organization that promotes reclamation of abandoned city lots. These organizations mobilize voters, distribute information, bring people together, and draw isolated citizens into the public realm. In short, the higher degree of state-sponsored activity in a large city like New York can foster more interest groups that create civil society.

Finally, as a result of the greater media markets of larger communities, local issues will be better publicized than in smaller places. Most large cities have their own television coverage and newspapers that focus on local issues. Such professional information services should keep residents more informed on public issues and interested in local politics. Smaller municipalities, particularly those that sit in the shadow of large cities, do not have these conduits of information. As a result, their residents are often less informed about political issues. For instance, it is likely that more people on Long Island can identify the mayor of New York City than can name their own municipal head. If interest and mobilization are the pillars of active citizen participation, the high-stakes politics of larger cities could be a bigger draw for citizens into public life.

COMMUNITY AS THE METROPOLIS

Thus we have good reasons for thinking that larger municipal populations can be both a benefit and a hindrance to civic participation. These reasons get further complicated if we conceive of community not in terms of local municipal boundaries but in terms of larger metropolitan areas. For suburbanization is the migration not simply to smaller places, but to smaller places *within* larger metropolitan areas. It is unclear whether the effects of municipal size outlined above are equally applicable for a metropolitan area. In other words, one may live in a smaller municipality like Bedford Park, but if it is embedded within a larger, contiguous metropolitan Chicago, the effects of a smaller population size may be completely overshadowed. In our metropolitan era, do municipal boundaries create community?

The answer to this question is uncertain. If city boundaries are unimportant amid a surrounding urbanized population, then the effects of metropolitan areas should both replicate and overshadow the effects of city size. In other words, if simply being proximate with more people makes one feel more alienated, then it should not matter whether those people are partitioned by the invisible walls of a municipal border. The crucial contextual element, in this instance, is the number of people in a given geographic region, not simply the number within a particular municipal jurisdiction. The effects of population size will be determined by the size of the metropolis, not the city, and the biggest differences in civic participation will occur between small rural places and large metropolitan regions.

If, on the other hand, city boundaries are important for defining the character of local political engagement or patterns of social interaction, then the effects of place size should occur irrespective of the size of the surrounding metropolitan area. In this case, differences between large and small places should occur because political engagement and mobilization arise primarily from the community as defined by the city boundaries. If this is true, small, rural places should have levels of participation similar to those of their counterparts that are embedded within a sprawling metropolis. Since past research has generally not compared the importance of city size relative to metropolitan area size, these speculations remain unresolved.

Differences in Civic Behavior

We can begin to settle these questions with some simple statistics comparing average rates of participation in several civic activities across several increments of city size. Figure 2.2 illustrates the average levels of participation in all five activities across a five-point place-size scale (less than 5,000, 5,000 to 50,000, 50,000 to 250,000, 250,000 to one million, and more than one million), showing separate figures for people in metropolitan and rural areas. For the first three civic activities (contacting officials and attending board and organizational meetings), steady declines occur as city size grows, although this effect is largely limited to residents of metropolitan areas. For example, 40 percent of residents of the smallest towns in a metropolis (under 5,000 in size) reported contacting locally elected officials, compared to only 30 percent in medium-size places (5,000 to 50,000 in size) and 25 percent in the biggest cities (over one million). Meeting attendance declines thirteen percentage points between the smallest and the largest metropolitan places for community boards and twelve percentage points for voluntary organizations. People in the smallest metropolitan places (under 5,000 in size) are also more likely to work informally with neighbors and report the highest rates of local voting, but among larger cities there are no consistent patterns.

In rural towns, those places outside of census-designated metropolitan

Metropolitan Areas

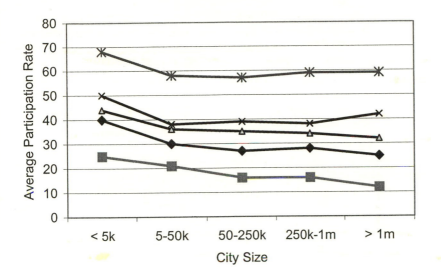

Rural Areas

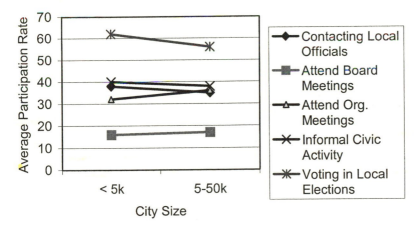

Fig. 2.2. Average Rates of Civic Participation by City Size for Rural and Metropolitan Areas (source: 1990 Citizen Participation / 1990 U.S. Census Dataset)

areas, there are few consistent differences in the effects of community size. Contacting and voting rates decline between small (under 5,000) and larger (over 5,000) towns, but attendance of community board or organizational meetings actually increases. Informal activism stays about the same. Most of the differences, however, between small and medium-size rural towns are not great enough to be considered statistically significant. For example, the differences in rates of contacting, meeting attendance, and informal activism between rural towns under and over 5,000 in size are all less than four percentage points. Interestingly, participation is lower in rural places than in those of the same size within metropolitan areas: the average rate of attending community meetings is 9 percent lower in rural towns under 5,000 in size than in their counterparts in metropolitan areas. The effects of city size are also much greater in metropolitan areas. The differences between small and medium-size towns in rural areas typically are within three or four percentage points but are often ten percentage points or more in metropolitan areas.

Thus, from these simple figures, it appears that civic participation diminishes in larger places, at least among those in metropolitan areas. In four of the five indicators of civic activity, steady declines occur with increases in municipal population size. The highest participation rates are among the smallest metropolitan places; the lowest rates are usually in the largest central cities. Yet in rural areas these patterns do not hold—participation does not seem to drop in larger rural towns compared to their smaller counterparts. What accounts for these rural anomalies? Why does participation drop with place size in metropolitan areas but not rural areas?

Part of the answer may lie in the differences between the types of people who live in small and larger places and in rural and metropolitan areas. In other words, the changes across city sizes and between rural and metropolitan areas may be due not to the social contexts but to demographic differences among people who live in these places. For example, as illustrated in table 2.1, people in rural and metropolitan areas differ in their education, age, homeownership, and median household income. Compared to residents of metropolitan areas, rural folk on average have completed almost a year less of school and live in places with median household incomes almost $10,000 a year lower. As both individual education and city-level income are important determinants of civic participation, these low resource levels may be the source of lower rural participation rates. Yet rural residents are also older and more likely to own homes, individual factors that correlate with higher civic participation. Furthermore, despite the steady decreases in civic participation within metropolitan areas, there are few demographic variations by size in the

Table 2.1
Average Education, Age, Homeownership, and Median Household Income by
Place Size for Rural and Metropolitan Areas

	Years of School Completed	*Age*	*Percent Homeowners*	*Median Income*	*ncases*
Rural areas					
Less than 5,000	12.4	44.9	72	$18,676	(243)
5,000 to 50,000	13.2	43.7	67	$19,990	(292)
Rural area average	12.8	44.2	69	$19,393	(535)
Metropolitan areas					
Less than 5,000	13.2	40.4	81	$28,527	(152)
5,000 to 50,000	13.6	41.1	72	$35,565	(477)
50,000 to 250,000	13.8	39.7	59	$28,719	(492)
250,000 to 1 million	13.9	40.6	53	$24,831	(298)
More than 1 million	13.7	39.8	42	$27,939	(240)
Metropolitan average	13.7	40.3	61	$29,283	(1659)

Source: 1990 Citizen Participation/1990 U.S. Census Dataset.

metropolis—residents of small metropolitan places have, on average, similar education, income, and age levels to people in large cities. The only demographic variance is that residents of smaller places in metropolitan areas are more likely to be homeowners. Given these confounding demographic characteristics, multivariate equations are in order to isolate the specific effects of city size.

Toward this end, I employ a logistic regression that allows the independent effects of city size to be estimated while simultaneously controlling for individual-level differences in education, age, income, and the like. Other city-level characteristics, affluence and racial composition, are also controlled, as well as whether the place is in a rural area or a large metropolitan area (over 2.5 million in size). Interaction terms also calculated the distinct effects of city size in rural and large metropolitan areas. To illustrate the full equations, I have listed them in table 2.2. However, as this book will contain a large number of such equations I will also translate the coefficients for city size into predicted probabilities and depict them figuratively. For example, figure 2.3 depicts the predicted rates of nonelectoral civic participation across five categories of cities, for residents of small and large metropolitan areas and rural areas, with the indi-

TABLE 2.2
The Effects of City and Metropolitan Area Size on Local Civic Participation with Controls for Individual and Contextual Population Characteristics (standard error in parentheses)

	Contact Officials		Attend Board Meeting		Attend Org. Meeting		Informal Civic Activity		Vote Local Elections	
City variables										
City size	−.133**	(.037)	−.165**	(.045)	−.047	(.038)	−.091**	(.035)	−.086*	(.015)
Med. hse. inc.	−.013*	(.007)	−.021*	(.009)	−.019**	(.007)	−.016**	(.007)	−.011	(.007)
Percent white	−.419	(.366)	−1.00*	(.426)	.886**	(.374)	−.267	(.433)	−.253	(.363)
Large metro area	−.669*	(.317)	.337	(.369)	−.395	(.318)	−.235	(.298)	−1.13**	(.322)
Rural	.039	(.236)	−.518	(.303)	−.189	(.247)	−.153	(.230)	−.216	(.247)
Large metro × city size	.102*	(.051)	−.032	(.062)	.069	(.051)	.078	(.047)	.168**	(.051)
Rural × city size	−.002	(.078)	.146	(.101)	−.005	(.082)	−.008	(.075)	−.075	(.081)
Other variables										
Education	.431**	(.047)	.394**	(.058)	.431**	(.049)	.430**	(.043)	.525**	(.048)
Income	.155**	(.035)	.199**	(.044)	.204**	(.054)	.183**	(.033)	.154**	(.036)
Age	.008**	(.004)	.008	(.005)	.007	(.003)	.006*	(.003)	.056**	(.004)
Homeowner	.354**	(.126)	.585**	(.174)	.419**	(.134)	.233*	(.115)	.452**	(.118)
Black	−.168	(.157)	−.299	(.199)	.321*	(.147)	.471**	(.135)	.083	(.143)
Female	−.230*	(.104)	−.188	(.128)	−.103	(.101)	−.011	(.097)	.097	(.105)
Length of residence	.368**	(.135)	.171	(.170)	.179	(.199)	.288	(.124)	−.089	(.128)
South	−.146	(.122)	−.285	(.153)	−.103	(.121)	−.021	(.115)	−.211	(.122)
Cox & Snell r-sq.	.12		.10		.13		.13		.22	
ncases	2,032		1,914		2,038		2,034		2,022	

Source: 1990 Citizen Participation / 1990 U.S. Census Dataset.
Note: Excluded category is metropolitan area under 2.5 million in size.

*p < .05 **p < .01

vidual demographic differences of the populations controlled.[11] In short, this is the predicted change in participation across the city size scale from the data listed in table 2.2. This is also a prediction of what figure 2.2 would look like if everyone in the population had the same education, age, income, and so forth, and every place had the same income and racial composition. For future purposes, the full equations for figures based on multivariate analyses will be listed in Appendix B.

Even when other individual and place-level characteristics are controlled for in the regression analyses, the same negative relationship generally occurs between civic participation and city size. For instance, among residents of metropolitan areas, the coefficients from logistic equations predict the following differences in civic participation between the smallest (under 2,500 in population) and largest places (over one million): contacting local officials drops by eight percentage points, attending community board meetings by nearly twenty percentage points, and working informally on community issues drops by fourteen percentage points for people in smaller metropolitan areas and five percentage points for residents of larger metropolitan areas.[12] Organizational meeting attendance declines in smaller metropolitan areas but slightly rises in larger metropolitan areas, although neither of these differences is statistically significant. Indeed, the only civic activity to increase in larger places is voting, among large cities of large metropolitan areas.[13] Otherwise, across all five civic activities, the pattern is the same—the larger the city size, the lower the level of civic participation. Even though civic activities like voting and attending organizational meetings are very different in their requirements and nature, the effects of city size are usually the same. Although larger cities may vary considerably by neighborhood, as a whole, compared to smaller municipalities, large cities have less civic engagement.

Several other characteristics of these findings are also noteworthy. One striking factor is that the differences between rural and metropolitan areas

[11] Probability estimates for the logit coefficients were calculated by evaluation of each coefficient on the logistic function. This generated a new figure, which was then subtracted from the probability estimate of the particular variable (calculated by evaluation of all the coefficients on the logistic function with the value of the coefficient for the particular variable set to its lowest value). The overall probability is derived by aggregation of these differences across the entire sample for each value on the city size scale. For a full description of this procedure, see Wolfinger and Rosenstone 1980, p. 123.

[12] I created a dichotomous measure of voting in local elections by recoding the frequency of voting in local elections scale so that a value of 1 signifies those who vote in every or most local elections, while a value of 0 represents those who never, rarely, or sometimes vote in local contests.

[13] Much of this is probably attributable to higher voting in very large cities like New York, Chicago, and Los Angeles, with high-profile and high-spending mayoral campaigns.

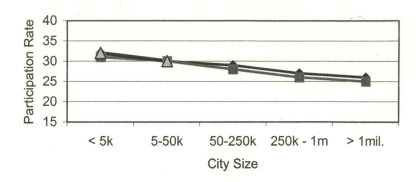

Contacting Local Officials

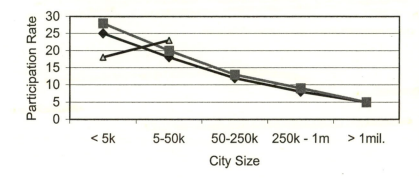

Attend Community Board Meetings

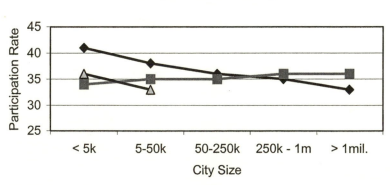

Attend Organizational Meetings

Fig. 2.3. Predicted Rates of Civic Participation by City Size for Rural Areas and Small and Large Metropolitan Areas (full equations in Appendix B)

Informal Civic Activity

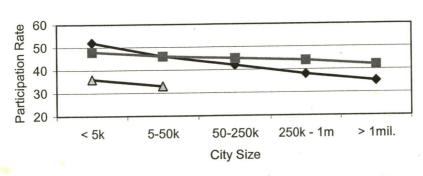

Voting in Local Elections

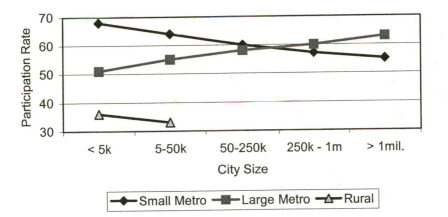

Fig. 2.3. *Continued*

come from the individual demographic characteristics associated with city size, specifically education and income. In all the multivariate equations, the coefficients for the rural term are generally small and have no statistical significance. Once the lower individual-level education and income levels of rural folks are taken into account, their nonelectoral participation rates are no different from those of people in metropolitan areas.[14]

[14] Subsequent multivariate analyses demonstrate that when just city size is controlled, rural residents have lower participation rates for attending board and organizational meetings and for voting. When additional variables measuring everything but education and income are included, people in rural areas continue to have lower participation rates, although the

The one exception is voting—people in rural areas report voting less frequently, although this difference is not statistically significant. Nor is the effect of city size in rural areas any different either. As illustrated in table 2.2, the equations contain interaction terms between city size and rural residence. These terms capture whatever extra effect a greater city size may have in rural areas. Outside of attending community board meetings, the coefficients for the interactive terms are small and negative. Thus we might predict that people in small, rural places are slightly more likely to participate than rural folks in larger places, although the low levels of statistical significance do not warrant much confidence in such predictions.

Another interesting finding is how much city size affects local civic activity. Political scientists typically focus on the differences between individuals based on their age or education; For instance, college-educated citizens are much more likely to vote than high school dropouts. But these results show large differences occurring by a city's size as well. The predicted difference in civic participation between the smallest and largest places are larger than most differences across individual-level demographic traits, except for education and income. In other words, the differences in contacting or board meeting attendance between small towns and large places are greater than those between renters and homeowners, men and women, or whites and blacks.

Also noteworthy is the fact that civic participation steadily declines with increases in a city's population. The predictions listed in figure 2.2 are what we would expect the average rates of civic participation to be for ten increments of city size. While not exactly linear, these civic declines are steady. For example, the model predicts that residents of a small suburb like Woodside, California (pop. 4,300), are 5 percent more likely to attend a local community board meeting than those in nearby Cupertino (pop. 41,000), who are 8 percent more likely than people in neighboring San Jose (pop. 750,000). The effect of city size is continuous: the larger a city becomes, the less likely it is that its citizens will participate in local affairs.

The other interesting findings from these tables come with respect to metropolitan areas. The depressing effects of municipal population size on nonelectoral civic participation occur irrespective of the size of the surrounding metropolitan area.[15] By itself, metropolitan area size has no

---

differences are no longer statistically significant. When the education and income measures are included, the rural coefficients attenuate greatly in size. This demonstrates that the lower levels of rural participation are due largely to socioeconomic differences. Interestingly, rural folks are always more likely to contact local officials, no matter what controls are added, although this difference is not statistically significant.

[15] For this test, interaction terms were created between the city size dummy variables and dummy variables for different increments of metropolitan area size (less than 1 million, 1

effect: none of the equations predict significant differences in nonelectoral participation between residents of rural areas or small and large metropolitan areas. Moreover, controlling for metropolitan area size generally has little impact on the magnitude of the city size effect.[16] Nor do the effects of city size grow with the size of the metropolitan area—the interaction terms between metropolitan area size and city size do not yield any significant coefficients for any civic activity. The one exception to this trend is with voting. Big-city residents of larger metropolitan areas are more likely to vote in local elections. This is probably a function of the high visibility campaigns in large cities like New York, Chicago, and Los Angeles. It may also be the consequence of mobilizing structures within the campaigns of larger cities. In smaller metropolitan areas, the equations predict lower rates of voting in medium-size cities. Nevertheless, the general trend is that civic participation declines in larger cities regardless of how big the surrounding metropolitan area may be. In other words, the model predicts that compared to those in Chicago, people in a city the size of Minooka, Illinois (pop. 2,563), are no less likely to participate in local civic activities than people in the rural and similar-size Muleshoe, Texas, even though the former are nestled within a metropolitan area of eight million people and the latter are isolated on the north Texas plains.

This last finding demonstrates the importance of city boundaries for shaping civic life. Most theories on the effects of city population size assume that people react to their municipality as a contained community, even if that city is contiguous to a larger metropolitan area. For example, the hypothesis that people in larger places are more psychologically disengaged is predicated upon the assumption that people view their city rather than their metropolitan area as their primary environment. We suspect that Minookans are more likely than New Yorkers to feel connected to their community or know their neighbors because the boundaries of Minooka somehow define a community that its residents identify with, even though those boundaries may be physically demarcated by nothing more than a street sign. The absence of any interaction effect based on rural or metropolitan area size validates this conjecture. From the models

---

million to 2.5 million, greater than 2.5 million). These terms were included in the regression equation. None of them yielded any statistically significant coefficients save for cities between 100,000 and 250,000 in size that were in metropolitan areas less than 1 million in size. Residents of the central cities of small metropolitan areas were 3 percent more likely to report an organizational affiliation than residents of similar-size cities in large metropolitan areas. These findings represent the only significant deviation from the negative, linear relationship between city size and participation, and the only difference by virtue of metropolitan area size.

[16] The predicted variations in participation by city size are roughly the same in the multivariate equations as they are in the cross-tabulations illustrated in figure 2.2.

above, we would predict Muleshoers and Minookans are equally more likely to participate in a wide variety of civic activities than Chicagoans. In sum, *city size is an important characteristic, in itself, for defining the civic behavior of its residents; for most civic acts, the bigger the city, the lower the level of civic involvement, even when that place is a small suburb nestled within a huge metropolis.*

CAUSES OF THE CITY SIZE EFFECT

Why does civic participation drop so sharply in larger cities? Borrowing insights from the civic voluntarism model, we can look to three possible causes: larger cities increase the importance of individual skills and resources, they make people more psychologically withdrawn, or they change the pathways by which people get recruited into civic life. To further understand why civic participation declines, we need to examine how each of these three determinants changes with the size of a municipal population.

Skills and Resources

The city of Houston, Texas, comprises over 1.5 million people spread over more than six hundred square miles, making it nearly half the size of the state of Rhode Island. For most Houstonians, attending a meeting of the city council or the local chapter of the Audubon Society involves a long journey. Since Houston has a very minimal public transportation system, active participation depends upon a car, which also involves the expenses of car maintenance, auto insurance, and finding and paying for parking. By contrast, nearby Bellaire has only 14,000 residents and is only eight square miles in size. While this does not make attending Audubon Society meetings any easier, for most other local civic events such as city council or school board meetings, this small size is an advantage. To attend a community board or council meeting, Bellairites need drive only ten minutes at most, and many can simply walk or bike. If individual skills and resources are an important determinant of civic voluntarism, then these factors may explain why participation drops so much in larger places. Faced with larger and more complex bureaucracies, greater distances to public offices, and larger-scale political organizations, residents of big cities may find even the most simple civic activities very difficult. For example, Houston has a large organizational structure handling street maintenance. If a Houstonian wants a pothole filled, he will have to work through myriad bureaucratic offices and file a request that will be handled with hundreds of others, and he must expect less personal accountability from public officials. By contrast, a Bellairite seeking a pothole repair has a smaller bureaucracy to negotiate, can more easily contact an official, and will probably have just one official responsible for the complaint. One could easily find analogous examples with other civic or organizational activities. It seems a safe bet that local civic participation is considerably easier in a smaller governmental unit such as Bellaire than in a large one like Houston.

But is this really the case? A good way to test this assertion is to compare people's sense of control over their political institutions, a characteristic typically known as efficacy. Many political scientists believe that efficacy is an important determinant of civic participation.[17] Researchers have found that when participation is too difficult or citizens feel their actions are meaningless, they have few reasons to get involved in public activities. These feelings of efficacy change with the population size of a city. For example, figure 2.4 illustrates the average scores on measures of citizen efficacy over both local and national government decisions. In the first box are measures of two four-point scales on how much influence respondents feel they have over local government decisions and how responsive they feel local governments are to their complaints. People in larger places report lower average levels of local influence than do those in smaller places. For example, respondents in cities of over one million score, on average, 0.4 points lower on this scale than residents of towns under 5,000 in size. Similar results occur for a measure of how responsive people feel local governments are to their complaints: people in larger cities report, on average, lower levels of responsiveness of local government, with people in small towns scoring 0.3 points higher than their counterparts in the largest cities. But, as illustrated in the second box, people in larger cities do not feel less empowered with respect to national politics. There are no steady or clear patterns between city size and national political institutions. Indeed, people in large cities (those between 250,000 and one million in size) report the highest levels of national political efficacy. Clearly, the size and complexity of big-city governments make residents feel disempowered about local politics.

But while this finding is suggestive, it is not conclusive. For if civic participation is really more costly or difficult in big cities, then the effects should be evident across different subpopulations. For example, in their study of electoral participation, Wolfinger and Rosenstone argue that the young or uneducated are less likely to vote where registration is more difficult, because these resource-poor groups find the bureaucratic hurdles of registering more consequential.[18] The size and scope of civic activity in big cities may cause a similar pattern. If contacting an elected offi-

---

[17] Verba and Nie 1972, Abramson and Aldrich 1982.
[18] Wolfinger and Rosenstone 1980.

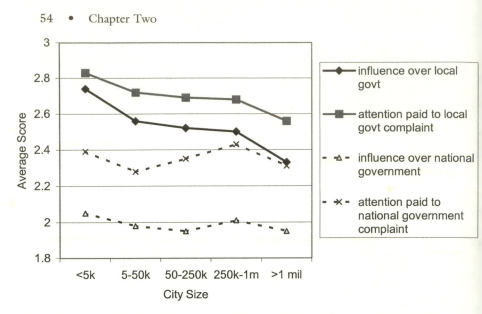

Fig. 2.4. Average Levels of Local and National Political Efficacy by City Size (source: 1990 Citizen Participation / 1990 U.S. Census Dataset)

cial or attending an organizational meeting is more difficult in Houston than it is in Bellaire, then the differences in contacting and meeting attendance between the two cities should be greater for citizens with fewer resources, such as high school dropouts, than for those with college degrees.

The data, however, provide no evidence of systematic differences in the effects of city size according to individual resources. Figure 2.5 lists the average rate of civic participation (from a measure that combines all five civic activities) across the five categories of city size for three individual education levels: those with a high school diploma or less, those with some college education but no degree, and those with a college degree or more. Although the average rates of participation across the civic activities are lower among the less educated, as we would expect, the differences across the city size scale are no greater. In fact, the effects of city size are larger for the more educated. For example, among the college educated, the average rate of civic participation on this five-point scale differs by more than an entire point. This would be a 20 percent difference in average civic participation; for those with a college degree, the effect is nearly the same. But for those with only a high school diploma or less, the effects of city size are not so consistent: the average civic participation score drops slightly from small to medium-size cities but then increases in the largest places. If civic participation is really more

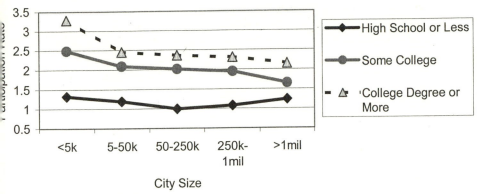

Fig. 2.5. Average Rate of Civic Participation by City Size for Three Educational Groups (source: 1990 Citizen Participation / 1990 U.S. Census Dataset)

costly in larger places, then we should find the greatest differences in the effects of city size among the less educated; instead, we find much larger differences among those subpopulations with higher overall participation rates. More sophisticated tests using multivariate equations also demonstrate similar findings: the effects of city size on civic participation are no greater for those who are less educated, younger, or poorer than for their resource-rich counterparts.[19]

Thus we have mixed evidence that skills or resources are important factors behind the lower participation rates in larger cities. On the one hand, people in larger cities do feel less efficacious with respect to local politics. This sense of disempowerment may reflect the difficulty of participating in large-scale democratic institutions and may increase the relevance of civic skills and resources. But, if civic action is more difficult in big cities, then the young, poor, and uneducated should be more deterred from participating in larger places. This, however, does not happen. Citizens with fewer skills and resources are no more affected by city size than those who are well endowed with civic knowledge. Indeed, the greatest effects of city size occur among those citizens with the most civic

[19] To test for these individual-level resource differences, I estimated the equations with interaction terms between city size and the three categories of education, three categories of age (under 35, 35 to 64, over 64), and four categories of annual family income (under $20,000, $20,000 to <$35,000, $35,000 to $60,000, and over $60,000). In none of the equations did the interaction terms between individual resources and city size yield any large or statistically significant coefficients. The equations predict that the effects of city size are no different among those with a high school diploma or less, those with some college education, and those with a college degree. Similarly negative results were also found when the other measures of individual resources (e.g., age and income) were substituted for the education measure.

skills. Participation maybe more difficult in a larger city, but that difficulty does not change the types of people who are participating.

Psychological Engagement

A second factor that explains civic participation has to do with people's interest in and attachment to their communities. To illustrate this point, let us detour slightly and compare two communities. Rhinebeck, New York, is a charming town of 2,800 residents a hundred miles up the Hudson River valley from New York City. It is also, by any measure, a much cleaner place than its large neighbor. Even along New York's nicest streets and avenues, small bits of trash, discarded cups and bottles, and cigarette wrappers seem to be perennial. Most of Rhinebeck's streets look clean enough to picnic on. Of course, with so many more people generating so much more garbage in such a small space, New York's filth, like that of most major cities, is an understandable consequence of its size. But population size cannot completely explain the trash: New York has an ample number of trash receptacles and squadrons of street-sweeping trucks running day and night; Rhinebeck's commercial streets, particularly on weekends, get a lot of foot traffic from strangers. Clearly, the behavior of average pedestrians must also be a contributing factor. After all, the average New Yorker is not imagined as someone who picks up random garbage on the street.

These impressions have been confirmed in numerous studies comparing urban and rural pro-social behavior. For example, psychologist Robert Levine conducted a series of experiments in helping behavior across dozens of American cities. In the experiments, the researchers take part in a number of behaviors that might require some public action: dropping a pen, requesting change for a dollar, feigning injury, and so forth. After repeated trials they found that residents of large and dense cities like New York, Los Angeles, and Chicago scored much lower in helping behavior, on average, than residents of smaller places like Knoxville, Rochester, and Canton, Ohio. Levine has concluded that people in dense, larger cities are less public regarding.[20]

So why might a city's size shape its residents' attachment to their neighbors and communities? Scholars have offered a variety of explanations. As noted above, early sociologists speculated that the size and social heterogeneity of large cities make their residents more psychologically disengaged from their community; yet later sociologists find little evidence that people in larger cities are any more alienated than

[20] Levine, Martinez, and Brase 1994.

people in small towns.[21] Across scores of studies of urban attitudes and behavior, there are few indications that urban residents have distinct personalities. People in big cities and small towns are equally likely to express the same levels of depression, isolation, and hostility.

Although people in big cities may not have a distinct "urban personality," their civic orientation may be altered by the *situation* of living in a larger place. Psychologists have found that the stress, crowding, and noise of many urban environments may provoke repeated types of *responses*, such as anger, hostility, and antisocial behavior. While these are factors present in most large cities, is there anything about the particular *size* of a place that generates withdrawal? Among the many theories that address how people respond to larger populations, probably the most plausible explanation is that because larger cities' inhabitants share civic responsibilities with so many more strangers, these places may create conditions for "bystander effects." A bystander effect is the phenomenon of someone's being less likely to help a stranger as the number of surrounding people gets larger. In scores of separate experiments, psychologists have found that while isolated individuals are usually willing to help others in need, when the number of other potential helpers increases, people become much more reticent.[22] Researchers believe this is because the presence of others makes individuals believe that someone else may be better able or more willing to take care of the problem—when people are by themselves, they are likely to take responsibility and act on their own. People in larger places may not work with neighbors, join organizations, or contact officials because they believe others will take care of the social problems these organizations address. Indeed, this is similar to the collective action dilemma faced by any organization. As Mancur Olson deduced, the size of an organization is directly related to ability to monitor this type of free-riding behavior—larger organizations have a more difficult time enforcing compliance, while smaller organizations have an easier time getting people to meet their responsibilities.[23] As bystanders to local affairs, people in larger places may lose interest in the well-being of their communities and withdraw into a private orientation.

Beyond looking at street cleaning, how might we tell whether a big city is filled with more bystanders? One good place to look may be in differences in local political interest. Political scientists often assert that politics is much more interesting in big cities than in small towns. With higher political stakes, a larger number of participants, and a greater visibility of politicians, it is generally assumed that bigger cities generate

---

[21] Fischer 1982.
[22] Latane and Darley 1970.
[23] Olson 1965.

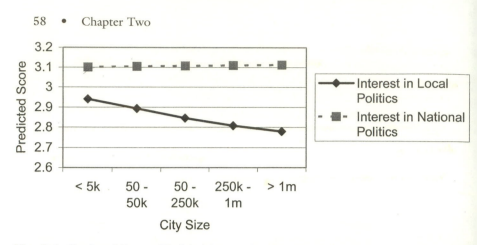

Fig. 2.6. Predicted Rates of Political Interest by City Size (full equations in Appendix B)

more interesting political controversies. But if people in larger places feel like bystanders to their communities, then their political interest may fall. Despite the greater stakes and visibility of local politics, residents may "tune out" as part of their psychological disengagement from their surroundings and be content to let others take responsibility for running their communities.

When we compare levels of political interest between large and small places, this seems to be the case. Figure 2.6 depicts the coefficients of two Ordinary Least Squares (OLS) regressions of national and local political interest on our standard set of predictors. The full equation is listed in Appendix B. When asked about their interest in local affairs, residents of larger cities are significantly less concerned than residents of smaller towns. Contrasted to people in places with populations below 5,000, people in places of more than one million score nearly 0.2 points lower on the five-point local political interest scale. But this negative relationship does not appear to reflect any generalized aversion to politics among residents of larger places. City size has no bearing at all on people's attention to national politics. When national political interest is regressed on the same set of predictors, the coefficient for city size is small and not statistically significant. As depicted by the dotted line, the regression equation finds virtually no linear relationship between national political interest and city size. In short, big-city residents do not appear any more alienated in general than their small-town counterparts. Whatever lack of interest big-city residents have in politics, it is limited to their own locale.

Clearly then, another possible reason for lower civic participation in larger communities is that people in such places are less interested in local affairs. Being surrounded by so many more people, citizens in big cities may simply feel compelled to let others take care of local community matters. In particular, the existence of more advocacy groups in larger cities may increase participation among members but stimulate more bystander effects among nonmembers. Or, as citizens in larger places feel less efficacious, the size and scope of big-city politics may simply be overwhelming. Feeling that the concerns of a distant city hall are not meaningful for them, big-city residents may simply tune out. Between the distractions of big-city life and feeling like one of millions of strangers, residents psychologically disconnect from their local community.

Mobilization

The final way that larger cities may depress civic involvement is by influencing the ways people are mobilized or recruited. One of the biggest factors influencing people's participation in voluntary or political activities is whether they are asked by others to do so. The likelihood that people are recruited depends, in turn, on their social connections.[24] Obviously, people who have more friends and acquaintances are more likely to be invited to join organizations than people who are shy and reclusive. In fact, some even consider these social networks to be the loosest form of civil society. After all, what is associational activity but another form of social connectedness? These patterns of social interaction may be sensitive to environmental effects. If a person is surrounded by people of different cultures or lifestyles, his or her ability to make friendships may be limited. The question for our purposes is whether or how these patterns of social interaction change systematically with a city's size.

Previous studies of social networks—the web of connections among individuals in a society—offer some suggestive findings. Social networks in small towns are typically portrayed as "close-knit": people are more likely to know their neighbors and to see acquaintances in public places. Think, for example, of Mayberry, the setting of the old *Andy Griffith* television show, a place where everyone is on a first-name basis and nothing escapes the watchful eye of Aunt Bea. By contrast, social networks in larger cities are typically "loose-knit": people know fewer of their neighbors, are less likely to run into friends in public places, and have less proximity and redundancy between their acquaintances.[25] The crowded streets of New York or the car-dominated highways of Los Angeles epitomize this urban social milieu where the vast majority of encounters are with strangers. Yet, like many other studies, most of this research has

[24] See Huckfeldt and Sprague 1995.
[25] Bott 1971, Fischer 1982, Janowitz 1952.

simply compared urban and rural places—we do not know whether people in small metropolitan places exhibit the socializing patterns of country
or of city folk.

It is also important to consider that social networks differ across various subpopulations; older, working, or better-educated people tend to
have a wider range of social contacts.[26] Perhaps the most interesting differences are those between men and women. As in most societies, American men and women vary considerably in their socializing patterns.
Women tend to rely on family and neighbors for more of their social
contact than men do and have more social contacts within the geographic vicinity of their homes—men tend to draw more contacts from
work, and their social networks are more geographically far-flung.[27] Although much of this gender difference is due to divisions of labor between men and women in employment and child rearing, these types of
behaviors are also rooted in earlier patterns of socialization. Even when
occupation, education, and parental status are taken into account,
women tend to have a more geographically bound range of social contacts and are much more likely to interact with either family or neighbors. These gender differences will be important for the effects of city
size. If women are more reliant than men on geographically proximate
neighbors for social contact, and neighbors are harder to know in larger
cities, then the civic effects of city size will be greater for women. In
other words, the socializing patterns of women may exacerbate the civic
consequences of city size.

The data show several differences in socializing patterns by city size.
First, people in larger cities know fewer of their neighbors. Figure 2.7
depicts the average rates of neighbor contact between men and women
across the city size scale; as the figure illustrates, people in cities over one
million in size are 8 percent less likely than people in the smallest places
to "speak regularly" with their neighbors. Despite the physical proximity
that comes from the population density of larger cities, residents of these
places are less likely to have neighborly contact. Yet most of the differences in neighboring across the city size scale are attributable to women.
Ninety-three percent of women in cities under 50,000 speak regularly
with neighbors, a figure that steadily drops to only 77 percent of women
in cities over one million in population. Men, on the other hand, show
fewer consistent patterns across the city size scale. Men in the largest
cities contact fewer neighbors, but men in medium-size cities report even
lower levels of contact. In short, women's neighboring behavior shows
consistent declines with city population sizes that men's do not.

[26] Fischer 1982.
[27] Campbell, Connidis, and Davies 1999, Pugliesi and Shook 1998.

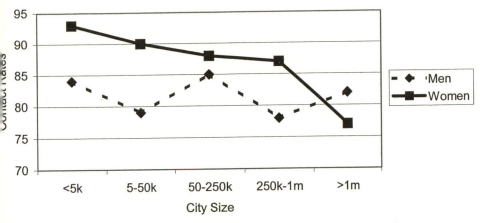

Fig. 2.7. Average Rates of Contact with Neighbors by City Size and Sex (source: 1990 Citizen Participation / 1990 U.S. Census Dataset)

Further evidence of the social consequences of city size is evident in patterns of political mobilization, with the greatest effects being, not surprisingly, for women. Figure 2.8 lists the average rates for two types of mobilization by city size for men and women. The first figure compares the probability that a respondent, in the previous year, had been asked either to take part in a campaign, to contact a public official, to take part in a protest, or to serve on a board. The second figure shows the percentage who were asked by a neighbor or acquaintance among the 58 percent who were mobilized. As expected, city size has little bearing on the likelihood that men will be politically mobilized and does not influence whether they were mobilized by an acquaintance. But among women city size is strongly related both to the likelihood of being mobilized for a political act and to the character of that mobilization. Women in big cities are 17 percent less likely to be mobilized, whereas for men this figure is only 9 percent. Moreover, differences in who is mobilizing them reveal how women's social contacts change in relation to their city's size. Compared to women in towns with fewer than 5,000 residents, women in cities with more than one million people are 20 percent less likely to be mobilized by a neighbor, whereas for men this difference is merely 6 percent. In short, the more proximate the social contact is to a woman's home, the more city size matters in determining the likelihood of her being mobilized.

These gender-based differences in social networks are also evident in certain types of civic behaviors. The absence of social contacts for women in bigger cities depresses their availability to be mobilized for civic activity, and, as we would expect, the effects of city size are greater for women

Percent Mobilized for Political Action

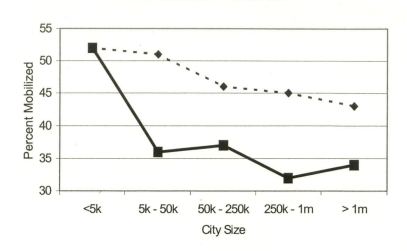

Percent Mobilized by Neighbors

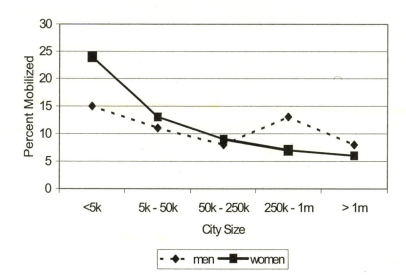

Fig. 2.8. Average Rates of Political Mobilization by City Size and Sex (source: 1990 Citizen Participation / 1990 U.S. Census Dataset)

in general and particularly among nonworking, married women of child-rearing ages. Of all the population, this group is the most constrained by their immediate social context for much of their social contact. These constraints are evident in one of the most community-oriented civic activities: attending meetings of voluntary organizations. Figure 2.9 illustrates the average rate of organizational membership by city size for three groups: men, women, and young, nonworking women. The greatest effects of city size on organizational participation are among young, female homemakers. Men living in cities over one million in size are five percentage points less likely to attend organizational meetings than people in cities under 5,000 in size; among women this figure is 18 percent; and among young, female homemakers, this figure is 23 percent! As we might expect, women with the most limited social contacts are least likely to be civically oriented, at least for one type of civic activity. Interestingly, however, these same gender effects do not occur for other types of civic activities, particularly others we might expect, such as informal action with neighbors or attending community board meetings. Other factors, such as political interest and efficacy, may be so strong as to eliminate gender differences in these types of civic acts. Nevertheless, among organizational activities, the participation of women with the most geographically circumscribed social networks is influenced most by the size of their community.

In sum, because social connections are more disparate in larger cities, the ability of neighbors to recruit each other for either political acts or organizational activities decreases. This effect is particularly acute for women, since they are more likely to be drawing social connections from their neighborhoods. The fact that women in smaller cities are more likely to be mobilized for political acts by neighbors reveals the higher degree of interconnection among neighbors that exists in smaller cities. The disjunction between social networks and locality poses a challenge to locally based organizations in large cities because they face a harder time disseminating information and drawing members within a given geographic proximity. The organizational action of women in larger cities, because of their constrained social contacts, is thus curtailed compared to that of their counterparts in smaller suburbs.

ACCOUNTING FOR THE CIVIC EFFECTS OF CITY SIZE

The evidence above suggests that people in larger cities (1) feel less efficacious with respect to local politics; (2) are less interested in local affairs; and (3) are less familiar with their neighbors and, hence, less likely to be recruited into civic activities. But while we find people in large cities exhibiting such qualities, are such factors *responsible* for their civic disen-

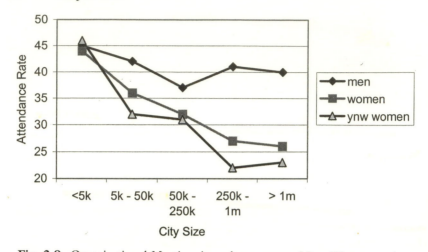

Fig. 2.9. Organizational Meeting Attendance among Men, Women, and Young, Nonworking Mothers

gagement? We can find the answer by reexamining the relationship between place size and local civic activity while controlling for local political interest and mobilization. If civic activity diminishes in larger places because their residents are less likely to be recruited by their neighbors or are more alienated, then the relationships between place size and participation should attenuate once the interest and mobilization items are included in the equations. To test this assertion, I reestimated the regression equations for a scale composed of the nonelectoral civic items before and after controlling for local political efficacy, political interest, and whether the respondent had been mobilized.[28] The results are depicted in figure 2.10, and the full equations are in Appendix B.

When political engagement and mobilization are taken into account, the negative relationship between place size and local civic activity shrinks considerably. For example, when just the standard controls are employed, the equations predict a twelve-percentage-point decline in the civic activity scale between the largest and smallest places. However, when the lower levels of interest, efficacy, and mobilization in larger places are taken into account, this decline attenuates by half, so that the difference is only six percentage points.

[28] Because of the anomalous findings around the interaction between city and metropolitan size and voting and the distinct nature of the voting act, I did not include it in the civic scale, although doing so would not change the results very much. Interestingly, residents of larger metropolitan areas are slightly more likely to score slightly higher on the nonelectoral civic activity scale after interest, efficacy, and mobilization are controlled. This might reflect the greater opportunities or motivating problems that occur in larger metropolitan settings.

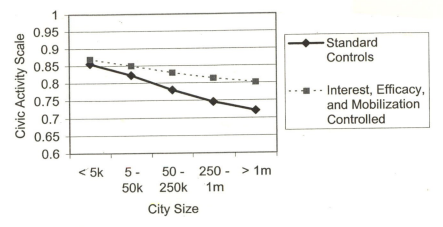

Fig. 2.10. Predicted Rates of Nonelectoral Civic Activity by City Size Before and After Controlling for Political Interest, Efficacy, and Mobilization (full equations in Appendix B)

Clearly then, civic participation is lower in larger cities partly because citizens are less politically interested, feel less efficacious, and are less likely to be mobilized. As the civic voluntarism model would predict, civic participation is lower in larger cities, not because the acts of participating are any different, but because the determinants of participation change. Smaller municipalities make participation easier, make citizens feel more empowered and interested in their communities, and bring neighbors together. While this does not rule out other reasons for the drop in civic participation in larger places, at least a big portion of the civic decline can be attributed to the social, political, and psychological character of big-city life.

CONCLUSION

In metropolitan America, civic participation is higher in smaller places than in large ones. Across a wide variety of activities, from contacting officials to attending board meetings to working informally with neighbors, people in larger places are less active than their counterparts in smaller places. As we have seen, big cities depress civic activity in numerous ways. First, the size and scope of activity in larger places can make civic action more difficult and make citizens feel less efficacious about local politics. People in larger cities report feeling that they have less control over political institutions and that local institutions are less responsive. Hence people in larger cities may drop out simply because they feel that their actions have so little impact. Second, despite the greater visibility and higher stakes of city government, people in larger places are less interested in local politics. This surprising finding probably arises from a psychological response to the urban environment: overwhelmed by the complexity and scope of big-city life, people in larger places may simply withdraw into a more private-regarding orientation and be content as bystanders to civic life. In detaching themselves from their communities, they also disassociate themselves from civic life. Finally, people in larger places are less likely to know their neighbors and less likely to have social contacts that are geographically proximate. When people are less familiar with those around them, local organizations and political movements face a harder time recruiting members and disseminating information, thus limiting many opportunities for participation. None of these explanations are mutually exclusive and all illustrate a general principle: as the size of a city increases, people are less socially connected with their neighbors, less interested in local politics, and, consequently, less active in local civic affairs.

This first step in exploring the civic consequences of suburbanization is quite suggestive: the political fragmentation of metropolitan areas into smaller, suburban governments has a big influence on American democratic life. A city's size is an important determinant of its citizens' civic activity, and city boundaries are very important for creating community in an era of metropolitan expansion. One might not expect an isolated place like Muleshoe, Texas, to have the same civic culture as a similar-size suburb like Minooka, Illinois. After all, Minookans are part of a large cosmopolitan area and have a larger social universe to draw from, while Muleshoers are somewhat isolated on the Texas plains. Yet the data indicate that there is no effect of the metropolitan area on the impact of city size on civic activity. In other words, from these statistical models, we would predict that Minookans, Muleshoers, or anyone else in a similarly small town, irrespective of its metropolitan location, is generally more likely to participate in civic life than a similar person in Minneapolis, Milwaukee, or Miami. In the American metropolis, municipal boundaries are as important for defining the social interaction and psychological orientation of its residents as they are for delimiting its land size. Despite the fact that city boundaries within many metropolitan areas are invisible amid a continuous urban sprawl, they nevertheless influence the behavior of the residents within.

So in at least one regard, suburbanization can benefit American civic life. As Robert Dahl speculated a generation ago, breaking up large urban areas into collections of small and medium-size municipalities creates communities, by virtue of their size, with more socially, psychologically, and civically involved citizens.[29] By the standard of citizen participation,

---

[29] Dahl 1967.

democratic government is more authentic in smaller places than in large ones. These findings support many of the speculations arising from past research. For example, public choice theorists have long argued that political fragmentation in metropolitan areas can benefit democracy by inducing competitive pressures between localities. Here, we might add that political fragmentation, in terms of size alone, also fosters more citizen involvement. Similarly, previous studies of community participation in larger urban areas emphasize that smaller, neighborhood-based institutions are effective at bringing citizens into public life.[30] Once again, the results here support such assertions. Although residents of larger places are more disengaged from local politics in general, the findings would suggest that where local institutions can be made smaller in focus and in more immediate reach of the citizenry, then people will become more involved. Thus neighborhood-based planning commissions, improvement zones, crime-watch programs, or representative boards will all be effective for empowering residents of larger cities. In short, smaller local institutions are better equipped for meeting the demands of the authentic governance principle stated in chapter 1.

Of course, these results should not lead to an immediate celebration of the civic virtues of suburbanization. Smaller places in metropolitan areas are rarely uniform in social composition and are highly differentiated in their affluence, racial composition, and other characteristics. In fact, smaller municipalities have strong incentives to differentiate themselves in the types of services they provide and the residents they seek to attract, and these differentiations have resulted in large amounts of social segregation. The consequence of dividing a single metropolitan area into numerous independent municipalities is a great deal of social segregation. As we will see in the chapters to follow, these other characteristics are not without their own consequences.

[30] Berry, Portney, and Thomson 1993.

CHAPTER THREE

Cities of Riches and Squalor

ACROSS THE Delaware River from Philadelphia reside two places of similar size that exemplify Dickens's adage about the best and worst of times. As one of the poorest cities in the country, Camden, New Jersey, is an effigy of industrial decay. Once a proud and strong manufacturing center, home to Campbell's Soup and RCA, Camden today has few employers. Its previously bustling factories are abandoned, ghosts of crumbling brick and broken glass. Nearby, block after block of once handsome brick row houses are empty and boarded up. With the decline in its manufacturing sector, the suburban migration of Camden's middle and upper classes left behind a city of the poor. Two in five of its adults live below the poverty line, and its median household income is under $18,000 a year. Camden's municipal government has few resources to deal with these problems. The annual city budget is less than $55 million, with most of that money coming from state and federal transfer payments. Hardest hit are its children. Fifty percent live in poverty and have few opportunities for social advancement. By any measure, Camden's schools are in poor shape—buildings are in disrepair, teachers are poorly paid, and student performance is weak. Fewer than one-third of Camden High School's freshman class will graduate in four years.

Cherry Hill, sitting next Camden, is an archetype of American prosperity. Composed mostly of single-family homes on quiet, wide streets, Cherry Hill fits the stereotype of a nice, middle-class suburb. Camden's rubble, decay, and social despair are nowhere to be found. Instead, neatly trimmed yards and shady trees surround comfortable homes. Children play on the streets or at neighborhood recreation centers, and, in general, the inhabitants know prosperity. Fewer than 2 percent of Cherry Hill's residents live in poverty, and the medium household income is over $60,000 a year. Its schools are clean and neat. Less than 1 percent of Cherry Hill high school students leave before graduation, and most go on to college. Beyond a common municipal border, Cherry Hill shares little with its impoverished neighbor.

Although Americans have grown accustomed to places like Camden and Cherry Hill, from a historical perspective the economic situation of both places is relatively new. Until quite recently, most cities like Camden contained a wide range of income groups. Cities and towns may have had rich and poor neighborhoods, but they were never dominated by only one social class. Indeed, throughout most of the nineteenth and early twentieth centuries, urban politics was defined by the struggle between different economic groups for control of city hall. Political machines, largely supported by working and poor residents, often came in conflict with middle-class reform candidates. But over the past fifty years, this situation changed. As Americans migrated to the suburbs and divided themselves into smaller places, rich and poor have become separated not just by neighborhood but also by municipal boundaries. With suburban-ization, wealth has come to differentiate not just America's citizens but its cities as well.

In fact, many commentators see economic segregation as *the* driving force in the politics of suburbanization. Many of the first truly suburban municipalities were incorporated by the middle and upper classes because they sought to resist annexation by "corrupt and inefficient" big-city gov-ernments, which were often dominated by working-class political ma-chines.[1] Consequently, towns populated exclusively by affluent citizens were born. Federal policies in the 1930s and 1950s helped further this economic distinction by providing mortgage subsidies for new homes in middle-class suburbs and promoted high-rise public housing in older ur-ban areas that served to further ghettoize the poor. Massive federal in-vestments in the interstate highway system rather than public transporta-tion encouraged the wider geographic split of the population, with those able to afford cars moving to more distant outskirts of the metropolis. Today, suburbs continue to use zoning laws, building codes, and other measures to exclude lower-income residents from their communities.[2] For example, in the 1970s and 1980s, several New Jersey municipalities spent millions of dollars in legal fees to fight court-ordered housing for the poor in their communities.[3] Today's metropolitan areas are a patch-work of economically differentiated communities.[4]

These patterns can be seen in almost any American metropolis. Take, once again, the example of Chicago. Map 3.1 depicts the median house-hold income of cities in the Chicago metropolitan area in 1990. The city of Chicago has a median household income of only $19,000 largely be-cause it has a substantial poor population, but, like most large cities, it also has its share of wealthy neighborhoods. For instance, along the Gold Coast of the city's north side, many homes and apartments sell for more than $1 million. Outside of the central city, the income ranges vary dra-

[1] Teaford 1979.
[2] One of the earliest and best works on economic zoning in suburbs is Danielson 1976.
[3] For an excellent history of the Mt. Laurel housing fight, see Kirp, Dwyer, and Rosenthal 1995.
[4] For more analysis of economic segregation, see Logan 1981, Massey and Eggers 1993.

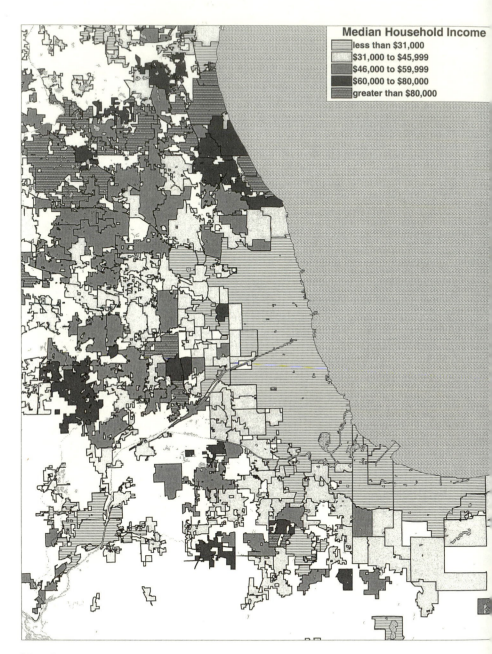

Map 3.1. Economic Segregation in the Chicago Area

matically. At one end, the Chicago metropolitan area has some of the wealthiest suburbs in the country; median household incomes in Winnetka and Kenilworth are above $100,000 a year. Meanwhile, a large portion of its suburbs are more middle-class. Aurora and Evanston have median household incomes near $40,000. Chicago also has some poor suburbs, such as Phoenix, a municipality with a median household income of less than $22,000 a year, over $10,000 below the national average.

Although the economic differentiation between central cities and suburbs is well known, what is not often recognized is how internally homogeneous many of these communities are. Many suburbs are distinct not just because they contain wealthier residents, but because they contain *only* wealthy residents. We can see this pattern by comparing a city's median household income level with its economic heterogeneity. Drawing from a sample of metropolitan area municipalities from the 1990 census, figure 3.1 depicts a scatterplot of places based on their median household income (x-axis) and their economic diversity (y-axis), which is measured with an index of qualitative variation (IQV). The IQV measures the distribution of residents in a city across several income categories; the higher the IQV score, the more widely a city's population is distributed across all income groups.[5] In other words, each point represents the score of a particular city on an income and economic diversity scale.

Two findings are immediately striking from this figure. First, as with the case of Chicago, American cities in general are highly stratified by income. From this random sample of cities, median household income levels range by more than $100,000, from impoverished cities with a median household income below $10,000 (e.g., Elsa, Texas) to posh cities with median incomes above $110,000 (e.g., Franklin Lakes, New Jersey). While most cities fall in between—$30,000 to $50,000—a significant portion exist at either end of the economic spectrum. Second, a city's economic heterogeneity has a curvilinear relationship with median household income. The most economically diverse cities (i.e., those with high IQV scores) are in the middle-income range; economically homogeneous cities (i.e., those with low IQV scores) are at either end of the

[5] I calculated the economic diversity of a city by counting the number of residents in each city that were within five categories of annual household income (less than $15,000, $15,000–<35,000, $35,000–<$55,000, $55,000–80,000, and greater than $80,000). The index of qualitative variation (IQV) measures the distribution of the population across these categories as the ratio of the amount of observed variation to the amount of variation that could actually exist. The scores range from 0 (no variation) to 1 (maximum variation across categories). The computational formula for the IQV is: $IQV = k(N^2 - \text{Sum}(f^2)) / N^2(k - 1)$ where k = number of categories (in this case the five income groups), N = sum of cases, and $\text{Sum}(f^2)$ = the sum of the squared frequencies.

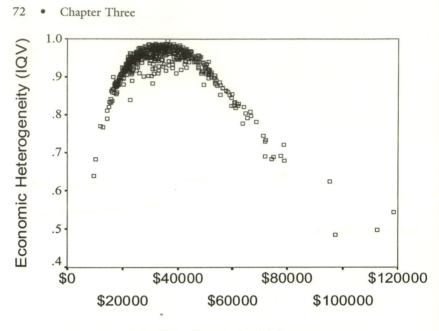

Fig. 3.1. City-Level Economic Diversity by Median Household Income among American Places (source: 1990 U.S. Census [STF 3] sample of six hundred cities)

economic spectrum. In other words, middle-income cities hold a wide range of income groups, but richer cities tend to have only rich people and the poorest cities tend to have mostly poor people.

In the context of urban housing markets, this curvilinear pattern is very understandable. With low taxes, high services, and zoning exclusions, posh suburbs maintain high property values, keeping out all but the affluent. Many impoverished areas, typically suffering from urban blight, a low tax base, and substandard public services, languish as middle and working classes depart in search of better and safer locales, leaving behind those too poor to exit. Poor cities thus become increasingly composed of just poor people. Middle-income cities can often provide housing available to some of the poor but contain wealthy neighborhoods as well, giving them a wider income range among residents. Consequently, cities at the polar ends of the economic spectrum tend to be homogeneous, while more heterogeneous, middle-class cities exist in the center.

Despite the prevalence of economic segregation in metropolitan life, we still have little understanding of how it affects democratic government. Most studies of urban politics assume divisions between residents based on their own class[6] or their relationship to property.[7] And while many scholars have investigated the *causes* of suburban economic differentiation,[8] few have investigated the civic *consequences*. The implications of economic segregation and homogeneity for mass political behavior have largely been ignored. As a result, many questions remain about how class differentiation in suburbia is affecting American civil society. How do citizens behave in a city comprising only rich inhabitants? Is civic life different in places where all citizens are poor? How does suburban economic segregation shape the contours of American democracy? This chapter examines these questions. A municipality's economic composition is an important determinant of its inhabitants' civic behavior, but in ways that are quite surprising.

NORMS, NEEDS, AND CONFLICTS

Upon casual inspection, Cherry Hill seems bursting with civic activity. Bulletin boards on the town library or town website are chock-full of announcements of local events and meetings. Mail carriers distribute thousands of announcements and letters daily from local organizations. Residents appear continually on the move, taking children to swimming practice or attending softball leagues or working on neighborhood food drives. At first glance, civil society in Cherry Hill seems quite strong.

Yet how much of this civic vitality is related specifically to living in Cherry Hill, and how much comes from the individual characteristics of its inhabitants? After decades of research into who participates in politics, political scientists have generally concluded that the single biggest predictor of whether people are active in civic affairs is their individual level of skills and resources. Educated and affluent citizens are far more likely to participate because they are typically more informed about public affairs, have more experience in organizations and democratic governance, and experience fewer costs of performing activities like registering to vote or contacting officials. That Cherry Hill appears to bustle with civic life is not surprising, because it has more educated and affluent residents who are also more likely to be civically active.

But does this mean that Cherry Hill is an optimally functioning democracy? Not necessarily. Given the higher participation rates of its inhabitants, Cherry Hill may seem civically vibrant but actually languish far below its potential. A Cherry Hiller may participate in a few local activities not because she lives in Cherry Hill but because she is educated and

---

[6] Katznelson 1981.
[7] Logan and Molotch 1987.
[8] For example, see Massey and Eggars 1993, Logan and Schneider 1984, Danielson 1976.

affluent. If she lived in a different type of community, she might be more engaged. The rate of civic involvement in Cherry Hill may be far below what it should be given the highly educated profile of its inhabitants. To determine the civic implications of suburban economic segregation, we need first to understand how a community's class composition itself inhibits or stimulates civic activity, independent of individual resources.

How Affluence Stimulates Civic Activity

Most commentators believe that civic participation will increase with both the affluence and the economic homogeneity of a community. Although previous research is not conclusive, many studies suggest that a community's economic composition can stimulate civic involvement in two ways. First, cities with greater affluence, by definition, contain more types of citizens with skills and resources, which can increase the opportunities for participation. People generally take part in civic activities when there are more civic events occurring or when there are friends and neighbors asking them to do so.[9] If I live in a community where my neighbors are recruiting me to join their clubs or vote for a candidate, or are posting announcements of board meetings, I'm more likely to take part than if I live in a place where such activities do not occur. The suburban ethnographies of the 1950s such as *Crestwood Heights* or *Organization Man* typically portrayed the affluent suburb as teeming with such opportunities. For instance, William Whyte described the affluent Chicago suburb of Park Forest as a place where neighbors were often enlisting each other into community activities.[10] People in more affluent places may participate to a greater extent simply because they are more likely to be surrounded by active people who are having meetings and creating organizations. Places like Cherry Hill have numerous community bulletin boards that are crowded with announcements because there are more Cherry Hillers organizing civic activities.

Second, the homogeneity of affluent places may turn civic participation into a social norm. People living in a wealthy place like Cherry Hill may feel compelled to join organizations or attend board meetings because this is what their friends and neighbors are doing. Civic action becomes a way of fitting into the community. Similarly, if more people in a place are of the same social class, a stronger community norm can be established, a norm that residents must either buck or embrace. These pressures have been noted in past research. Both Whyte and Herbert Gans saw the ho-

---

[9] See Verba et al. 1995, Rosenstone and Hansen 1994, Huckfeldt and Sprague 1995.
[10] Whyte 1956.

mogeneity of suburban communities as important for establishing norms of behavior, one of which was joining local civic activities.[11]

More recent studies based on survey data report similar results, particularly Robert Huckfeldt's comparisons of people in different neighborhoods. After controlling for the respondent's individual levels of education and income, Huckfeldt examined how much variation in people's participation rates could be explained by their neighborhood's affluence. He found people in affluent neighborhoods more likely to participate in a variety of political acts, a trend that he attributed to neighborhood social norms. As Huckfeldt describes, "the high status environment encourages participation through the informal transmission of group-based norms which turn participation into a social obligation."[12] Although Huckfeldt never directly measured such norms with his surveys, this assertion remains a powerful and intuitively plausible explanation for higher participation in affluent places.

How *Affluence Can Harm Civic* Engagement

Even though the majority of studies suggest that higher levels of affluence and homogeneity are beneficial for civic life, there are many reasons to suspect that the opposite may be true—that civic participation may be lower in wealthier places. To begin with, the *tranquillity* of affluent suburban municipalities may reduce the incentives for civic involvement. Partly this arises from the sorting of people along economic lines. Exclusionary zoning practices and relatively low tax levels in affluent places attract residents whonot only are similar in income but favor such policies and seek similar government services.[13] In other words, people may move to affluent suburbs because they want better schools and do not want to subsidize programs for poorer residents, such as public transportation, health, or housing. This political homogeneity may limit the number of local issues drawing people into the public realm. Suburban politics becomes something of a vacuum, as affluence and homogeneity in a community eliminate the conflicts that stimulate citizen interest. As Robert Wood commented forty years ago, "where the suburb approaches true homogeneity and the income and social status of the residents is high . . . conflicts and issues of great moment simply do not arise . . . apathy ensues, not from frustration, but from contentment."[14] Satisfied that the policies that maintain their city's economic composition are secure, residents of affluent cities may have few incentives to participate in local civic

[11] See Whyte 1956, Gans 1967.
[12] Huckfeldt 1984, p. 106.
[13] Weiher 1991, Plotkin 1987, Danielson 1976.
[14] Wood 1959, p. 63.

activity. In short, civic life may be weak in an affluent place because the politics in such places is relatively boring.

Furthermore, a community's affluence in itself may limit the reasons for neighbors to come together. Past research in urban politics has shown that some types of civic activities are higher in poorer areas because of greater social needs. For example, residents of poorer neighborhoods are more likely to contact their elected officials than are those in affluent ones,[15] despite the fact that affluent neighborhoods contain more of the types of people who are likely to contact government officials. Why is this case? Unlike people in poor places, residents of affluent neighborhoods typically face fewer social problems such as homelessness, crime, or unemployment. Residents of poor neighborhoods must deal with more local difficulties and, therefore, have a greater need for public action. These differences in social problems should pertain to affluent and poor cities as well. Because affluent places like Cherry Hill have an ample tax base to keep the roads paved and have fewer citizens requiring public assistance, there is simply less reason for citizens to be involved in local politics. In poor suburbs, such as Camden, New Jersey, crime, pollution, and health and welfare concerns will be greater, and so will the necessity of citizen action.

Finally, according to some economists, the market competition between suburbs for certain types of citizens also reduces the need for civic participation. In what is often called the "public choice" model of urban politics, local governments tailor their policies for particular constituencies to attract the optimal balance between citizen service demands and revenue capacity.[16] Because local governments are often afraid of losing their tax base, they work to keep tax rates low and maintain efficient government services. Citizens maintain a tight leash on government officials not through their vote at the ballot box but by threatening to vote with their feet and move to a new locale. This exit option forces public officials to craft policies, not in response to electoral pressures or public demands, but from fear of losing an optimal tax base. Citizens and municipal leaders thereby engage in a segregating dance—leaders target policies for particular constituencies, which are enlarged as citizens move to those places with the most advantageous benefits. Although such economic models are overly simplistic portrayals of urban politics, they do provide a compelling logic for how, in a politically fragmented metropolitan area, cities will become increasingly homogeneous, and how this homogeneity will further reduce the need for public activity.

---

[15] Jones, Greenberg, and Drew 1980; Haeberle 1985.
[16] The seminal article on the public choice perspective is Tiebout 1956; and this view is well represented in the works of Ostrom, Bish, and Ostrom (1988) and Parks and Oakerson (1989). For a review of this literature, see Keating 1995.

Thus we have two strikingly different expectations about how a municipality's economic composition may shape its citizens' civic behavior. If being surrounded by people who are more educated or wealthy increases the social pressures or opportunities to engage in civic activity, then civil society should be stronger in more affluent and homogeneous places. But if the absence of political conflict and social problems limits the incentives of residents for getting involved, then civic participation may be lower. To see which of these hypotheses is correct, let us return to the data.

EMPIRICAL TESTS

A simple comparison of average participation rates by median household income reveals few differences between people in rich and poor places. As depicted in figure 3.2, participation rates are generally highest in the most affluent cities, but there are few steady or linear increases with a city's income level. In fact, apart from attendance of community board meetings, there are no steady or linear increases in civic participation as the affluence of a city increases. For instance, 30 percent of respondents in places with median household incomes under $20,000 reported contacting locally elected officials, compared to 28 percent in places between $30,000 and $40,000 and 30 percent in places over $50,000. Similar patterns occur for rates of voting, working informally with neighbors, or attending organizational meetings. Board meeting attendance is the only activity that changes between residents of poor and wealthy places—only 15 percent of residents in the poorest cities (i.e., those with median household incomes under $20,000 a year) reported attending a board meeting, compared with 25 percent in the most affluent places (i.e., places with median household incomes above $50,000 a year). When we just compare average rates of civic participation, there seem to be few differences between rich and poor and places.

In many ways these findings are quite curious. With a simple cross-tabulation, we would expect that civic participation would continually rise with a city's affluence because the respondents who live in these cities are more educated and affluent themselves and are therefore more likely to vote, contact officials, or attend organizational meetings. The absence of any steady increases is therefore somewhat puzzling—residents of wealthy places have over five years more education, on average, than those in the poorest places. This fact alone should be contributing to higher overall participation rates. Yet the rates do not steadily increase. Clearly, the differences between individual resource levels and the affluence of the community need to be sorted.

As in the previous chapter, a more sophisticated estimation procedure can isolate the distinct civic effects of a city's affluence. Using a series of

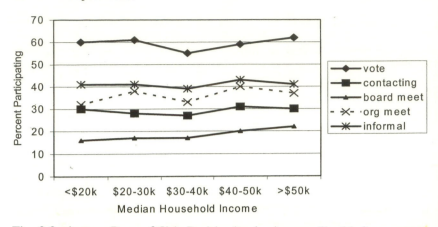

Fig. 3.2. Average Rates of Civic Participation by Average City Median Household Income (source: 1990 Citizen Participation / 1990 U.S. Census Dataset)

regression analyses, I calculated the distinct effects of city-level income on civic activity, while holding constant individual differences in education, income, homeownership, and other factors. I also included measures of the other city-level characteristics, such as size, racial composition, and age. Figure 3.3 depicts the predicted rates of five civic activities across the city income scale based upon the coefficients from the regression model. A full description of the estimation and the equations are presented in Appendix B.[17]

Once we hold individual-level differences in education and income constant, the equations predict a curvilinear relationship between civic participation and a city's median household income. As illustrated in the figures, the predicted rates of informal neighboring, voting, and attending community board or organizational meetings rise from the poorest cities to middle-income places but then fall quite dramatically between middle-income cities and affluent ones. For example, compared to people in middle-income cities (median household income of $35,000), residents of the poorest cities (incomes below $15,000) are 10 percent less likely to attend community board meetings, 14 percent less likely to at-

[17] I derived the aggregate marginal effect of city affluence by taking the logit coefficient for the log of median household income (and the log of median household income squared) and calculating a probability estimate by evaluating each number on a logistic function. I then derived the overall probability estimates by aggregating these differences across the entire sample for each value above the lowest value where both log income terms were divided into ten-point increments. I calculated the predicted effect for any particular city's affluence level by estimating where it was on the ten-point log scale and the probability difference of that point relative to the lowest value in the scale.

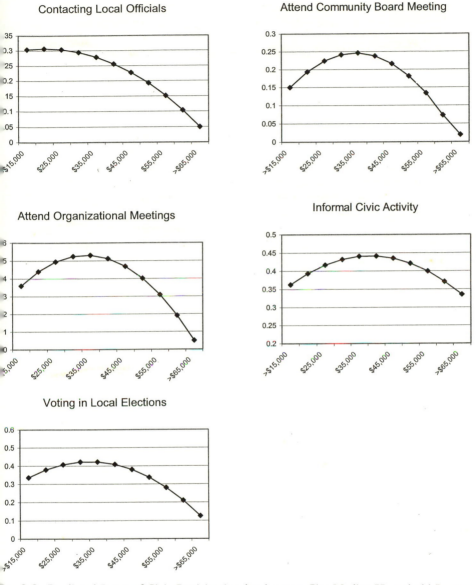

Fig. 3.3. Predicted Rates of Civic Participation by Average City Median Household Income (full equations in Appendix B)

tend organizational meetings, and 13 percent less likely to work informally with neighbors; they score eleven percentage points lower on the voting scale. Yet compared to people in middle-income cities, people in the richest places are also less likely to be civically active: the models predict a twenty-percentage-point drop in board meeting attendance, a twenty-five-percentage-point drop in organizational meeting attendance, an eighteen-percentage-point drop in informal activism, and a seventeen-percentage-point drop in the voting scale. Indeed, the only civic activity to demonstrate a steady and linear decline across the city income scale is in contacting local officials. People in the poorest places are more likely to voice complaints than those in either middle-income or wealthy cities. Nevertheless, across most of the civic activities, a curvilinear pattern remains. Participation may be lower in poor than middle-income cities; the biggest differences, however, are not between poor and rich but between rich places and middle-income cities. Such steep differences in civic participation indicate that a city's affluence is a strong determinant of its civic vitality.

These results contradict the conventional wisdom about how a place's affluence can influence its civic life. Both Robert Huckfeldt's previous quantitative studies and the ethnographies of the 1950s report higher levels of civic participation in more affluent settings because of increased social pressure. Conventional wisdom also would suggest that opportunities to participate are higher in wealthier settings, but comparing participation across a wide range of places shows that this is not the case. The predicted participation rates rise slightly from the poorest people to those in middle-income cities, but the absolute lowest rates are among residents of the most affluent towns. Interestingly, this pattern is evident across all kinds of civic activities. Whether we examine voting in local elections, informally working with neighbors, or attending community meetings, people in affluent places are less civically involved than their counterparts in middle-income places. On a municipal level, simply being surrounded by more people who are likely to participate (i.e., the affluent and educated) does not necessarily make a person more likely to participate. In fact, it seems to decrease the likelihood of their participation!

Given that these findings so strongly contradict both the past research and our own expectations about the influence of affluent contexts, we may wonder about the consequence of unmeasured effects. For instance, might these patterns be the consequence of some other city-level characteristics, such as size or racial composition? Probably not. For although affluent municipalities tend to be smaller in population size and less racially diverse, the multivariate equations control for these other city-level characteristics. Nor can these results be attributed to the types of governments in affluent places. While affluent cities tend to have "reform-style" governments (i.e., council-manager or commission govern-ments, at-large elections), these factors do not influence whether citizens work informally with neighbors or attend organizational meetings. If we include measures of city institutional arrangements in the multivariate equations, the coefficients for the city affluence measures are largely unaffected.

Nor can these results be attributed to any individual-level characteristics in the inhabitants of affluent or poor places either. When we do not control for an individual's education or income level, as in the cross-tabulations in figure 3.2, few clear relationships emerge between civic participation rates and a city's median household income. Such findings initially were surprising: we would expect steady increases in civic participation because the respondents who lived in more affluent settings are more educated and wealthy and should be more likely to participate in civic activities; indeed. this is one reason why multicollinearity between individual-level affluence and place-level affluence does not influence these results.[18] After individual-level characteristics are controlled for, it becomes clear why such increases were generally not evident: people in affluent cities, once their higher status is taken into account, are actually participating at rates below what we would expect. In the simple cross-tabulations, their higher individual education and income levels were masking their relative underachievement.

Of course, one may argue that the decision to live in a very poor or affluent city, irrespective of one's demographic characteristics, is symptomatic of some other individual-level trait that corresponds with reduced civic participation. For example, people who choose to live in places like Cherry Hill might also be the type who avoid working with their neighbors. Civic activity declines in affluent places because the people who are drawn to these places are also seeking refuge from civic life. As compelling as this argument may be, it is implausible that people move to an affluent place simply to flee from civic responsibilities. People move to wealthy places to get a nice home, to enjoy a quiet neighbor-

---

[18] One concern among those with knowledge of statistical analysis may be the multi-collinearity between the explanatory variables. In other words, in the statistical equations many of the predicting variables, such as education, income, and homeownership, are significantly correlated with the median household income of the place. There are several reasons, however, why this is not apparent in these findings. First, the direction of the coefficients for the place-level affluence variable is different from that for individual-level measures of income and education. If place-level income were simply another way of measuring individual-level affluence, such directions would not be apparent. Second, with a large number of cases and the diversity of income levels across all but the richest and poorest cities, the correlation between place- and individual-level income is not as high as one might suspect. Finally, the large number of cases in the CPS sample should also help mitigate against the multicollinearity that does exist between variables.

hood, or to have better schools for their children, not because the obligations of voting or attending voluntary organizational meetings are too
onerous. While working informally with neighbors or attending community board meetings may involve contact with a diverse population, voting, contacting officials, and volunteering in local organizations do not.
Given that the educated and affluent people who populate well-off suburbs tend to be civically active, their potential for harboring some latent
aversion to any civic participation seems unlikely. And, even if their
movement to a suburb represents an unwillingness to live with people of
different social classes, races, or backgrounds, it is not self-evident why
this would result in decreased civic involvement *after* they move to a
more homogeneous environment. As we shall see, a more likely possibility is that by choosing a quiet, tranquil, affluent suburb, residents are
also choosing a political environment that gives them few reasons to get
involved in local affairs.

THE CIVIC CONSEQUENCES OF SOCIAL TRANQUILLITY

The statistical models predict that a city's civic participation level rises
and falls with its income. Civic participation increases from poor to middle-class cities but then drops precipitously at the upper end of the income scale. Yet we still do not know what accounts for this curvilinear
pattern. According to the civic voluntarism model (see chapter 1), the
answer is in the ways a city's economic composition changes either the
importance of skills and resources, patterns of mobilization, or citizen
interest in politics. In other words, civic participation is lower in affluent
places because civic acts are more difficult, there are fewer opportunities
to participate, or residents are simply less interested. So which of these is
a factor? It seems unlikely that civic participation is more "costly" in
affluent settings; if anything, being surrounded by more educated or affluent neighbors and having well-funded local institutions would decrease
the costs of local actions. With so many people likely to be organizing
community events, civic activism in places like Cherry Hill should be a
relatively easy activity. Nor is there reason to suspect that mobilization
opportunities would decline either. Once again, residents of affluent settings live among highly skilled and resourceful people who typically participate in civic actions; such people are likely to be organizing events and
recruiting their neighbors. If anything, mobilization should be higher in
affluent places. Consequently, the most likely explanation is that civic
participation rises and falls across the city affluence scale because citizen
interest in local affairs is also rising and declining.

  As noted above, one reason citizen interest may wane in affluent places
is that there are fewer of the civic problems that draw residents into

public affairs. Communities that have substandard housing or poor streets or a lack of green space, or that suffer from more social problems, also have more compelling political issues. Since poor cities often lack the fiscal resources to address these problems, it is often up to citizen-initiated efforts to meet these needs. In attempting to solve their community's problems, citizens can come together either through informal efforts or by creating civic organizations. Interest in local affairs may be stronger in a poor place because there are more pressing local issues. And, for at least one civic activity, this pattern occurs. People in poorer cities are the most likely of any group to contact local officials, and contacting is the most direct form of civic activity related to addressing particular needs. But for most civic activities, there are no steady declines from the poorest to richest areas. Rather, civic participation rises from poor to middle-class cities and then drops off on the upper end of the economic scale. If social needs were the primary factor in bring neighbors together in any regularized fashion, we would expect linear decreases in participation across *all* the civic items, and this does not occur. While social needs may explain some of the changes in civic participation, some other factor is also affecting civic life, particularly between poor and middle-income cities.

In searching for another explanation, we should reconsider what a city's median household income really indicates. At one level, it measures the income level of a place, but, as illustrated in figure 3.1, it also relates to the *distribution* of income among the residents: cities at both ends of the income scale tend to be more economically homogeneous than those in the middle. In other words, poor cities (i.e., those with median household incomes below $25,000) tend to be composed of mostly poor people; wealthy cities (median household incomes above $60,000) have mostly affluent residents. Middle-income cities contain the widest possible range of income groups and have the highest degree of economic diversity. Interestingly, the curvilinear pattern between economic diversity and city affluence (depicted in figure 3.1) closely resembles the curvilinear relationship between civic participation and city affluence (depicted in figure 3.3). Just as a city's economic diversity rises and falls across the income scale, so does its predicted level of civic participation. Perhaps this economic diversity is the real source of civic variation among poor, middle-income, and wealthy cities.

To understand how a city's economic diversity can shape its civic life, we need to reconsider first the relationship between political and civic life. Civic participation is often viewed as independent of the state in "the space of uncoerced human association."[19] Few writers, however, either

---

[19] Walzer 1995.

see civic participation within the political conflicts of a community or understand how the two relate. Typically, it is assumed that democratic polities have a constant and uniform need for active citizen participation.[20] Yet this assumption is questionable. After all, one might just as easily argue that, from the standpoint of democratic governance, the necessity of civic participation exists in direct proportion to the diversity of its population's political interests. Communities with internally homogeneous political desires have little need for high levels of civic activity because their residents' preferences are so easily represented. If citizens all want the same ends from their political institutions, then there is little need for independent, nongovernmental structures to organize and articulate citizen preference. Any citizen can easily speak for the whole, and citizen concerns can be represented by the most minimal of civic actions. If, however, a community contains a greater diversity of opinions, needs, or interests, the importance of civic participation increases. For when citizens live amid people who seek different political ends, they need to find others with whom to unite. Lone voices may be faint amid a cacophony of political voices, but brought together, they can make their political wishes heard. Civic participation is thus more crucial in a politically heterogeneous setting, because in such places citizens will need to do more to make their political preferences known.

But just as a community with more political conflict has a greater need for civic participation, it also has more lures to draw citizens into public life. In places where different interests struggle to form and organize, gain adherents, and overcome their opposition, political life is more lively. Attracted by the spectacle of conflict, citizens become interested in political issues and are drawn into public action. Since citizen interest and mobilization are key factors determining civic involvement, political conflict—by stirring up political interest—can also strengthen civic life. For example, citizens who oppose a city's decision to cut social spending may unite together, establish an organization, and forge deeper social bonds among themselves, while those who may want lower taxes can do the same. The conflict between groups within the same political institutions stimulates civic action. A diverse polity not only has the need for strong civic participation to facilitate its democratic process but also provides the political competition that fuels citizens' involvement. This is also in accordance with the authentic governance principle: The places where civic participation is most necessary are, by virtue of their heterogeneity, also the most politically lively and provide the most compelling reasons for citizens to get involved.

The strength of a community's civic sector thus relates, in part, to its

[20] Verba and Nie 1972.

diversity. Communities that have more competing political interests provide the conflict to draw citizens into the contest. Of course, this leads to an interesting question: what exactly makes a community diverse? This question is not as easy as it may first seem. Social psychologists have found that people are quite willing to divide and distinguish themselves along the most minimal lines.[21] Even in the most homogeneous and affluent of communities, citizens may find differences among themselves. How, then, can we determine whether a community is truly heterogeneous?

While we must acknowledge that people can and do find the most minimal basis for division, in politics some characteristics typically arise that are more important than others. Of these, perhaps no factor is more important than material conditions. Political theorists from James Madison to Karl Marx have argued that differences in wealth are the primary cause of political division.[22] This is especially the case with respect to local politics. In Paul Peterson's influential book on the limits of city government, the economic composition of a municipality directly relates to the political pressures it experiences and the policies it seeks to implement. According to Peterson, local governments must choose among three types of spending: (1) allocational—spending on public goods that are nondivisible, such as parks or fire protection; (2) developmental—spending that promotes future growth, such as road and water systems; and (3) redistributive—spending that transfers resources from the collective to particular citizens, such as welfare payments or public housing.[23] Obviously, allocational public services—such as a minimum level of public safety, fire protection, clean air and water, and public health—are desired by all citizens. Beyond this, however, citizen requests from local political institutions vary in relation to their economic position. Wealthy people have the resources to secure good housing, better home security, or education for their children. Consequently, they seek to limit their tax expenditures by restricting public services. Middle-class citizens may want a wider range of programs but may also seek to protect the property values

[21] Tajfel and Turner 1979, Brown 1985.
[22] In *Federalist*, number 10, Madison writes, "The latent causes of faction are sown in the nature of man and we see them everywhere brought into different degrees of activity. But the most common durable source of factions has been the various and unequal distribution of property. Those who hold and those who are without property have ever formed distinct interests in society . . . The regulation of these interests forms the principle task of modern legislation." (Hamilton, Madison, and Jay 1982 [1789], p. 18). But where Marx saw class conflict as inevitably leading to revolution, Madison understands it as a permanent feature of social existence and something thus necessitating a particular structuring of government—that is, the sharing and distribution of political power among different branches of government.
[23] See Peterson 1981, pp. 8–45.

of their homes. Poor citizens typically are limited in their selection of residential locations and typically must contend with substandard housing stocks and neighborhoods with greater social problems; therefore, they will be less concerned with local tax rates and more directed toward securing redistributive types of programs.

From this standpoint, economic diversity is a primary determinant of local political competition. Political conflict in relatively homogeneous cities at the poles of the economic spectrum will be low. In poor cities, most citizens will want more redistributive types of spending programs and will be less concerned with tax rates. In affluent cities, few will need redistributive spending, and most will want a high level of allocational services and low tax rates. Although rich and poor places will seek different political ends, the character of political life in both types of places should be similarly consensual. In marked contrast will be the political life of economically diverse, middle-income cities where a greater range of political interests pursue mutually incompatible goals: the affluent may want to keep taxes down, the middle-class may want better schools or to protect property values, and the poor may want more public services for housing, transportation, or health care. Facing greater political competition, residents of diverse, middle-income places have greater incentives to come together, form civic organizations, and take part in local politics. Such organizations, in turn, stage public events, try to mobilize other citizens, and publicize their positions. Consequently, citizens of diverse cities have more public issues that can attract their attention and more reasons to get involved in public life. Civic participation should thus be stronger in a more diverse city because there are more compelling issues and struggles stirring the citizenry.

To a certain extent, these syndromes are evident in Cherry Hill, New Jersey. Take, for example, the bulletin boards on the town's website. Organizational activity clusters largely around children's groups and particular events. The biggest mobilizing activity is the Spring Bloom Festival, and the most political event is the notice of a tax break for senior citizens. There seem to be few indications of groups contesting the construction or development of an office building, or political rallies for candidates. If the bulletin board is any indication, political life in Cherry Hill is very tranquil.

NEEDS, CONFLICT, AND CIVIC PARTICIPATION

If conflict is essential for fueling civic participation, we should find evidence in the national data. Let us begin with the idea that civic participation is affected by a city's economic heterogeneity. We can do this by reestimating the regression analyses used above with a measure of a city's economic diversity. These equations allow the civic influence of a munici-pality's economic homogeneity to be specified while its other aggregate characteristics and the respondents' individual-level traits are held con-stant. Figure 3.4 portrays the relationship between the five civic activities and a municipality's economic diversity (the full equations are listed in Appendix B). Once again, apart from citizen contacts with public offi-cials, civic participation is lower in more homogeneous cities than in eco-nomically diverse ones. For example, the equations predict that residents of the most homogeneous cities are 8 percent less likely to attend com-munity board meetings, 14 percent less likely to attend voluntary organi-zational meetings, 11 percent less likely to work informally with neigh-bors, and 12 percent less likely to vote in local elections than those in the most heterogeneous places.

It appears that the curvilinear relationship between city income and civic participation is partly attributable to economic diversity. Just as eco-nomic heterogeneity rises and falls across the city income scale, so does civic participation. Indeed, the only civic activity that does not decline in more homogeneous places is contacting public officials; residents of het-erogeneous and homogeneous places are equally likely to contact. The absence of any effect of diversity on contacting corresponds with the lin-ear relationship between contacting and median household income in figure 3.3. Where no curvilinear relationship exists between city income and civic participation, there is no effect of economic diversity.

Of course, this does not mean that differing social needs have no effect for other types of civic activities. Even with a measure of a city's eco-nomic diversity, we still find lower civic participation rates in cities with higher median household incomes. But now we find a steady, linear, and negative relationship. As indicated in the corresponding tables in Appen-dix B, the effects of city-level income on civic participation are still strong and negative once a city's economic diversity is also taken into account. Informal activism, organizational meeting, and voting all drop from poor to affluent cities. Clearly, the absence of social problems in affluent places is a factor accounting for the relatively lower participation rates.

So economic homogeneity is just as important as affluence in shaping citizen participation. This corresponds well to the expectations from the conflict model of civic participation, which identified citizen interest in local affairs as the operative factor linking civic action and a city's income and heterogeneity. Where social needs are greater or where wider groups of citizens compete for political resources, citizen interest in local politics will be greater. But so far, these propositions are merely assumptions. While previous scholars have speculated about this point, no one has ever tested this proposition with real data. Using the same political interest items used in chapter 2, we can compare people's interest in local and

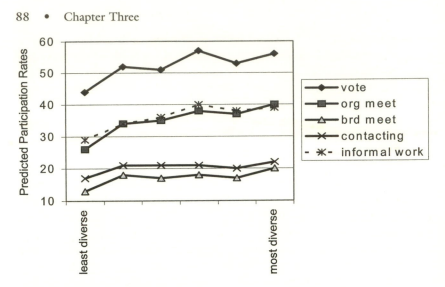

Fig. 3.4. Predicted Rates of Civic Participation by City-Level Economic Diversity (full equations in Appendix B)

national politics by their city's economic composition. Figure 3.5 depicts the predicted levels of the two political interest measures across both the city income and city diversity scales from OLS regression analyses (the results are listed in Appendix B).

As expected, people in economically homogeneous cities are less interested in local politics than people in diverse places. The equations depicted in figure 3.5 predict that people in the most homogeneous cities score 0.8 points lower on a four-point interest-in-local-politics scale than those in the most heterogeneous places, a difference that is large in magnitude and statistically significant. In fact, compared to the other variables, the coefficients for the city diversity measure are greater in magnitude than any other factor save the individual respondent's education level. In other words, a city's economic diversity is a primary determinant of its inhabitants' local political interest. But interest in local affairs also relates to a city's overall level of affluence. Residents of cities with median household incomes above $59,000 a year score 0.4 points lower on the four-point political interest scale than do those in the poorest cities, also a large and statistically significant difference. People in richer cities are simply less interested in politics than people in poorer ones.

However, just as with a city's size, so once again, there are no significant differences in national political interest among residents of either poor and rich cities or diverse and homogeneous places. People who live in rich, homogeneous places are just as interested in national politics as

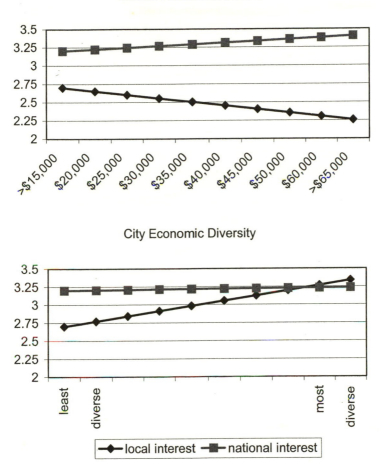

Fig. 3.5. Interest in Local and National Politics by City-Level Income and Economic Diversity (full equations in Appendix B)

people who live in diverse middle-income places. This finding indicates that the low civic participation rates in affluent places are probably not due to the types of people who choose to live in such locales. If people who moved to wealthy suburbs were also the type to flee from civic engagement and politics in general, we should find lower interest in national as well as local activities. But this does not occur.[24] The effects of a community's economic composition are limited to local affairs.

[24] Nor is there any relationship to national-level civic participation. If we were to substitute measures of national civic activity, such as voting in national elections, contacting national

So is this local political ennui in affluent and homogeneous places responsible for the lower rates of civic participation? We can answer by reestimating the relationship between a city's economic composition and the civic participation items, while also taking into account the individual respondent's interest in local politics. Figure 3.6 depicts the predicted rates of civic participation by a city's median household income and its economic composition before and after the respondent's interest in local affairs is controlled for; figure 3.7 portrays a similar pattern between economic diversity and three types of civic activity. Once again, the full equations are listed in Appendix B.

When interest in local politics is controlled, the steep relationship between economic composition and civic participation greatly attenuates. For example, the predicted rates of civic participation are still lower in wealthy cities than middle-income places, but for all activities except organizational attendance, these differences are no longer statistically significant. Low political interest accounted for most of the declines in voting, informal activity, board meeting attendance, and contacting officials. Before political interest was controlled, the models predicted that people in middle-class cities would be 20 percent more likely to attend community board meetings; once their lower political interest was factored in, the model predicts them to be only 8 percent more likely. Similar patterns also occur with the measures of economic diversity. As illustrated in figure 3.7, the new relationship between economic diversity and civic activity is much weaker, compared to the earlier estimates. The predicted differences in contacting officials, informal activity, and local voting attenuate by over fifteen percentage points once lower political interest is factored into the equation.

Thus civic participation rises and falls across the city income scale partly because people in affluent and economic homogeneous places are less interested in local affairs. As the civic voluntarism model predicts, interest in politics is a key determinant of whether citizens will involve themselves in public activities. But political interest is not randomly distributed across the population—it varies systematically with a person's education, income, and age, and with the character of politics in a given jurisdiction. In other words, political interest varies across localities because politics is simply more interesting in some places than in others. A city's economic composition is a major determinant of just how engaging local politics can be. At the upper end of the economic spectrum, wealth and social homogeneity keep affluent suburbs from facing the problems and con-

---

political leaders, or working on national political issues, we would find no effects of community economic composition.

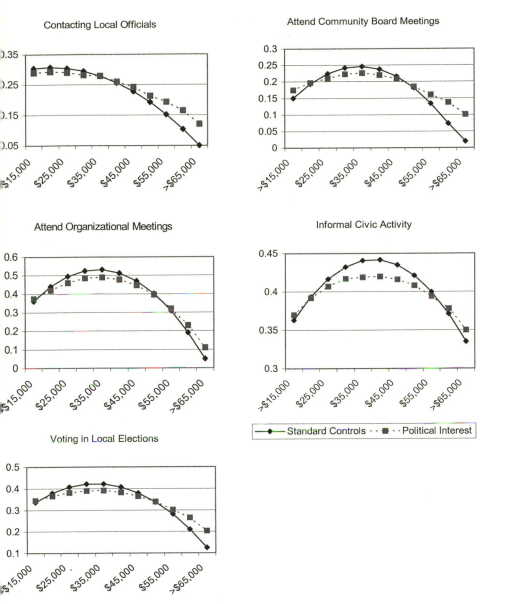

Fig. 3.6. Predicted Rates of Civic Participation by City-Level Income with Controls for Political Interest (full equations in Appendix B)

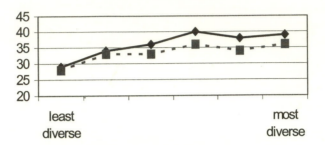

Informal Civic Activity

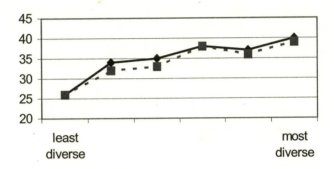

Attend Organizational Meetings

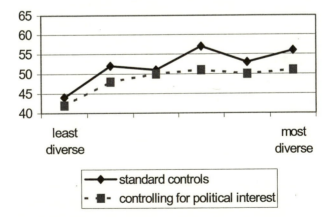

Voting in Local Elections

Fig. 3.7. Predicted Rates of Civic Participation by City-Level Economic Diversity with Controls for Political Interest (full equations in Appendix B)

flicts that make local politics lively. With a relatively homogeneous and affluent population, cities with high median incomes have fewer social needs. Presumably, residents of affluent cities also share, to a high degree, in a consensus about exclusionary municipal policies that keep their property values high and taxes low. Fewer social problems and greater political consensus translates into less public interest; with little reason for residents to attend to community affairs, civic engagement will generally decline. As Robert Wood speculated a generation ago, suburbanites' contentment with local politics breeds apathy toward their communities and less civic engagement.[25]

At the lower end of the economic scale, poverty and social homogeneity reduce conflict, limit local capacity to enact change, and discourage citizen involvement, a conclusion that has been drawn in previous studies of poor, inner-city communities.[26] While the social needs of places like Camden can stimulate some activities, like contacting officials or working informally with neighbors, their homogeneity reduces political action. The concentration of the poor in homogeneous poor places also undermines their ability to construct the healthy civic capacity that is so crucial for solving many of their social problems.

Politics is most lively in those places that contain a wide range of income groups, places that tend to exist in the middle of the economic spectrum. In middle-income cities, a greater set of economic interests compete for local services—wealthy residents want lower property taxes, middle-class inhabitants may seek playgrounds for their kids or better allocational services, and poorer residents work for more redistributive spending. As different classes contest public spending, political conflict increases and more citizens are recruited into the fray.

CONCLUSION

Economic segregation has profoundly altered the character of America's metropolitan areas. Not so long ago, most of America's cities were vibrant, diverse places. In places like Newark or Oakland, civic leaders once envisioned grand public projects such as libraries, universities, parks, and esplanades, places that not only represented the vitality of the city but would provide common areas where its residents could mingle. But such visions began to fade in the 1950s as the American economy began to change. Urban manufacturing jobs disappeared, and new types of companies increasingly sought suburban locales. The automobile and new highway systems enabled the middle classes to migrate to the suburbs,

---

[25] Wood 1959, pp. 53–95.
[26] Cohen and Dawson 1993, Parenti 1970, Skogan 1990.

and, consequently, many older cities became "warehouses for the poor." Once-proud cities like Trenton, New Haven, Gary, and Cleveland suffered from having too many poor people and too few tax revenues to assist them. By the 1970s, fiscal crises became commonplace and many cities were forced to dramatically reduce public spending levels. Residents of these places were left not just with higher concentrations of poverty and its accompanying social ills, but with fewer resources available to solve their community's problems and often limited options for leaving. Many affluent and middle-class suburbs explicitly prohibited the construction of lower-income housing, effectively keeping the poor trapped in impoverished areas. Even in the rare case where such economic zoning was prohibited by the courts, opening up the suburbs to lower-income residents has continued to be an elusive goal.[27]

The social consequences of this economic segregation have been profound. By any social indicator, the quality of life for residents of poorer areas is far below that for people in affluent settings. For instance, health researchers have found that life expectancy among people in poor areas is far below that of people in wealthy areas.[28] In places with high concentrations of the poor, one finds higher rates of crime, violence, malnutrition, depression, and infant mortality.[29] William Julius Wilson has argued that this concentration of the poor creates "cultures of poverty" in inner cities.[30] According to Wilson's famous argument, the departure of many working people from low-income neighborhoods undermines a culture of work and hope in these areas. Children raised in a climate of hopelessness and economic despair are not exposed to social norms that value work and neighbors. Indeed, no group in American society has suffered as much from this economic segregation as children. In many poor cities, one in two children live below the poverty line, suffer from malnutrition, have higher risks of accidental or violent death, and enjoy fewer prospects for social advancement.[31] This gap is nowhere more evident than in rates of spending for public schools.[32] The impoverishment of central cities has left an inner-city public school system that is chronically underfunded and incapable of meeting both the educational and the social needs of the population it serves.

The findings in this chapter demonstrate that economic segregation has consequences not just for those populations trapped in poor inner

---

[27] Kirp, Dwyer, and Rosenthal 1995.
[28] See Holosko and Feit, 1997.
[29] Waitzman and Smith 1998, Jones and Duncan 1995, Duncan and Brooks-Gunn, 1997.
[30] Wilson 1987.
[31] Foster and Furstenberg 1999, Brooks-Gunn, Duncan, and Aber 1997, Duncan and Brooks-Gunn 1997.
[32] See Duncombe and Yinger 1997, Orfield, Eaton, amd Jones 1997, Kozol 1991.

cities but for those in homogeneous, affluent suburbs as well. The data indicate that a city's economic composition strongly influences whether its citizens participate in local civic activities. However, in contrast to the conclusions of previous researchers as well as the conventional wisdom, I do not find a positive relationship between affluence and participation. Instead, civic participation is significantly lower in cities with higher median household incomes and in cities that are more economically homogeneous. Once the differences in both individual characteristics and other city-level traits are taken into account, the predicted rates in all types of civic activities steadily decline between diverse middle-income cities and those homogeneous cities at the tail ends of the economic spectrum. Ironically, the cities with the lowest participation rates (the most affluent) are also places that, by virtue of the individual characteristics of their inhabitants, should have the highest rates of civic activity. Nevertheless, *once these individual differences are considered*, large declines in civic participation become apparent, declines that far outstrip differences between such groups as homeowners and renters, single and married people, or new and old residents.

Civic life languishes in homogeneous and affluent cities partly because their residents are less interested in local politics. The exclusionary practices that help create and sustain a suburb's affluence also limit the range of social problems and political conflicts within their borders. In doing this, however, they also reduce their residents' incentives for civic action. Residents of affluent cities are less likely to vote, contact local officials, or attend meetings of organizations or community groups because they are generally less concerned with the affairs of their community. While a few scholars have suspected that economic segregation might produce civic apathy in an affluent suburb, they have not recognized how segregation also harms the civic life of poor, homogeneous cities. With a similar uniformity of political interests and a lack of political resources, civic participation in poor places also declines. This is not to say that the aggregate rates of civic participation will be lower. Due to the fact that affluent places have more educated and affluent residents, their participation rates will be high. But, as demonstrated in figure 3.2, the rates will be below what we would predict given their inhabitants' individual-level status. As in Cherry Hill, civic life may seem rich, but it might actually be languishing far below its potential.

Such findings do more, however, than simply demonstrate that economic contexts influence civic participation—they also indicate how the economic segregation of metropolitan areas that has accompanied suburban growth is harming American democracy. Although the fragmentation of metropolitan areas into many smaller municipalities may encourage participation by making smaller civic communities, this fragmentation also fosters economic segregation. By creating politically separated pockets of affluence, suburbanization reduces the social needs faced by citizens with the most resources to address them; by creating communities of homogeneous political interests, suburbanization reduces the incentives for citizens to join the public realm. Economic segregation is harmful for civic life. This is one of the central tenets of authentic governance theory: local governments need to actually articulate and resolve the social conflicts that exist within a geographic area; they should not serve as instruments for certain groups of people to wield unchallenged in their struggle against others.

This conclusion stands in sharp contrast to many positive assessments of intergovernmental competition that comes with municipal economic differentiation. According to public choice theorists, economic segregation is a benefit because it helps promote greater efficiencies in the administration and delivery of local public services. In an economically segregated metropolis, local governments can tailor their policies to a particular constituency to optimally balance between revenue capacity and service demands. But such analyses do not take into account the political consequences of segregation. By creating little democracies of like-minded citizens, municipal specialization and segregation limit the political conflicts that typically arise in heterogeneous communities and lower the incentives for civic involvement.

Of course, some may argue that the relocation to affluent suburbs is itself a civic act. By choosing an affluent city, residents may be "voting with their feet" for a set of policies. With this exit option, citizens force public officials to craft policies, not in response to electoral demands or public pressures, but from fear of losing a tax base. Market mechanisms thus relieve citizens of the necessity of political participation. In the politically fragmented metropolis, civic participation is rendered obsolete by market competition. From this standpoint, low civic participation in affluent cities is not problematic but indicates the success of political institutions at meeting citizen demands. People in affluent cities forgo participation not from apathy but from contentment.

This argument may hold some intuitive appeal, but it overlooks three important issues. First, despite their political separation, residents of affluent cities are still economically interconnected with their surrounding areas for employment, services, and goods. By creating affluent, homogeneous communities that are politically separated from the larger and more diverse metropolitan economy, affluent suburban municipalities effectively distance their residents from the problems and conflicts of the greater economy on which they depend. An artificial distinction is created between local civic and economic life. Suburban municipal autonomy allows wealthy communities to externalize conflicts generated within the larger economic context. Struggles over land use and public resources are transformed into contests between municipalities rather than among citizens. Consequently, community-based solutions to metropolitan social problems such as urban blight or transportation that depend on citizen involvement and intergovernmental cooperation are undermined. The political separation of affluent cities incapacitates many citizens with skills and resources to address the civic needs of the contemporary metropolis.

Second, the mobility envisioned by public choice theorists is not a neutral reward of the "best services at the best price" but a political act that is steeped in racial and class politics. As democratic institutions, America's local governments, by definition, must be accessible to all citizens. By allowing the affluent to incorporate themselves as a municipality and maintain zoning and land-use policies that effectively bar lower-income groups from being able to reside in their community, suburbanization is creating governments that service only the upper classes. This is not simply a market-driven decision but a political action on the part of certain groups to maintain and protect their wealth. The "market" for municipal services is not really a market but an instrument in maintaining social difference and class privileges.

Third, the negative civic consequences do not occur only among places at the upper end of the economic spectrum but among poor cities as well. The notion that people should influence local government by voting with their feet assumes that all citizens are equally mobile. Yet poor people typically do not have such options. For a family of five with a household income of $20,000 a year, options within a metropolitan housing market are limited. Most public choice economists do not consider the social or political implications of people with limited mobility who get trapped in poor cities. Not only must such people suffer from the by-products of higher concentrations of poverty, they must deal with local political institutions commanding limited resources to address their collective problems. Unable to exit their situation or shape city policies, residents of poor cities lose interest in politics and disengage from local civic life. Economic segregation not only distances the affluent and resource-rich from social problems, it limits the capacity of poor areas to sustain a strong civic culture.

Finally, there are the larger civic implications that arise from having large portions of the population, particularly those with skills and resources, disengaged from the practice of local democracy. Although this point will be elaborated on in chapter 8, we should begin to consider what it would mean if we were to treat local government as a product of consumption rather than citizenship. According to Alexis de Tocqueville, a key element sustaining America's democratic practices was the educa-tion its citizens received in local government.[33] Participation in local civic activities and associations is essential for democratic governance not sim-ply because it helps citizens aggregate their preferences but because it alters their conceptions of themselves and their relationship to society. By joining with others, citizens learn to see through their narrow, parochial, and egoistic concerns and acquire what he terms "self-interest rightly understood." In other words, civic activity alters one's political prefer-ences, bringing them more in line with more collective goals. If public decisions become regulated by quasi-market mechanisms rather than democratic processes, and if people in affluent suburbs lose interest in local politics and drop out of public life, then the essential skills of citi-zenship erode and civic identity becomes overly tied to parochial con-cerns.[34] For example, if people no longer need to debate, organize, or compromise on local issues, then their capacity to act as citizens is re-duced. If intramunicipal political conflict is minimized by market selec-tion, local democracy becomes artificially consensual, and political insti-tutions that aggregate more diverse sets of interests (i.e., the state or nation) may lose support. And if citizens understand their community or choose where to live based on a particular set of economic policies, their sense of connection and obligation to the larger society may diminish.

[33] Tocqueville 1969 [1835], pp. 189–95.
[34] For more on this point, see Frug 1999.

CHAPTER FOUR

The Civic Paradox of Racial Segregation

AT FIRST GLANCE, one might expect Sterling Heights, Michigan, to be a racially mixed city. With 120,000 residents, Sterling Heights is a large place, and, in the United States, most big cities traditionally have been ethnically diverse. It is also in the Detroit metropolitan area, which has one of the largest African American populations of any urban area in the country. Sterling Heights, however, is not so multifarious—among its 120,000 residents, fewer than 500 are black, less than one-half of 1 percent. Amid a large and racially diverse metropolis, Sterling Heights sits as a suburban citadel of white racial segregation. Yet no one protests at its borders or challenges its municipal charter. Despite its striking level of racial exclusion, most people simply tolerate Sterling Heights as an all-white community. Why, over thirty years after the civil rights movement, is there such acquiescence in this high degree of racial segregation?

Well, outside of its size, Sterling Heights is not that unusual. In Detroit, as in most metropolitan areas, solely white suburbs and racially mixed cities are the norm. Since 1900, the overwhelming majority of suburban migrants have been white, and, for various reasons, the vast majority of suburban places have evolved as solely white communities. Although African Americans and other minorities have begun to suburbanize in greater numbers since the 1970s, this has not changed the racial character of suburban life.[1] Rather, black and, to a lesser extent, other minority suburbanization has mimicked earlier patterns of racial separation that occurred within city neighborhoods. Most African Americans have migrated to predominantly black places, which are often in older, industrial areas such as Elizabeth, New Jersey, Richmond, California, or East St. Louis, Missouri. In their poverty and high housing density, many of these "suburbs" more closely resemble central cities than bedroom communities.[2]

---

[1] Farley 1996, Schneider and Phelan 1993.

[2] Other minority groups, such as Latinos and Asian Americans, are far more suburban and less segregated than African Americans. Roughly half of the Latino and Asian American metropolitan populations live in suburbs, a relatively high percentage considering that large portions of both of these groups are immigrants, who tend to locate in larger cities. Asian Americans and Latinos are also far more likely to live in predominantly white suburbs than are blacks (Massey and Denton 1993). Racial exclusion in suburbia has come largely at the expense of African Americans.

The prevalence of suburban racial segregation is evident in the national census data. Compare, for example, the data in figure 4.1, a simple distribution of American municipalities within metropolitan areas by two categories of size. The upper part of the figure shows, for all cities in metropolitan areas under 100,000 in size, the number of places by the percentage of their population that is white. In other words, of the 5,277 metropolitan places under 100,000 population (most of which are suburbs), it depicts how many are over 95 percent white, how many are 80 to 85 percent white, and so forth. As is evident in the first histogram, the vast majority of smaller metropolitan places are predominantly white; in fact, nearly two-fifths are at least 98 percent white, and nearly three-fourths are at least 90 percent white. Considering the fact that whites constitute only 73 percent of the American metropolitan population as a whole, these figures are quite striking. If the cities were distributed relative to the white proportion of the population, the histogram would show the vast majority of cities between 70 and 80 percent white.[3] Instead, most smaller metropolitan places are almost entirely white, with a very low percentage containing significant proportions of minority populations.

Larger cities, as the second histogram demonstrates, are much more evenly distributed across the percent white scale. A small number of larger cities, like Sterling Heights or Madison, Wisconsin, are predominantly white, and a few, such as Detroit, Michigan, and Inglewood, California, are disproportionately nonwhite. But most larger cities are grouped in the middle of the scale, and most of these have a lower proportion of whites than in the population as a whole. Yet, as with smaller cities, the patterns for large cities demonstrate a skewed distribution. If whites were parceled across larger cities in proportion to the population as a whole, the largest categories in this histogram would be in the 70 to 80 percent white range, with a more narrow distribution at the tail ends. Instead, the bulk of larger cities fall in the range between 40 and 70 percent. In other words, the vast majority of larger cities hold disproportionately large minority populations.

The spatial reality of this racial segregation is even more evident if we consider again the example of Chicago. Map 4.1 shows the percentage of white residents among places in the greater Chicago metropolitan area. Despite the fact that blacks constitute 20 percent of the metropolitan area population, the vast majority of its 284 suburban places contain few

---

[3] This segregation is even more pronounced for the black percentage in these places: more than 50 percent of American metropolitan places are less than 1 percent black, and 75 percent are less than 5 percent black. In short, only a quarter of American places have a proportion of minorities at or above their representative numbers in the population.

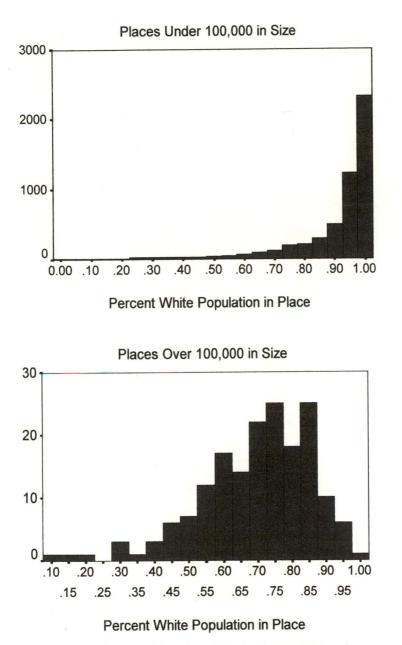

Fig. 4.1. Distribution of American Cities by Percent White of Population (source: 1990 U.S. Census [STF 3] places in metropolitan areas)

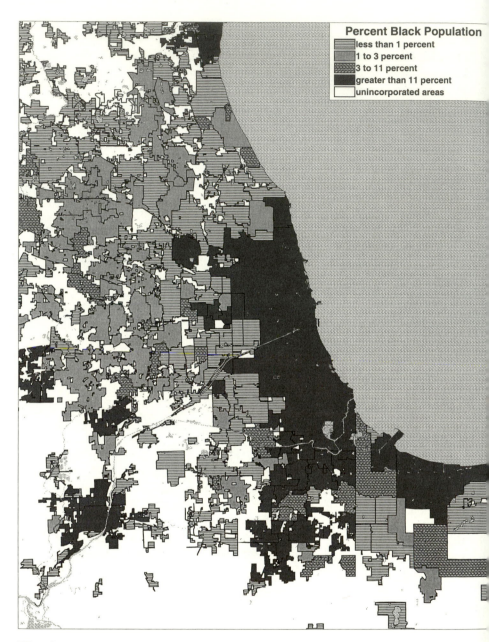

Map 4.1. Racial Segregation in the Chicago Area

African Americans—over 200 are over 95 percent white. Meanwhile, Chicago itself and many of its proximate suburbs have a high proportion of African Americans. Chicago, for instance, is roughly 40 percent black; Dixmoor, Phoenix, and Bellwood are over 60 percent black; Robbins and Ford Heights are over 90 percent black. Although Chicago may have a particularly high level of segregation, it is by no means exceptional.[4] Maps of almost any major metropolitan area in the United States would show similar trends: high percentages of minorities concentrated in central cities, with many suburbs almost exclusively white.

As with the phenomenon of class segregation related in chapter 3, the "hypersegregation" of African Americans is a relatively recent phenomenon. Throughout most of American history, blacks and whites in urban areas lived in close proximity. Colonial New York, for example, had a large black population (at times 20 percent of the city), composed of both slaves and free blacks, yet no black ghettos as we think of them today.[5] In the eighteenth and nineteenth centuries, blacks in most large cities, such as New York, Philadelphia, and Boston, lived in neighborhoods that were racially and ethnically mixed.[6] Although blacks faced severe discrimination and political disenfranchisement, and were often targets of racial violence, they were not segregated from whites in distinct racial ghettos.

The current patterns of intense racial segregation started at the beginning of the twentieth century. Drawn to factory jobs and seeking to escape the harsh discrimination of southern life, African Americans began moving to northern cities in large numbers; between 1910 and 1930 nearly 1.5 million African Americans migrated from the South to cities like Cleveland, Detroit, Chicago, Philadelphia, and New York.[7] But rather than being evenly distributed across northern cities, most of the migrating black populations were relegated to a handful of neighborhoods. Through violence, deed restrictions, social pressures, and discriminatory real estate practices, whites effectively cordoned blacks off in densely populated, racially defined ghettos. Racial segregation was furthered in the 1940s and 1950s by federal housing programs that denied mortgage assistance to black neighborhoods and subsidized the construction of high-rise public housing units in predominantly black neighborhoods.[8] As whites began moving to suburbs in the 1950s and 1960s, neighborhood racial differences became institutionalized with municipal

---

[4] See Massey and Denton 1993.
[5] Burrows and Wallace 1998.
[6] Massey and Denton 1993.
[7] Massey and Denton 1993, pp. 17–59.
[8] Jackson 1985.

boundaries. In suburbs, all-white neighborhoods were recast as all-white cities. Despite landmark legislation and court decisions in the late 1960s and early 1970s that outlawed race as a criterion for public housing finance and construction, high levels of racial segregation continue to be perpetuated by discriminatory housing practices of banks, real estate agents, and insurance brokers, and by white racial antagonism. Consequently, most black and white Americans still live apart, either in highly segregated urban neighborhoods or in suburban municipalities.[9]

For decades, scholars have been examining the social and economic consequences of this racial bifurcation, and the conclusions have generally pointed in one direction: racial segregation has had a grave and negative impact on African American populations. Arguably, the biggest effect has been on public education. Nearly fifty years after the Supreme Court ruled that racial segregation in schools was unconstitutional, most black children are still educated in predominantly black schools: 64 percent of black children attend schools that are majority black; 30 percent of black children attend schools that are 90 percent black.[10] These patterns of racial segregation in education persist because local school districts are geographically situated and often coterminous with suburban municipal boundaries. Predominantly black schools are usually located in poor central cities; they are underfunded compared to their suburban municipal counterparts and typically have fewer resources to meet the additional needs of children from impoverished households. While every child in the United States may be guaranteed a public education, not every child receives an education of equal quality, and racial and class segregation in the American metropolis gives this inequality a racial tone. Racial segregation has also been shown to have effects on health, employment, crime, and quality of life.[11]

But while the social and economic consequences of racial segregation are well documented, the civic consequences are virtually unknown. Most research on race and local democracy has focused on either individual-level racial differences in political participation, black empowerment in central cities, or questions of descriptive representation in legislative districts.[12] Virtually no research has examined the impact of racial segregation on citizen participation in civic affairs, particularly among all racial

[9] Phelan and Schneider 1996.
[10] Orfield, Eaton, and Jones 1997.
[11] Shihadeh and Ousey 1996.
[12] For studies of individual racial differences in participation, see Verba, Schlozman, Brady 1995, Verba and Nie 1972; the best overview of black empowerment is in Browning, Marshall, and Tabb 1997; Swain 1993 and Cannon 1999 provide a good summary of the debate over black representation.

groups.[13] In the midst of a racially diverse nation, we have little understanding of how living in an all-white or all-black city shapes the average citizen's involvement in democratic government. This chapter explores how civic participation varies by a city's racial composition.

THE HISTORICAL CONTEXT OF RACE AND LOCAL POLITICS

Problems of racial discrimination have haunted America's democracy since its beginning. From constitutional fights over the status of slaves to contemporary debates over census enumeration, race continues to define America's most pressing questions of citizenship and civic identity.[14] This long history of racial controversy has significant bearing on our inquiry into the civic implications of racial segregation. Considering that African Americans, Latinos, and Asian Americans were often barred from political participation until the 1960s, race and ethnicity are civically important characteristics in themselves. Many of the same forces that contributed to the political disenfranchisement of minorities also contributed to the drastic patterns of residential segregation outlined above. Given this interconnection among race, segregation, and civic participation, it is important to first pay heed to the ways that racial and ethnic identity has been a key factor for either integrating various groups into American civic life or excluding them from it, particularly at the municipal level.

Prior to the 1860s, most large American cities were both populated and controlled by what Robert Dahl calls "a Yankee elite," successors to the men of British lineage who came to power following the Revolutionary War—other ethnic and minority groups, whether they were Catholic, Jewish, or African American, were generally excluded from political power.[15] Anglo-Saxon dominance of urban politics began to wane, however, by the second half of the nineteenth century as a large migration of European Catholics prompted the creation of urban political machines, partisan organizations that used political patronage to secure votes of new immigrant groups.[16] Not only did these machines challenge the power of the Yankee elite, they also integrated politically marginal ethnic groups into American civic life. Political machines registered immigrants to vote, mobilized them into social clubs and local political life, and pro-

---

[13] The little research on civic participation, race, and context has focused either on the effects of state-level racial composition on voting (Hill and Leighley 1999) or on the local behavior of just African Americans (Bobo and Gilliam 1990, Cohen and Dawson 1993). I could find no research that examines the impact of neighborhood- or city-level segregation on the civic life of all citizens across a variety of civic behaviors.

[14] Smith 1995, Shklar 1991.

[15] Dahl 1961.

[16] Erie 1988.

vide lessons, albeit distorted ones, in democratic politics.[17] The informal social networks and ties among these immigrant groups were a key factor enabling political machines to disseminate benefits and mobilize voting behavior.

Political machines, however, did not confer these same benefits on other nonwhite racial and ethnic groups. Chinese immigrants in the nineteenth century were not only highly segregated in Chinatowns, they were denied most basic voting rights and political power.[18] Similarly, when southern blacks migrated to northern cities in the 1910s and 1920s, they were typically not enveloped into political machines as equal partners. While some machines controlled predominantly black wards, patronage benefits such as municipal jobs, contracts, and city services were not equally distributed. Machine politicians, such as Richard Daley in Chicago, purposely sought to segregate blacks into highly concentrated urban neighborhoods to effectively limit their political power.[19] Blacks in northern cities did not face the same discriminatory Jim Crow laws as their southern counterparts, but they were nevertheless similarly disenfranchised from political power.

When minority political empowerment finally occurred, the setting and potential of urban politics had radically changed. The civil rights movement of the 1950s and 1960s not only put an end to politically sanctioned discrimination against minorities, it also helped foster a politicized identity among African Americans and other minority groups. From voter registration drives to the political activism of the Black Panthers, African Americans and Latinos in urban areas began to organize themselves politically and gain political power. The massive white out-migration from central cities also made minority groups larger voting blocks. By the 1970s, blacks and Latinos were finally able to overcome decades of discrimination in urban politics and achieve elected office. The election of Maynard Jackson in Atlanta, Carl Stokes in Cleveland, and Henry Cisneros in San Antonio ushered in a new era of black and Latino political representation. At the same time, blacks and Latinos were able to make inroads against discrimination, increasing as a percentage of the municipal workforce and acquiring a greater proportion of municipal contracts.[20]

Yet the history of recent minority political empowerment has unclear implications for processes of democratic governance. By the time blacks were finally gaining access to elected offices in many cities, the white population of these places was dramatically decreasing, as was their mid-

---

[17] Wolfinger 1974.
[18] Chan 1991, Takaki 1989.
[19] Pinderhughes 1994.
[20] Browning, Marshall, and Tabb 1997, Eisinger 1982, Mladenka 1989.

dle-class tax base. Many black leaders came to office facing massive concentrations of poverty, high degrees of social disruption, and few public resources. As a result, black leaders have been constrained in the political agendas they have been able to pursue. A few, such as Marion Berry in Washington, D.C., created extensive patronage organizations, but most other black leaders have not replicated the ethnically based political machines of a century ago. Nor did most black mayors build political coalitions along class lines. Social problems of unemployment, housing, and education may fall disproportionately on black urban populations, but with little control of the productive resources in the economy, black leaders have limited power to solve these problems. Rather, many black city leaders have pursued the strategy of promoting economic growth by working with white economic elites, in the hopes of creating jobs and opportunities for minority advancement.[21] Mayors such as Coleman Young in Detroit, Tom Bradley in Los Angeles, and Andrew Young in Atlanta prioritized economic development over any massive redistributive programs targeted at minority populations. The major impact of black political incorporation has been to correct racial imbalances that had existed in municipal hiring and contracting, rather than to make any significant changes in the material conditions of most urban black populations.[22]

Consequently, the style of today's minority politics differs considerably from earlier types of ethnic mobilization. Without material incentives to coordinate group-based political and civic activism, minority political incorporation in many cities has resulted in a basic pattern of ethnic politics that Raymond Wolfinger has described as "symbolic benefits for the many and real benefits for the few."[23] In other words, most black and Latino civic participation has revolved around the appeals of leaders to a sense of group identity. Lawrence Bobo and Franklin Gilliam, for example, find that blacks participate largely on the basis of feelings of group consciousness stimulated by black leaders, rather than because of material expectations of race-based political rewards.[24] These symbolic appeals have not been without effect. Overcoming a long history of political disenfranchisement, the affirmation of group pride has mobilized blacks and Latinos and righted the imbalances in electoral participation within a very short time. Whereas in 1960 black political participation was much lower than that of whites, today blacks and whites participate at roughly equivalent levels.[25] Although Asians and Latinos vote at slightly lower levels,

---

[21] Stone 1989.
[22] Eisinger 1982, Mladenka 1989.
[23] Wolfinger 1974, p. 85.
[24] Bobo and Gilliam 1990.
[25] Verba, Schlozman, and Brady 1995.

this results in large part from the presence of a high proportion of immigrants in these communities.[26] Barring isolated cases, individual race itself is no longer the barrier to participation in the local democratic process it once was.

Nevertheless, the high degree of racial segregation, particularly between cities and suburbs, calls into question whether American democracy has achieved race neutrality. Discrimination against citizens according to race or ethnicity may no longer be legally sanctioned, but most local American political institutions, including cities, counties, and school districts, are highly bifurcated along racial lines. The civic consequences of this racial separation are unclear. In a polity committed to principles of racial equality yet divided into racially distinct political entities, do its democratic institutions provide an equal voice in politics for all citizens? In other words, is racial segregation distorting the process of self-governance in the United States?

Most answers to these questions have focused on the issue of minority representation and empowerment, with particular attention to whether the racial composition of a particular electoral district inhibits minorities from effectively gaining access to public office. Given the reluctance of whites to vote for minority political candidates,[27] many have debated whether political districts should be drawn to create majority-minority constituencies, thus greatly increasing the odds of minority representation. Indeed, the Supreme Court has ruled that although race cannot be the *primary* factor determining how districts are drawn up, it has also ruled that cities with minority populations must provide by-district as well as at-large city council races to ensure that minorities have equal access to office.

But the question of representation is plagued by a central dilemma: are minority candidates essential for representing minority interests? Given America's long history of racial segregation and discrimination, proponents of purely descriptive representation (i.e., the profile of elected leaders should mirror demographic differences in the population) have a compelling case. As long as whites continue to resist voting for minority candidates because of racial biases, minorities will face a difficult time achieving elected office.[28] We can overcome this bias in outcomes, it is argued, only by creating electoral districts with disproportionate minority populations. On the other hand, one may argue that the color of a candidate's skin is no longer important for advancing minority interests. Some congressional scholars have asserted that white candidates with significant

---

[26] Uhlaner 1989, Cain, Kiewiet, and Uhlaner 1991.
[27] Citrin, Reingold, and Green 1990, Sigelman et al. 1995, Terkildsen 1993.
[28] See Welch and Bledsoe 1988.

minority constituencies often do as good a job of representing minority interests as minority candidates, although others have strongly disagreed and most questions of representation remain unresolved.[29]

Since we cannot ascertain the consequences of racial segregation for either white or minority populations by focusing solely on representation, other aspects of democratic governance should be examined. In this respect, no factor is more important than minority political participation. The color of a political leader's skin may not ensure that a minority group's interests are represented, but active political participation by a minority group can. For instance, in a city that is only 20 percent black, African Americans may have a harder time electing blacks to public office, but if they are politically active and unified, they can be a strong and decisive political bloc.[30] In the absence of any clear guideline on whether descriptive representation is essential for democratic governance, the best way to gauge the civic impact of racial segregation is to see how it influences citizens' ability to represent their own interests through participation in the political process.

Moreover, examining civic participation also enables us to evaluate how whites respond to racial segregation. Most writings on representation understandably have focused largely on minority populations because of their long history of political disenfranchisement and their smaller populations. In the vast majority of American electoral districts, whites do not face racially based barriers to election and do not suffer from underrepresentation. Yet racial segregation may affect the process of democratic governance for white populations in other ways. By focusing on civic participation, we can evaluate how the racial bifurcation of America's cities and suburbs affects the process of self-governance for *all* its residents.

How Segregation Shapes Civic Involvement

Most research on race and civic involvement has focused primarily on the effects of *individual* race or ethnicity and has largely ignored the racial *environment*. It is still unclear whether living among people of one race makes people more or less likely to be civically involved than if they live in a racially mixed setting. As noted in chapter 1, the best way to identify whether a social context, like a city's racial composition, influences civic activity is to see how it shapes the determinants of participation. In other words, how does a city's racial composition affect its residents' attachment to their communities, their interest in local politics, their social

[29] See Swain 1993, Cannon 1999.
[30] For articulation of this classic pluralist argument, see Dahl 1961.

connections with their neighbors, or their experiences of the costs and benefits of participation? Given the history of race relations in America, we might also wonder how the dynamics of participation vary between white and minority communities. In addressing these questions, we will find existing research in related areas to be of some assistance. Although past scholars have not specifically examined racial environments, previous studies of racial attitudes and political behavior offer some important suggestions about how a city's racial composition opens the pathways to public life.

Ethnic Community

One of the primary determinants of individual political participation arises from feelings of "ethnic community." Race, like any defining personal characteristic, can stimulate civic activism as members of a racial group both identify with fellow group members and seek to better their group's position. When citizens understand politics relative to an important and defining social characteristic like race, such issues gain more pertinence or feel more compelling—blacks, Latinos, and Asian Americans are more likely to engage in various types of political activism in response to such feelings of strong group identification and solidarity.[31] For example, Thomas Guterbock and Bruce London find that blacks who feel a greater sense of ethnic community and greater political efficacy are more likely to vote and take part in voluntary organizations than blacks who do not.[32]

The salience of ethnic identity is very dependent on the social context. Situations defined primarily by race, such as racially segregated residential areas, are more likely to evoke a sense of racial consciousness than situations defined by other group cleavages.[33] Thus a black resident of Brooklyn may find the racial dimension of his identity more salient in a racially defined neighborhood like Bedford-Stuyvesant but less salient in the context of a Yankees baseball game, where being a Yankees fan is the more overriding social identity. The social environment, by demarcating the salience of racial identity, also determines the psychological motivation to become civically active relative to racial concerns.

In addition, these patterns of ethnic community can also influence civic engagement by shaping patterns of social interaction. People living in racially similar environments may also feel more familiarity, trust, and communication between neighbors, which can facilitate civic action.

---

[31] Bobo and Gilliam 1990, Shingles 1981, Gurin, Miller, and Gurin 1980, Lien 1997, Uhlaner 1989, Leighley 1996.
[32] Guterbock and London 1983.
[33] Brown 1985.

Community homogeneity has long been recognized as important for developing strong ties between neighbors, bonds that can facilitate the transmission of political information and mobilization into public affairs.[34] Indeed, one of the biggest concerns of early scholars such as Tonnies and Wirth was that the social heterogeneity of cities fostered alienation and anomie among residents. Similarly, communitarian political theorists often view the homogeneity of values in a polity as important precisely because trust and commonality between neighbors is so easily transmitted.[35] Whites living in an entirely white suburb may feel more in common with all of their neighbors and share racially situated beliefs, particularly compared to those outside of the setting, and thus have stronger social ties.[36] Blacks or Latinos may also find greater commonalities among neighbors if they live in settings with higher proportions of minorities. These social ties are crucial for civic action, particularly for less formal civic activities such as working with voluntary organizations and with neighbors.

The question remains, however, about where and how racial environments can trigger these feelings of racial or ethnic consciousness. For minorities, feelings of racial identification depend largely on the size of the proximate minority population. According to most studies, feelings of racial consciousness increase with the density of the group in an immediate environment.[37] Researchers have found that African Americans identify more strongly as "black" as the black percentage of the population continues to grow until blacks are an overwhelming majority.[38] Thus we may expect that for blacks and Latinos, increases in the proportion of minorities will also increase feelings of racial solidarity. In places with large concentrations of minorities, blacks and Latinos may be more willing to think of themselves in terms of their racial identity or express feelings of ethnic community. Conversely, in places that are overwhelmingly white, blacks or Latinos may disassociate from stronger racial identities and instead think of themselves in terms of more individual traits, such as personality, occupation, or interests.[39]

For whites in metropolitan areas, the capacity of the environment to foster a sense of "ethnic community" is less clear. Given that America is still a majority white society, living among more whites may not necessarily give whites a greater sense of racial consciousness the way the anal-

---

[34] See Fischer 1982.
[35] See Sandel 1998, Taylor 1992.
[36] Fischer 1982.
[37] Lau 1989, Bobo and Gilliam 1990, Shingles 1981, Gurin, Miller, and Gurin 1980, Bledsoe et al. 1995.
[38] Bledsoe et al. 1995.
[39] Brown 1985.

ogous situation affects minority populations. In fact, past research suggests just the opposite. White racial consciousness, as evoked in feelings of racism or racial prejudice, typically grows in relation to the size of proximate minority populations. For example, looking at opinion data from the past twenty years, Marylee Taylor finds strong and consistent evidence that a larger black metropolitan population generates a much higher degree of antiblack sentiments among whites, including the invocation of racist stereotypes and opposition to race-based public policies.[40] According to her research, white racial consciousness increases as the minority population increases. Furthermore, since so many whites are segregated in racially defined suburbs, the environment that is important for shaping white racial consciousness may not be their particular neighborhood or even their municipality but the greater metropolitan area. Whites living in an all-white suburb may feel a greater sense of in-group solidarity, particularly compared to the more racially diverse metropolis. Intense suburban racial segregation may demarcate the municipality itself as the racially defined community. Citizens may thus involve themselves in community affairs or work politically as a means of reaffirming their own racial identification or as a means of ensuring the integrity of their city's racial exclusion. Furthermore, social patterns may vary for whites in all-white or predominantly white versus racially mixed places—whites who live amid more minorities may feel less commonality with neighbors, have fewer proximate social ties, and be less civically involved.

Ethnic Conflict

A second perspective on the civic implications of racial segregation focuses on the "real conflict" between racial groups. Many social scientists have sought to explain feelings of racial bias and resentment as originating in the conflict between races over material resources. According to the "power-threat" hypothesis, whites engage in racial violence and other acts of racial discrimination partly in response to the threat that living among many blacks poses to their political and economic privilege.[41] Numerous studies have validated this claim: whites' negative racial attitudes increase with higher percentages of blacks in their immediate area.[42] This racial antagonism putatively arises because people understand economic and political competition between races in zero-sum terms: any gains for one group comes at the expense of another and all its members. Indeed, the fires of racial competition are often stoked as candidates and groups

[40] Taylor 1998.
[41] Key 1984 [1949], Blalock 1967.
[42] Glaser 1994, Wright 1977, Taylor 1998.

jockey for political power and invoke racial messages as a means of building support. Municipal policies, whether they concern the placement of a garbage dump or fire department funding, may be portrayed in racial terms to draw the attention of constituent groups. For example, in 1999, police shootings in New York City of a black immigrant garnered the attention of Al Sharpton and other African American political leaders, while a shooting of Jewish man in Brooklyn attracted the response of the Hasidic community. Each incident arose from causes that police argued had nothing to do with the race or ethnicity of the victims, yet both served to mobilize the particular ethnic communities, which saw the incidents in racial terms: both stimulated letters to public officials, rallies at city hall, and other forms of organized political action.

The impact of ethnic conflict on civic participation is not well understood. On the one hand, we might expect that intergroup competition will motivate political activism as members of different racial groups struggle for public resources. Generally, it seems reasonable that whites, blacks, and Latinos will be more likely to vote or engage in other civic activities as a means of ensuring that their group gets political rewards. On the other hand, racial conflict may prompt whites to erect barriers to participation. As was demonstrated in the South prior to the Civil Rights and Voting Rights Acts, the political threat of large black populations prompted whites to demobilize minorities and institute racial hurdles for electoral participation.[43]

Given these considerations, any expectations about how racial environments shape the parameters of ethnic conflict and civic participation will depend upon the role of municipal boundaries. It is plausible to assume that intracity racial competition will be higher in racially mixed municipalities. Since many of these places are also larger and more urbanized, the stakes of this competition involve greater public resources. Although political leaders in many cities may not control enough economic resources to significantly affect urban unemployment and poverty, they still command a large amount of public funds. Municipal decisions in the funding of services and the administration of land-use decisions can have large impacts on a particular neighborhood or group's material position. Because electoral politics in most racially mixed cities is driven so much by racial and ethnic considerations, it is also likely that citizens will understand the competition for public resources in racial terms. Like gender or partisanship, race is often a heuristic used by voters with limited information to determine their preferences and understand the alternatives represented by candidates. In other words, in the absence of information or other meaningful divisions, voters may presume that candidates or

[43] Key 1984 [1949], Hill and Leighley 1999.

officials who are of their race are more likely to represent their interests; such voters are thus more inclined to become involved in local politics and more likely to be mobilized by racial appeals.[44] According to theories of realistic conflict between races, members of one race may view any decisions that benefit another as coming at their expense. Ordinary political decisions in a racially mixed setting, therefore, may be more likely to take a racial tone. Conversely, the social homogeneity of a white suburban municipality eliminates the potential for intracity political struggles to be understood in racial terms. Without salient racial cues, many citizens may see fewer reasons to follow local politics or listen to appeals from local leaders.

Yet residents of homogeneous places, particularly the all-white suburbs in racially mixed metropolitan areas, may view their municipal institutions as instruments in racial conflict and may be motivated to take part in local politics as a means of maintaining their racial prerogatives. Many criticisms leveled at suburbs point specifically to the way in which whites use suburban boundaries to exclude minorities not simply from their neighborhoods but also from sharing their public resources, such as education, police protection, or public beaches.[45] The imperative of this racial exclusion may prompt local political action. For example, whites in Sterling Heights may view nearby African American populations in Detroit as potential competitors for public goods and may thus use their municipal institutions to ensure their prioritized access to public resources. Even though intracity racial conflict may be minimal, the intercity racial conflict may be so great as to prompt citizens to maintain a civic vigilance.

Correlates of Racial Segregation

A third way that metropolitan racial segregation may shape civic participation comes less from individual psychological or political responses to the race of neighbors than from the social conditions that correlate with racial environments. As a result of a long history of discriminatory practices in both the private and the public housing domains, places that are older, more dense, and varied in land use also contain a higher proportion of minorities, and places that are more economically homogeneous and solely residential in land use are disproportionately white. Indeed, even as blacks and other minorities have suburbanized, they have been more likely to move to "inner ring" suburbs, places that often resemble central cities in land-use patterns and history. The racial composition of a place may therefore also be an indicator of the types of social needs and

---

[44] Terkildsen 1993.
[45] Danielson 1976, Kirp, Dwyer, and Rosenthal 1995.

concerns a community may face. Older and more industrial places have a larger number of social problems, including those of substandard housing, decaying public infrastructure, hazardous waste, and an outmoded employment sector. As Bryan Jones and others have argued, this greater concentration of social needs may be a major incentive for civic participation.[46] All residents of racially mixed places, putatively facing more problems in their community, may have more incentives to become politically involved.

•   •   •

In sum, as with other aspects of a social environment, past research indicates that the racial composition of a municipality may affect citizen participation, but that the direction of this effect depends largely on how citizens view local institutions in relation to their own racial consciousness and identity. For racial minorities, feelings of ethnic community increase with the percentage of fellow group members and also promote interest in politics, feelings of political efficacy, and civic participation. For whites, the interaction between the racial context and civic participation is more complicated. The presence of more minorities may make whites identify more strongly as "white," but the question remains as to how close these minorities need to be to produce this effect. If simply the presence of nearby minorities is enough to generate concerns of ethnic conflict, then white civic participation may increase with the percentage of minorities not only in a city but also in the greater metropolitan area. But if the only way that racial environments shape white participation is by determining the number of neighbors with whom whites might socialize, then racial heterogeneity in a smaller environment, such as a municipality, might depress civic activism. Finally, racially mixed environments may stimulate more civic participation not because of interracial social dynamics but because of the greater problems that arise from their physical and social condition. Since previous research has not examined the effects of racial environments on civic participation, it remains unclear which, if any, of these hypotheses are valid.

EMPIRICAL TESTS

To sort through these competing hypotheses, let us return to the national data and compare some simple statistics. Figure 4.2 lists the average rates of civic participation across places by the percentage of their population

[46] Jones, Greenberg, and Drew 1980.

Blacks

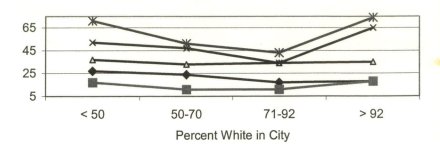

Whites

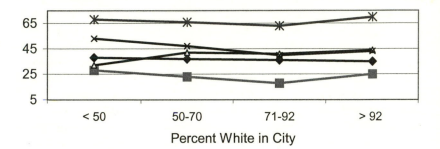

Latinos/Other

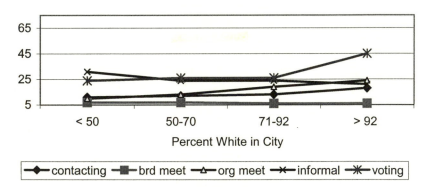

Fig. 4.2. Average Rates of Civic Participation by Percent White in City for Three Racial Groups (source: 1990 Citizen Participation / 1990 U.S. Census Dataset)

that is white for three racial groups: whites, blacks, and Latinos.[47] Among whites, there are few clear or consistent patterns linking civic engagement and the racial composition of a municipality. For example, the frequency of voting is roughly the same in nonwhite places (i.e., places under 50 percent white), 66 percent, as it is in mixed-race places, although it jumps up to nearly 70 percent in predominantly white places (i.e., places over 92 percent white). Board meeting attendance and informal civic activism among whites generally declines from nonwhite to mixed cities, while organizational participation increases with the percent white in a community. Contacting stays relatively constant. For the white population as a whole, it is difficult to draw any conclusions about the relationship between racial segregation and civic activism from simple cross-tabulations.

For African Americans, on the other hand, the effects of racial context are more consistent. Across all four civic activities, there are steady declines in participation between blacks in nonwhite and racially mixed cities. For example, both informal activism and the average score on the local voting scale drop by roughly twenty percentage points between nonwhite cities and mixed cities with a white population between 70 and 92 percent. Smaller drops also occur for contacting and board meeting attendance. Organizational participation seems largely unaffected by the racial context. Curiously, participation is highest among blacks in predominantly white cities. The rates of voting, informal activity, and board meeting attendance are all at their highest rates in predominantly white cities, although it must be noted that only 17 of the 352 African Americans in the sample live in this places. Among Latinos, there are also few recognizable patterns. As a group, Latinos' participation levels are far below those of whites and blacks, owing largely to language and citizenship differences, and the changes in participation across the percent white scale are generally small as well. Voting, organizational attendance, and contacting all seem to rise with the percent white in the city, while informal activism declines.

From the simple cross-tabulations, it is difficult to know exactly how a community's racial composition shapes its residents' civic activity. On the one hand, there appear to be strong group differences in participa-

[47] Since suburbanization has been primarily a white phenomenon, I have chosen to measure the racial differentiation of metropolitan places largely in terms of their white population. The major racial divisions captured in the 1990 Citizen Participation Study are whites, blacks, and Latinos. Of the 1,690 cases in metropolitan areas, only 37 identify themselves as Asian American, American Indian, or as being from some other racial group. Because of their proportionately small numbers they are excluded from the 285 respondents who identified themselves as Latino. Three hundred and fifty-five of the remaining respondents identified themselves as black.

tion. African American civic behavior responds consistently across the percent white scale, generally decreasing from nonwhite to white places; whites and Latinos, while less consistent across civic acts, seem less adversely affected and may even be encouraged by increases in the percent white in a community. On the other hand, it is difficult to know whether the cross-tabulations are masking some unmeasured effects. As we saw in figure 4.1, most predominantly white places are also smaller in size. Smaller places stimulate more civic activity, but it is unclear whether the differing participation rates in the cross-tabulations are the result of the city's size or of its racial composition. Similarly, people who live in predominantly white places, on average, have higher education and income levels and are older and more likely to be homeowners. For example, homeowners constitute 75 percent of those in predominantly white places but only 48 percent in nonwhite places. Since the elderly, homeowners, and the more educated are all more likely to be civically active, it is hardly surprising that rates of civic participation would be higher in predominantly white places, particularly among minority groups.

To properly estimate the distinct effects of a city's racial composition, we must take these other characteristics into consideration. Toward this end, as in the previous chapters, I employ a series of logistic regression analyses. Figures 4.3 and 4.4 display the predicted rates of participation for four categories of places by their white racial composition: places less than 50 percent white (nonwhite cities); places 50 to 70 and 71 to 90 percent white (racially mixed cities); and places over 90 percent white (predominantly white cities).[48] The logistic regressions also controlled for the standard set of individual characteristics (age, education, income, etc.) as well as for measures of city size and the log of median household income. Because the effects of white racial composition are likely to be different for whites, blacks, and Latinos, separate estimations are offered for all three racial categories. The full equations are listed in Appendix B.

The regression equations indicate that the racial composition of a municipality shapes its residents' civic behavior even when the other

[48] To calculate these figures, I ran logistic regressions with a term measuring the percent white in a city (ranging in value from 0.04 to 1) and an interaction term between the percent white and a dummy variable measuring whether the individual respondent was black or Latino. To calculate the predicted probabilities, I employed a procedure similar to the one described in chapter 2, where the distinct effects of the coefficients for the percent white, individual black or Latino dummy, and interaction terms were estimated with all other variables set to their means and then the differences aggregated across the four points of percent white in a city listed in figure 4.3—that is, less than 50 percent white, 50–<70 percent white, 70–92 percent white, and greater than 92 percent white.

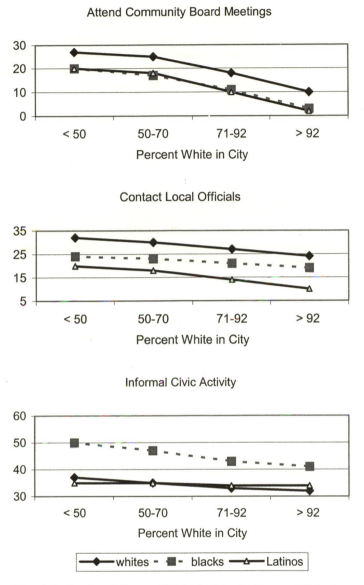

Fig. 4.3. Predicted Rates of Civic Activity by Percent White in City for Three Racial Groups (full equations in Appendix B)

characteristics of the respondents and their communities are considered, although now the direction and relationship are decidedly mixed. As illustrated in figure 4.3, when all other variables are held constant, the equations predict that people who live in predominantly white cities, no matter their own individual race, are much less likely to participate in three types of civic activity than residents of racially mixed places or nonwhite cities. Other factors being constant, whites, blacks, and Latinos in predominantly white cities are all 15 percent less likely to attend community board meetings and all at least 5 percent less likely to contact local officials than their counterparts in nonwhite cities. Blacks in predominantly white places are also less likely to work informally with neighbors than blacks in nonwhite places, although for whites and Latinos these differences are not statistically significant.

For the other two types of civic activity, these same patterns do not hold. As illustrated in figure 4.4, whites in predominantly white cities are significantly *more* likely to attend organizational meetings or vote in local elections than whites in mixed or nonwhite cities.[49] The equations predict that whites in predominantly white places are more likely to vote in local elections than whites in nonwhite places and attend organizational meetings at rates that are more than fifteen percentage points higher. For blacks, the effects of racial environments are nearly as strong, although they work in the opposite direction. Blacks in predominantly white cities are 15 percent less likely to take part in voluntary organizations and score over ten percentage points lower on the local voting scale than blacks in nonwhite cities. Latinos, like whites, are more likely to engage in organizational activity if they live in predominantly white cities, and slightly more likely to vote regularly than Latinos in nonwhite places.

There are several important characteristics to note about these findings. First, as with the other defining characteristics of a place, racial composition is an important determinant of civic activity. There are sizable and statistically significant differences in many of the civic activities between residents of nonwhite and predominantly white places. The biggest differences occur for board and organizational meeting attendance and voting in local elections, with smaller differences for contacting and informal activism, but the magnitude of the differences in the former activities is quite large. For example, the fifteen-percentage-point differences in board and organizational participation are larger in magnitude than the differences between high school dropouts and college-educated citizens, between homeowners and renters, or between men and women.

---

[49] These findings correspond with those of Hill and Leighley (1999), who find that racial diversity at the state level corresponds with lower turnout, less mobilization, and more barriers to registration.

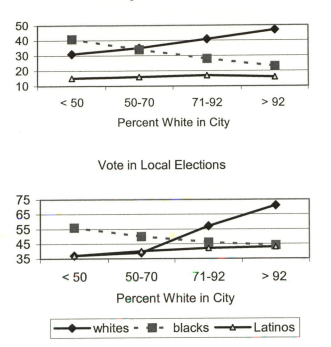

Fig. 4.4. Predicted Rates of Voting and Organizational Activity by Percent White in City for Three Racial Groups (full equations in Appendix B)

Second, unlike size or affluence, a place's racial composition does not affect all five types of civic participation in consistent ways. Where civic activity uniformly declines in both larger and more affluent places, only three types of civic activity decline in predominantly white places for all racial groups: contacting, informal civic work, and board meeting attendance.[50] Blacks, Latinos, and whites are less likely to engage in these

---

[50] Another reason why all types of civic activity do not respond consistently may lie in the differences between a city's racial diversity and its white racial composition. Since whites constitute the majority of the American population, it is easy to presume that the white percentage within a municipality is also an indicator of its racial diversity: the greater the percentage of whites, the greater the racial homogeneity. But this is not always the case. If we compare the racial diversity of a city with the percent of the population that is white, we find that racial homogeneity also exists at the bottom end of the percent white scale. Many cities with low white populations, such as Detroit, are composed mostly of one minority group, a pattern that occurs across the country as a whole. Since Asians tend to be more residentially integrated with whites, one is less likely to find solely Asian communities. High

three activities as the percentage of whites in a city grows. For the other two civic activities, the effect of a place's racial composition changes both in direction and in its interaction with individual race. Whites in predominantly white places are more likely to vote and be active in local organizations. For blacks, the opposite effect occurs—blacks living in predominantly white cities are much less likely to work in organizations or vote. Latinos are much less affected by their racial surroundings, partly because their overall levels of participation are much lower.

In sum, these findings suggest that white racial segregation in the suburbs tends to depress most types of civic activity, particularly for African Americans. Among both whites and blacks, a greater white percentage in a municipality corresponds with a lower propensity to contact officials, attend community board meetings, or work informally with their neighbors. Minorities in predominantly white places (i.e., suburbs) are also less likely to engage in voluntary organizations or to vote. The only exceptions to this trend are with white organizational activity and voting. In predominantly white cities, whites are more likely to attend organizational meetings and vote frequently in local elections.

RACIAL SEGREGATION, POLITICAL INTEREST, AND MOBILIZATION

In chapter 1, I suggested that social environments shape civic participation primarily by influencing the determinants of participation, such as political interest and mobilization. For example, chapters 2 and 3 demonstrated that residents of larger and economically homogeneous cities were less likely to be civically active partly because they were less interested in community affairs, were less likely to be mobilized by their neighbors, or found participation less efficacious. These same factors should also drive the relationship between civic participation and a place's racial composition. From the standpoint of an *ethnic community* argument, political interest, efficacy, and mobilization among minorities should all increase with the proportion of minority group members in a community—people who live among people of their own race, the thinking goes, are more likely to identify with their fellow group members and get involved in community affairs.[51] Proponents of an *ethnic conflict* argument may argue that similar effects hold for whites: the greater the size

---

levels of Latino integration reduce the number of predominantly Latino places as well. Cities that are at the ends of the percent white scale, particularly those that are predominantly white, tend to be very racially homogeneous. Cities that contain between 40 and 80 percent white hold a much wider range of racial groups and score much higher on the racial diversity scale. The percent white in a city is not a linear proxy of its racial homogeneity; rather, racial homogeneity is highest in places at the *ends* of the percent white scale.

[51] See Lau 1989, Bledsoe et al. 1995.

of the minority population, the more racialized the political conflict, and the more whites may get involved as a means of expressing their own racial identity.

Yet the findings above do not immediately suggest that the same processes work in identical ways for all racial groups, as blacks, whites, and Latinos respond to racial environments in different ways. Among blacks, there are consistent patterns of civic participation—all five civic behaviors decrease as the percentage of whites in their city grows. Among whites and Latinos, however, there are inconsistent patterns across the percent white scale—participation drops for acts like contacting and community board attendance in predominantly white places, but it rises for acts like voting and organizational activity. This prompts the question of the extent to which civic participation is driven by feelings of ethnic community, conflict, or some other source, and whether these feelings are the same for all racial groups.

One way to sort through these issues is to examine the interracial differences in the determinants of participation across the percent white scale. Figure 4.5 depicts the predicted average levels of local political interest, feelings of political efficacy, and patterns of political mobilization across the percent white scale derived from OLS regression equations that controlled for the same set of variables listed above. For blacks, feelings of both political interest and efficacy decline as the percentage of whites enlarges. The equations predict that blacks living in a nonwhite city score, on average, 0.5 points higher on a four-point political interest scale and nearly 1 point higher on an eight-point efficacy scale than blacks living in a predominantly white city. Whites and Latinos are slightly more likely to express political interest and efficacy as the percentage of whites in a city increases, although the differences in efficacy are small and not statistically significant. Interestingly, there are almost no differences in patterns of political mobilization across the percent white scale for any of the three racial groups—the mobilization patterns of whites, blacks, and Latinos, while occurring at different levels, seem largely immune to the racial composition of the municipality.[52] Nevertheless, for the other two determinants of civic activity, there are large differences across the percent white scale, particularly for African Americans.

These differences in political interest and efficacy largely account for the changes in black participation. Figure 4.6 depicts the predicted rate of overall civic participation (by aggregating all five civic participation items) for African Americans first, as regressed on the standard set of

[52] This may be the consequence of the unit of analysis employed. In other words, political mobilization may be more influenced by neighborhood racial composition than by city-level racial composition.

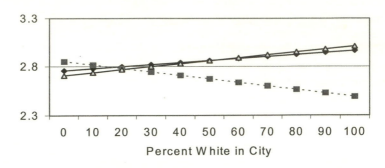

Interest in Local Politics

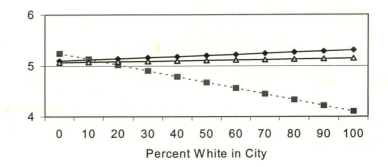

Efficacy

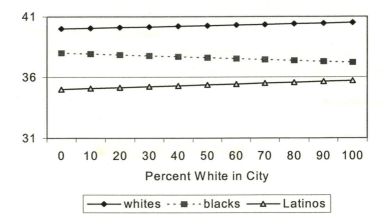

Mobilized for Local Politics

— whites · · ■ · · blacks — △ — Latinos

Fig. 4.5. Predicted Levels of Political Interest, Efficacy, and Mobilization by Percent White in City for Three Racial Groups (full equations in Appendix B)

controls, and then when controls for political interest and efficacy are added. When we take into account only individual differences in education, age, income, and the like, and city size and median household income, there is a sharp drop in the average number of civic acts across the percent white scale. The equation predicts that blacks in predominantly white places participate in 0.7 fewer civic acts than those in nonwhite places. However, when lower interest and efficacy are also controlled, the difference shrinks, nearly in half, to only 0.37 civic acts, a divergence that is no longer statistically significant. Much of the changing rates of civic participation between blacks in white and nonwhite cities is attributable to these feelings of interest and efficacy.

The evidence in figure 4.6 thus suggests that feelings of ethnic community are at the heart of the relationship between black civic participation and the racial environment. Blacks in predominantly white places are less likely to engage in a host of civic activities because they feel less empowered and less interested in community affairs. Consider, for example, the five hundred African Americans living in Sterling Heights, Michigan. Insofar as they represent a tiny fraction of their city's population, it is unlikely that their feelings of racial community can be evoked in any politically meaningful way. As Roger Brown has speculated, in these circumstances, blacks are more likely to express loyalty to existing social norms or "exit" into personal characteristics rather than act according to racially based concerns. As the percentage of blacks in a community increases, blacks gain a greater sense of racial solidarity, as past research has shown, become politically engaged, and involve themselves in local activities.

It is difficult to know, from the data presented, whether Latino civic participation is affected by feelings of ethnic community and racial environments. The levels of political interest and efficacy among Latinos are far below those of the other racial groups and mirror their generally low levels of civic participation. Moreover, Latino civic participation does not vary nearly as much with the racial composition of the community as it does for either whites or blacks. To whatever extent Latinos are experiencing a sense of ethnic solidarity, it does not seem related to the white racial composition of their surroundings.[53]

Nor does the ethnic community hypothesis explain white civic participation, as whites' feelings of political interest and efficacy are not greatly affected by their environment.[54] Moreover, these determinants do not

---

[53] Latinos may be more active with a greater proportion of Latinos in their city. Unfortunately, the small number of Latinos in the Citizen Participation Study do not allow for this assertion to be tested.

[54] It is also unclear from these data how well ethnic community can explain Latino partici-

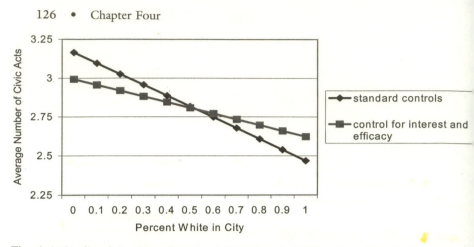

Fig. 4.6. Predicted Average Number of Civic Acts for African Americans by Percent White in City Before and After Controlling for Political Interest and Efficacy (full equations in Appendix B)

really explain the differences in participation between whites in racially mixed and predominantly white cities. For example, if the equation depicted in figure 4.6 is run for whites, the effects of political interest and efficacy have virtually no impact on the relationship between the racial environment and civic participation. Although a sense of racial group solidarity may account for the differences in organizational activity, as I will discuss below, feelings of ethnic community do not explain most differences in white civic participation across racial environments.

Of course, theories of ethnic community may not be well suited for explaining the behavior of a predominant racial group in society, such as whites. Feelings of group identity may be present only for minority or disempowered groups such as blacks, women, or gays, or specific ethnic populations that have suffered discrimination, such as Irish or Jewish Americans. A better explanation of white civic behavior may come from the ethnic conflict model, which states that whites in more racially mixed places are putatively stimulated by racial competition to get more interested in public affairs.

Yet the data provide little evidence that ethnic conflict is behind the differences in white civic behavior. First, white voting patterns do not perform in accordance with an ethnic conflict model—whites are much more likely to vote if they live in predominantly white places than if they

pation. Given the low rates of Latino involvement and the relatively small differences across the percent white scale, it is difficult to know how Latinos are responding to environmental cues. Clearly, larger sample sizes with more data are required to unearth the contextual effects on Latino civic behavior.

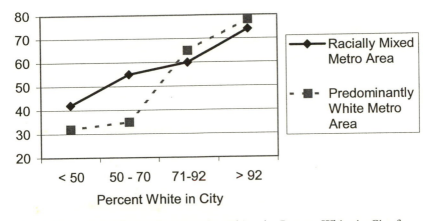

Fig. 4.7. Predicted Rates of Voting for Whites by Percent White in City for Racially Mixed and Predominantly White Metropolitan Areas (full equations in Appendix B)

live in racially mixed cities. According to the ethnic conflict model, voting should be higher in settings where racial conflict is greater. Now, a proponent of conflict theory may argue that the voting patterns do reflect racial struggle, but the domain of this struggle is intermunicipal rather than intramunicipal. In other words, whites in white suburbs are voting more as a means of affirming their racial prerogatives as defined by local municipalities amid the threat of nearby black populations. If this theory is correct, then we should find higher voting in white suburbs of racially mixed metropolitan areas than in predominantly white metropolitan areas. The data, however, do not support this contention. Figure 4.7 compares the predicted rates of voting for whites by the percentage in their city that is white between predominantly white metropolitan areas (populations over 80 percent white) and racially mixed metropolitan areas (populations under 80 percent white). As is evident in the figure, there are virtually no differences in predicted voting rates. White voting in white metropolitan areas behaves almost identically to white voting in racially mixed metropolitan areas, across the percent-white-in-the-city scale.

Second, it does not appear that the higher rates of white board meeting attendance, contacting, or informal civic activity in racially mixed cities (see figure 4.3) are the consequence of greater racial conflict either. Whites in racially mixed cities are slightly less interested in local politics. If the conflict theory were correct, these whites should be exhibiting greater attention to local affairs; instead, they are less interested. Furthermore, for these three civic activities, participation falls at relatively equal levels for all three racial groups. Whites, blacks, and Latinos are all equally more likely to attend board meetings and contact officials in places with fewer white residents. If theories of racial conflict were correct, these results would vary across racial groups.

So why are white residents of racially mixed places, who are also less interested in local affairs, also more likely to work in their communities, just as their black and Latino neighbors do? The most likely explanation is that a city's racial composition brings the differences between the various civic acts more sharply into focus. The three civic activities listed in figure 4.3—contacting officials, attending board meetings, and working with neighbors—are instrumental types of behavior, that is, they are directed toward a particular goal. Citizens usually contact leaders or get involved in community boards in response to particular problems or concerns in their surroundings, such as getting a pothole filled, addressing school safety, or lobbying for better street cleaning.

The higher and uniform rates of citizen action in nonwhite cities may reflect the types of social needs present in racially mixed places. As noted above, racially heterogeneous places, being older, larger, and more urbanized than predominantly white places, also harbor a larger number of social problems requiring citizen action. For instance, racially mixed cities like Yonkers, New York, or Hayward, California, as more industrialized and urban places, are also more likely to face problems of traffic, housing, and waste than a predominantly white suburb of equal size. Hence residents of these places may be more likely to attend community meetings, contact officials, or work with neighbors (the most immediate and direct forms of political involvement), because they are faced with a greater number of social problems. The combination of greater social problems, fewer public resources, and higher racial heterogeneity may also serve to further racialize political conflict and stimulate civic action.[55]

The other civic activities are much less instrumental. Voting, for example, is not an efficient mechanism for communicating specific policy preferences. Even in small municipalities the likelihood that an individual vote can be decisive for the outcome of an election is quite small. Consequently, the motivations for voting often may come from the symbolic rewards, such as reaffirming one's membership in a particular group. People in homogeneous communities may be more likely to vote or attend organizational functions as a means of bolstering a group identity. It is also likely that nonwhite cities are more likely to produce minority candidates, thus bolstering black voting and depressing white turnout.

---

[55] Unfortunately, nothing in the data allows for these last speculations to be tested directly. The complete causal mechanisms between racial segregation and the varying types of civic participation await future tests with more complete data.

Organizational attendance is also more of a social than an instrumental activity. Although many local organizations function to address social needs in a community, many are simply places to interact with like-minded people. Voluntary organizations are also more related to personal connections and social networks than other civic activities. Organizational participation, unlike other civic acts, may reflect strong intraracial socializing preferences. Whites in predominantly white surroundings may be more likely to know their neighbors and have acquaintances nearby; they are more likely to engage in social activities with those with whom they feel they have more in common. Blacks who live in predominantly black areas may be more organizationally active for the same reasons.

In sum, the effects of racial segregation on civic participation arise from disparate sources for different racial groups. For blacks, it appears that feelings of ethnic community drive some of the heightened participation levels in racially mixed places. Such feelings of racial solidarity may also drive the increased voting and organizational activity of whites in predominantly white settings. However, another factor also explains the participation differences between nonwhite and white places—the existence of social problems and concerns. All people in racially mixed cities are more likely to participate, no matter what their individual race, because of the greater social needs that arise in urban areas. This demonstrates the other political reality of racial segregation. Blacks, Latinos, and other minorities are disproportionately concentrated in poor urban centers that have higher population densities, higher levels of crime and social problems, and greater need for citizen activity. The reality of these problems defines metropolitan political life and patterns of civic action. They also create the civic paradox of racial segregation.

CONCLUSION

In the 1960s, racial segregation in America's metropolitan areas was at the forefront of national political concern. Following riots in Detroit, Newark, Watts, and other cities that cost hundreds of lives and billions in property, the federal government proclaimed that the racial division of cities and suburbs was a primary threat to the nation's well-being. In their famous pronouncement, the 1968 National Advisory Commission on Civil Disorders (also known as the Kerner Commission) concluded that suburbanization was fostering the "division of our country into two societies: one, largely Negro and poor, located in the central cities; the other, predominantly white and affluent, located in the suburbs."[56] Left unchecked, the continuing problems of urban violence, poverty, and ra-

[56] As quoted in Berger 1960.

cial discrimination, the commission concluded, would be perpetuated, with grievous implications. The commission recommended that America needed to do more than simply accept the status quo or pour money into poor, urban areas; America needed to promote the racial integration of its suburbs.

For a brief time, many government and nongovernmental organizations pursued this goal. In 1968, Congress passed the Fair Housing Act, which banned racial discrimination in the sale or rental of housing units. Public interest organizations, such as the NAACP, used the law to challenge racially biased practices in various municipal housing authorities as well as private real estate agencies. Scores of local organizations set about designing and building subsidized housing to encourage black settlement in suburban areas.[57] Yet, over thirty years later, America's cities and suburbs remain as racially divided as ever. Despite the efforts of the federal government, federal and state courts, activists, and voluntary organizations, most suburbs continue to be almost entirely white, while most larger central cities hold a disproportionate share of minorities.

What implications does this continued racial segregation hold for American democracy? Are the mechanisms of democratic government distorted by imbalances in a city's racial composition? Such questions do not have easy answers. Some scholars look at the continued disparities between blacks and whites with regard to health, income, education, and employment and argue that America's political institutions, particularly the ones in cities and suburbs, are not serving minority interests.[58] One need only consider the Los Angeles riots of 1992 as an indication of the social tensions that still exist within America's inner cities. Yet race and class segregation in America's metropolitan areas are highly correlated. Although the class situation of many minorities doubtless results from continued practices of discrimination, it is difficult to ascertain whether the scarcity of public resources and the lower quality of public services in many racially mixed places is the consequence of their poverty, their racial composition, or some combination of the two. Outside of education, it is hard to attribute any policy outcomes to racial segregation alone. Similarly, from the standpoint of representation, it is unclear whether racial segregation is a benefit or a hindrance to the articulation of minority political interests. Higher proportions of minorities within political jurisdictions may ensure that minority candidates have a fair chance of being elected; yet, given the fiscal limitations of most municipal leaders, it is by no means guaranteed that minority interests will thereby be advanced,

---

[57] See Boger 1997.
[58] West 1994, Cloward and Piven 1974.

assuming that such distinct minority interests could be readily identified in the first place.

And, as we have seen in this chapter, the particular effects of racial segregation on patterns of civic participation do not lend themselves to any simple conclusions either. On the one hand, racial segregation seems to boost certain types of civic activities, particularly those involving more symbolic gestures or social connections between residents. Both whites and blacks are more interested in local politics, are more likely to take part in local organizational activity, and are more likely to vote in local elections when surrounded by people of their own race. Blacks living in predominantly white places report feeling less empowered and less politically interested. Denizens of racially homogeneous places seem to be more socially entangled in their communities than people in diverse locales.

On the other hand, this greater social connection does not translate into more politically active citizens across the board. Residents of predominantly white cities, both white and nonwhite, are much less likely to contact officials, attend community board meetings, or work informally with their neighbors than people in racially mixed places. Although the sources of these differences cannot be precisely determined with existing data, the most likely cause is the social condition of racially mixed places. Racially diverse municipalities in America are also more populated, dense, and urbanized than most predominantly white cities. Just as many predominantly white suburbs are underpoliticized (i.e., through intense racial and class segregation they effectively preempt many of the political conflicts brought about by the economic and social diversity of a metropolis), so many racially mixed cities may be overpoliticized. In other words, most racially mixed cities not only contain a disproportionate share of minority populations, they also contain a disproportionate share of social problems requiring collective solutions. If racial heterogeneity also gives these conflicts a racial flavor, then the social circumstance of racially mixed places can stimulate other types of political involvement.

Ironically, suburban racial segregation may benefit American civil society yet distort its processes of democratic governance. Many contemporary political observers bemoan the putative loss of community and the norms of trust over the past forty years.[59] Such commentators view the breakdown of American society as undermining the potential of its democratic institutions to allow for meaningful self-governance by its citizens. For example, in his famous "bowling alone" argument, Robert Putnam locates the decay of American civic life in the declining levels of organiza-

---

[59] Putnam 1995, Ehrenhalt 1995, Suarez 1999.

tional membership.[60] While Americans are still bowling in great numbers, they are no longer bowling in organized leagues and are losing the experiences that help build social trust and sustain community.

From the results in these chapters, those seeking a "return to community" may find themselves in the awkward position of advocating racial segregation. If social capital is a crucial mechanism for the success of democratic institutions, then political theorists must grapple with the paradox of a multiracial society: as long as race and ethnicity continue to be a predominant characteristic by which people differentiate themselves socially, democracies wanting higher stocks of social capital will benefit from greater spatial racial segregation. Indeed, the recommendation of the Kerner Commission may be disadvantageous for the civic life of minorities. If nonwhites living in white areas feel less interested or efficacious with respect to local politics, then integration may serve only to demobilize and disempower those groups that have long suffered discrimination. In a racially conscious society, where racial differentiation defines patterns of social interaction so sharply, segregation also facilitates greater social contact among citizens and interest in local affairs.[61] From the social capital perspective, the segregation of metropolitan populations may be the optimal situation for generating stronger ties between residents.

But to value racial segregation in the name of civil society is like cutting off one's head to spite one's face—segregation may boost social connections between citizens but cause distortions in the nature of local democracy. Segregation does not increase participation in all types of civic activities, only those involving socially based contacts among citizens (participation in voluntary organizations) or symbolic political gestures (voting). The other ways that citizens voice their opinions, such as through contacting officials or working with neighbors to solve prob-

---

[60] Putnam 1995.

[61] Obviously, the best solution to the social capital dilemma is not to gladly accept segregation along racial lines as a means of boosting community but to address those factors that keep people from different races or ethnic groups from interacting more freely. Unfortunately, the means for doing this are not simple. The difficulties of promoting racial harmony through interpersonal contact are monumental. A vast literature on interracial contact has shown that the benefits of interracial mixing arise only under very constrained circumstances. Proximity and contact alone are no guarantee that racial antagonisms will attenuate (Brown 1985). Indeed, many argue that racial mixing contributes to higher levels of antagonism (Blalock 1967). Nevertheless, in a democratic society committed to the principle of racial equality, the current pattern of racial segregation must be viewed as intolerable. While promoting integration may have some costs to American democracy in feelings of community and its stock of social capital, the current alternative of embracing the status quo threatens to further balkanize the nation's metropolitan areas and inhibit the cooperation necessary for addressing the most grievous of social problems.

lems, uniformly increase in racially heterogeneous places largely because of the political reality of these places. Residents of racially mixed cities, no matter their own individual race, are more politically active because such places often shoulder more social problems requiring collective solutions. The greater social capital fostered by racial segregation cannot justify the social and material imbalances that currently exist within America's metropolitan areas. According to an authentic governance principle, local governments need to share in the social problems of a geographic area. To have some instruments of the state solely responsible for facing the legacies of industrial development is to violate the democratic imperatives of local government.

As I will discuss in chapter 8, if local institutions are to address the problems that threaten the well-being of the metropolis—a threat looming over all residents, regardless of their skin color—racial integration must be promoted, even if this means sacrificing a sense of ethnic community and social capital in the short run. Otherwise, problems of poverty and postindustrial urban decay will continue to fester and to be cast in racial tones. In the 1960s and as recently as the early 1990s, these realities exploded in racial violence and urban riots; the continuing reality of racial segregation in the American metropolis makes such urban disturbances a likelihood in the future. As with class segregation in suburbia, white racial segregation is a means by which local political institutions serve to exclude and separate citizens of a common metropolitan community: a separation that may boost some kinds of social involvement but will ultimately impede democratic governance in a metropolitan era.

CHAPTER FIVE

A Bedroom *Polis*

THE LOCATION OF A furniture store is not the type of issue that generally arouses political passion, nor is Westchester County, New York (a suburb of New York City), the type of place typically equated with political controversy. Yet both are at the center of a political maelstrom. Mamaroneck, an affluent bedroom suburb, recently passed a law to block the construction of a large furniture store in nearby New Rochelle. This move has divided the whole county into two factions. On one side are the smaller bedroom communities like Mamaroneck, Rye, Pelham, and Larchmont, which want to restrict development and maintain the residential character of Westchester. On the other side are larger, more diverse communities such as Yonkers, Mount Vernon, and Port Chester, which are seeking jobs and economic growth. What started as a plan for a furniture store has mushroomed into an intense political struggle involving protests, lawsuits and countersuits, and the entire political organization of a county. Why is there so much vehemence over a furniture store? At one level, this fight is about class politics: affluent suburbs trying to impose their will on larger, less affluent communities. As Mayor John Spencer of Yonkers notes, "Those of us in big cities face problems that smaller communities do not. We need jobs, we need revenues and opportunities for people."[1] But at a deeper level, this conflict is so fierce because it speaks to an issue at the heart of local politics—the ability of municipalities to determine land usage within their own borders.

Land is, as any observer of city politics will tell you, at the center of local politics. From Fargo to Fresno, city council meetings are dominated by issues of property development, road and infrastructure construction, zoning, and tax abatements. Most average citizens' concerns about local politics center on either their own property or others' property development plans that might impinge on their quality of life. The lion's share of local political contributions come from interests tied to real estate.[2] Many local political candidates, particularly from smaller constituencies, are drawn from the ranks of developers, real estate agents, or other land-

---

[1] As quoted by Lisa Foderaro, "Suburbs Try to Limit Projects outside Their Borders," *New York Times*, March 11, 2000, p. B1.

[2] For documentation and examples, see Logan and Molotch 1987, pp. 230–31.

oriented businesses with a keen interest and expertise in municipal ordinances.

This land-centered character of local politics derives largely from the subordinate position of municipal government. Local governments are creatures of state government and are thereby limited in the powers they can wield. In most states, the broadest powers given to localities concern land use (e.g., zoning policies, property tax rates, and infrastructure investments in roads, sewers, and water lines).[3] Municipal politics also tends to focus on land use because it is there that local governments can, in theory, exercise the most control. As Paul Peterson has argued, local politics is limited because land, unlike labor or capital, is immobile and thus is one of the few realms easily subject to local dominion.[4] For all these reasons, land development and regulation is the primary mechanism in municipal government for stimulating economic growth, defining a community's composition, and shaping a town's quality of life.

The importance of land use is also central for our inquiry into suburban democratic life. With suburbanization, America's cities have become increasingly differentiated not only by their affluence and racial composition but by the character of their land usage. Prior to the twentieth century, limited transportation technologies forced people to live within walking distance of their work, and most older cities held a dense concentration of residential, commercial, and industrial sites.[5] As is still evident in the historic sections of Boston, Williamsburg, or many European cities, many eighteenth-century urban buildings were designed to be places not just of residence but of employment. Although the early nineteenth century saw an increasing differentiation between home and work, most homes continued to be nestled close to industrial areas. It was only with the advent of the streetcar and the automobile that the proximity between work and home began to widen and an entirely new type of place arose, the bedroom suburb.[6]

Bedroom suburbs are distinct from either central cities or rural towns because they are often large communities composed solely of homes. Whereas large cities traditionally have had commercial and industrial sites within their dense settlements, today this is no longer the case.[7] Across

---

[3] Logan and Molotch 1987.

[4] Peterson 1981.

[5] Mumford 1961.

[6] Throughout this chapter I use the terms "suburbs" and "bedroom suburbs." Although most popular references conflate the two terms, in this study they have separate meanings. Suburbs are all the places within a metropolitan area that are not part of the central city. Bedroom suburbs (a.k.a. residentially predominant cities) are a particular type of suburb that I will define shortly.

[7] Although residential enclaves located outside of large urban areas have existed for thou-

the United States, hundreds of larger municipalities, often with as many as 50,000 residents, contain virtually no designated work sites or businesses. In fact, since 1945, the development of residentially predominant places has been the primary catalyst of metropolitan growth.[8] Although industrial and commercial activity outside of central cities also increased during this time, it is primarily the creation of bedroom suburbs on the outskirts of large central cities that has driven the expansion of the American metropolis.[9] Today, nearly one in four Americans lives in what could be called a residentially predominant place or bedroom suburb.[10]

The democratic implications of this shift, however, are ambiguous. Most studies of urban political life have rightly focused on the struggle between groups defined by their relationship to the land. For example, John Logan and Harvey Molotch distinguish between the political desires of those who seek to maximize the exchange-value of property (such as commercial developers, banks, real estate agents, etc.) and those who also seek use-value from the property they inhabit (i.e., renters and homeowners).[11] Because the effects of local policies have quantifiable impacts on the value of property, commercial interests have strong incentives to be keen observers of, and players in, local politics. Their smaller number and their control over the productive resources in a capitalist economy also make them ideal coalition partners for local officials, who typically seek to promote employment and enhance municipal tax revenue.[12] In these growth regimes, the concerns of average citizens are often passed over. Most homeowners and renters face collective action problems in expressing their preferences, since most have limited, enumerable property interests and often seek more use-value from their property than exchange-value. In other words, the average citizen has few incentives to be attentive to municipal decisions unless a particular threat arises to her immediate environment, a fact that is consistent with our understanding of public opinion in general—that is, most people are inattentive to politics unless a dominant or salient issue grabs their attention.[13] Given the imbalances of resources, interest, and attention between average citizens and major property holders, local democracy is generally characterized as the domination of growth-oriented developers who occasionally are

---

sands of years (Jackson 1985), it is only in the past two centuries that large settlements devoted primary to residence have emerged.

[8] Muller 1981.

[9] Jackson 1985.

[10] This figure was calculated from the 1990 Census as the percentage of Americans living in cities where less than 25 percent of the employed population worked in their city of residence.

[11] Logan and Molotch 1987.

[12] Stone 1989, Elkin 1987.

[13] Zaller 1992.

thwarted by mass uprisings of the citizenry, often in response to threats to their quality of life.[14]

Yet this characterization of growth-dominated politics derives largely from the observation of big cities. Most research on urban politics focuses on larger cities like Atlanta, New Haven, New York, Chicago, or Los Angeles. In these places, the desires of renters, homeowners, and real estate developers are often in sharp contrast with each other, and, because of the advantages of commercial interests, local democracy is often distorted in favor of growth regimes. Yet such a framework says little about democracy in places where such struggles are, by definition, preempted. If a suburban municipality has strict zoning forbidding commercial development, then growth-oriented interests are necessarily excluded from city politics. Political conflicts may occur less frequently within a bedroom suburb, but, as the case of Mamaroneck reveals, they will arise between municipalities. Growth or regime models of local politics are not very applicable in a city where all residents have a similar relationship to the land. To study how democracy functions in residential communities, we need to look beyond the machinations of city hall and focus on how citizens actually involve themselves in local affairs when they live in a city of homes.

Given the direction of past research, this would seem an easy task. Although not always recognized as such, residential predominance has been a central focus of most research on the suburbs. In other words, most studies of suburbs in general have been of bedroom suburbs in particular. These studies provide very mixed assessments about the influence of suburban social contexts. Early views tended to characterize bedroom suburbs as minirepublics with superinvolved residents. Several ethnographies of the 1950s and 1960s that focused on solely residential communities, such as Gans's *The Levittowners*, Seeley et al.'s *Crestwood Heights*, Whyte's *Organization Man*, or Berger's *Working Class Suburb*, generally concluded that such places made residents more engaged in community affairs. As Berger summarized: "A new kind of hyperactive social life has apparently developed in suburbia. This is manifest not only in the informal visiting or 'neighboring' that is said to be rife, but also in the lively organizational life that goes on. Associations, clubs, and organizations are said to exist for almost every conceivable hobby, interest, or preoccupation."[15] Later critics, however, have argued that bedroom suburbs foster isolation and withdrawal.[16] Unlike the public and interactive spaces accorded by urban neighborhoods, the "privatized" lifestyle generated by the architecture and design of the typical bedroom suburb put-

[14] Stone 1989, Ferman 1996.
[15] Berger 1960, p. 6.
[16] Langdon 1994, Schneider 1992, Kunstler 1993.

atively inhibits spontaneous social contact and citizen involvement in local politics.[17] This indictment of the typical bedroom suburb is epitomized by Phillip Langdon's conclusion: "We need to develop [bedroom] suburbs that foster neighborhood and public life rather than squelch it. This requires designing suburbs so that public areas throughout the community are enjoyable to occupy. Houses need to treat the public areas as important, congenial places. Instead of glorifying interior and private spaces while leaving the public environment dominated by uncommunicative facades and garage doors, we need to reorient houses so that they dignify and enliven the places where neighbors and strangers come in contact with one another."[18] According to most contemporary critics, today's residential suburbs are stifling the public engagement and civic activism fostered in an earlier, urban era.[19]

As with most assertions about suburban life, these critiques of bedroom suburbs are either dated, overgeneralized, or not substantiated with any firm evidence. The ethnographies of the 1950s may provide interesting descriptions of individual places, but they cannot specify whether categorical differences exist between the behaviors of suburban and nonsuburban residents or what the sources of these behaviors may be. It is unclear whether the patterns described by individual researchers are attributable to the bedroom suburb's residential character, its economic status, or the types of people who chose to live there. Moreover, if their generalizations are valid, it is unclear whether they continue to hold in a time when, for example, a larger percentage of women are employed. Meanwhile, contemporary architectural criticisms of bedroom suburbs are based largely on speculation and echo a nostalgia for a time and place that may exist only through a filtered memory. In truth, we have no strong evidence that citizens living in a city composed solely of homes behave any differently from or are any more or less interconnected than their counterparts in a city with mixed land use. Nevertheless, given the primacy of land to local politics and the heap of speculation about bedroom suburbs, we have many reasons to suspect that democracy may function differently in solely residential places.

DEFINING A BEDROOM SUBURB

The first step in exploring democratic life in a bedroom suburb is to determine which places belong to this category. This is not a straightforward task. Although the defining characteristic of a bedroom suburb may

---

[17] Jacobs 1961, Popenoe 1985.
[18] Langdon 1994, p. xiii.
[19] Suarez 1999.

be the absence of work sites (as the name implies, bedroom suburbs are primarily places of residence), most studies do not attribute the contextual effects of suburban residence to the dearth of indigenous workplaces. Rather, other social or physical characteristics, such as the prevalence of garage facades or the absence of public spaces, are typically accused of alienating the citizenry.[20] It is unclear, however, which of these factors are unique to bedroom suburbs. Many bedroom suburbs have public meeting areas, group facilities, or physical designs that encourage social interaction. Many urban areas have high-rise apartments that, as Jane Jacobs pointed out, seem more isolating than any neighborhood.[21] From the design criteria, it is virtually impossible to develop a quantifiable measure of how "suburban" a community really is. Moreover, from the perspective of urban politics, the more important aspect of suburban life is the arrangement of property interests within a community. According to growth machine models, what matters most for a local democracy is not what types of homes citizens live in, but what type of use- or exchange-value they desire from their property and whether there are groups with large financial investments seeking to manipulate local politics, often at the expense of neighborhood quality of life.

Consequently, in examining the effects of the bedroom suburb, I focus primarily on the residential quality of the place, that is, what percentage of its buildings are dominated by homes. The best available measure of this quality comes from two place-level items in the U.S. Census: the percentage of the workforce composed of commuters; and the percentage of residents who are homeowners. The first measure is used because the census provides information not on all the buildings within a community but on domiciles alone. Hence existing data do not allow for the percentage of land-as-residential to be directly calculated. Nevertheless, the percentage of commuters (i.e., the percentage of the workforce employed in other cities) can be used as a good proxy, since it seems reasonable to assume that a place with a higher commuting rate will have fewer work sites than a place with lower one. Of course, some places may have as many residents commuting out as commuting in: a city may have many commuters but not necessarily be solely residential. Consequently, other measures are also needed to verify a place's residential character. The percentage of homeowners provides a good supplementary measure. Not only is it highly correlated with the percentage commuting, it also indicates the types of domiciles in a city, since more than two-thirds of all owned dwellings are single-family homes.[22]

---

[20] See Baldassare 1992, Langdon 1994, Popenoe 1985, Jackson 1985.
[21] For the classic appraisal of the human impacts of urban environments, see Jacobs 1961.
[22] Jackson 1985.

TABLE 5.1
Average Percentages of Commuters, Families, and Homeowners by City Size
(standard deviation in parentheses)

City Size	Percent Commuter	Percent Homeowner
Suburb		
< 50,000	79 (14)	68 (14)
50,000–200,000	71 (13)	60 (13)
Central city		
< 250,000	37 (11)	52 (8)
> 250,000	30 (11)	47 (9)

Source: 1990 U.S. Census, sample of 1,620 cities within metropolitan areas.

In examining data on actual cities, we find that these two characteristics distinguish bedroom suburbs not just from large central cities but from other suburban cities as well. Table 5.1, based on the 1990 Census, displays the average percentages of commuters and homeowners by city size and central city status.[23] Central cities have low percentages of both traits: for places over 250,000 in size, on average, only 30 percent of the workforce is employed in another city and only 47 percent of domiciles are owner-occupied. In central cities under 250,000 in size, these figures are only slightly larger, with 37 percent commuting and 52 percent homeowners. Moreover, the averages for central cities have smaller standard deviations. In other words, cities like Baltimore, Chicago, and San Diego are relatively similar in their low rates of homeownership and commuting. Suburban places, on the other hand, have higher percentages of these characteristics and are more widely differentiated by them. In cities under 50,000 in size, on average, 78 percent of the workforce commutes to another city and 68 percent of residents are homeowners, all percentages much higher than their central city counterparts. Even larger suburban cities (those over 50,000 in size) have relatively higher percentages of commuters (71 percent) and homeowners (60 percent). Wider standard deviations also reveal the greater differentiation among these smaller cities and reflect the increasing diversification of metropolitan areas. In other words, while some small suburbs are very residential in character, others are what Joel Garreau has famously called "edge cities," commercial areas on the outskirts of a metropolis that have a dense concentration of office and retail space.[24]

[23] "Central city" is defined as the largest core city within a metropolitan area (e.g., San Diego) or core cities within a consolidated metropolitan area (e.g., Oakland, San Francisco, and San Jose).

[24] Garreau 1991.

Yet residential predominance is not totally distinct from the other characteristics of metropolitan places. Most residentially predominant places are smaller in size, and there is a logic to this correlation: cities grow in population typically because of the imperatives of economic activity—for example, many people move to New York City because of employment opportunities. Smaller places, with a smaller retail market and limited labor pool, will have a harder time sustaining work sites. Although most big cities are mixed in their land use, cities under 50,000 in size show a much greater differentiation. Some are solely residential, others are solely industrial, and still others are a combination of the two. Considering this fact, subsequent analyses will focus on the effects of residential predominance only among cities under 50,000 in size.

Bedroom suburbs also tend to be correlated with racial and economic segregation—many bedroom suburbs are of one social class and composed largely of one race. Despite this correlation, land use is distinct from racial and economic homogeneity. Affluent places tend to be more solely residential, but not all residentially predominant places are more affluent. The average household income in a residentially predominant place (i.e., over 65 percent of workers commuting) is approximately $36,000, although this figure has a standard deviation of $18,000; for less residential places, the average income is lower, $26,000, but so is the range (the standard deviation is only $7,000). Whereas mixed-use places are roughly similar in their income level, bedroom suburbs come in all price ranges. Similarly, most bedroom suburbs are predominantly white, but racial homogeneity is not a characteristic unique to residentially predominant cities.[25] Racial segregation is pervasive throughout the entire metropolis. Blacks within metropolitan areas are still concentrated within central cities that have mixed land uses, but residential land use is not a solely white phenomenon either. Blacks are also moving into bedroom suburbs, and predominantly white suburbs are not all singularly residential; many "edge cities," like Stamford, Connecticut, are predominantly white.

The distinctiveness of residential predominance as a defining characteristic of metropolitan places can be illustrated once again in a map of the Chicago area. Map 5.1 displays all the places in the greater Chicago metropolitan area by the percentage of homeowners. Compared to the maps in chapters 3 and 4, this map reveals that not all the places in Chicago which are affluent or white are also solely residential, nor vice

---

[25] On average, bedroom suburbs are 90 percent white compared to mixed-use communities, which are only 83 percent white; yet the standard deviation for both types of communities is roughly 16 percent. So both more and less residential communities have an equal range of racial variation, even if the mean of bedroom suburbs is somewhat higher.

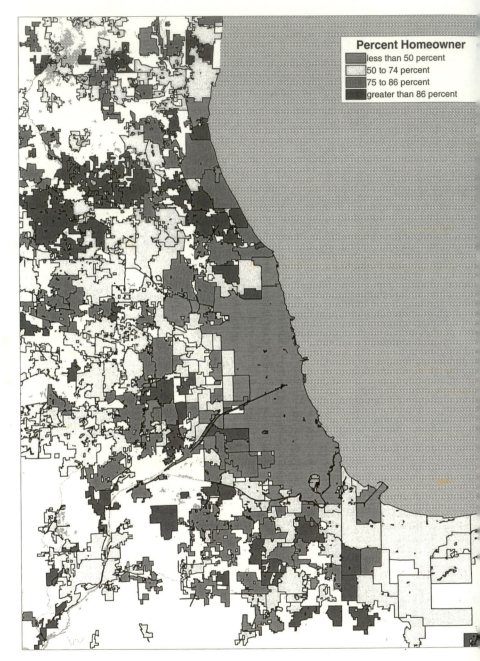

Map 5.1. Homeownership in the Chicago Area

versa. For example, Dixmoor, Illinois, has a very low median household income and a large black population, but it is much more residential than nearby Chicago, which has a higher income and more whites. Similarly, a suburb like Evanston is very affluent and predominantly white, yet it has a relatively low level of residential predominance. Thus using commuting and homeownership as measures, we can distinguish land use from the other traits that differentiate cities and suburbs.

PREVIOUS SPECULATIONS ON RESIDENTIAL PREDOMINANCE

So how might this quality of residential predominance influence individual civic behavior? Previous research, while lacking sufficient empirical rigor, offers a cornucopia of suggestions about how residential environments shape the incentives and opportunities for civic participation. These speculations fall roughly into three categories.

First are the early sociological studies asserting that residentially predominant contexts stimulate civic involvement.[26] These works—mostly ethnographic studies from the 1950s—note a common phenomenon: in the suburbs that were studied, residents were continually preoccupied with local civic activity. As William Whyte observed in Park Forest, Illinois, "every minute from 7 a.m. to 10 p.m., some organization is meeting . . . sometimes it seems that the residents are drawn to participation just for participation's sake."[27] This participatory frenzy was attributed, in part, to the high proportion of homeowners in the suburban environment.[28] Municipalities with many homeowners are places where more residents are invested in their communities: socially, financially, and historically. These investments may have cumulative effects. High rates of homeownership can stimulate higher levels of social contact between neighbors.[29] Such neighboring can boost civic participation by helping local organizations transmit information and recruit new members. In his ethnography, Whyte argued that the high rates of homeownership in Park Forest contributed to social norms that made civic participation a prerequisite for "belonging" to the community.[30]

Theories of urban politics can also be read to imply that communities with large percentages of homeowners will be more civically active places. Logan and Molotch's deductions about the economic imperatives of urban politics suggest that a community with more homeowners will have a

---

[26] Whyte 1956, Seeley, Sim, and Loosley 1956, Wood 1959.

[27] Whyte 1956, p. 251.

[28] It is unclear how much of this affect was also due to the lower female workforce participation rates during this time.

[29] Kingston 1994, Fava 1975.

[30] Whyte 1956.

greater percentage of people with financial investments in their locality and, given the property-centered nature of local politics, will be more interested in the affairs of city hall.[31] This higher aggregate level of political interest may create a climate of civic activism, as residents form organizations, publish newsletters, create phone trees, and facilitate the mobilization of their neighbors into political action.

By contrast, other qualitative[32] and quantitative[33] studies have argued that residential suburbs have little or no independent effect on social behavior. According to this viewpoint, social behavior derives mostly from the individual characteristics of the bedroom suburbanite rather than from anything endemic to the bedroom suburb. For instance, Herbert Gans criticized researchers like Whyte for "failing to see that the behavior and personality patterns ascribed to suburbia are in reality those of individual class and age."[34] The few quantitative studies seem to support Gans's claim. Comparing the behavior of survey respondents in central cities and suburbs, researchers find little difference in social or political behavior once an individual's personal characteristics are taken into account.[35] Although these quantitative studies did not estimate the particular effects of citywide homeownership or commuting and did not define suburbs in any but the crudest terms, they nevertheless conclude that differences in suburban behavior are mostly attributable to individual characteristics or individual self-selection. Furthermore, one might also read the urban politics literature to have a similar view. According to a growth machine model, what is most important for individual civic participation is the *individual* relationship to the land. Once the tenure of the citizen is taken into account, it may not matter whether a city is filled solely with homeowners or with businesses.

Despite these types of findings, many writers still believe that residentially predominant social contexts can influence civic behavior; however, unlike earlier scholars, they see this influence as negative. For example, some scholars conjecture that necessary commuting deprives bedroom suburbanites of time and resources available for social interaction and civic work.[36] In addition, cities that have more commuters also have fewer work sites and, as a result, may have a limited range of local activities.[37] For example, cities with homogeneous land usage will probably lack many of the political struggles between seekers of exchange- and

---

[31] Logan and Molotch 1987.
[32] Gans 1967, Berger 1960.
[33] Fischer and Jackson 1976, Wirt et al. 1972.
[34] Gans 1964, p. 641.
[35] Wirt et al. 1972, Fischer and Jackson 1976.
[36] Langdon 1994, Martin 1956, Dobriner 1963.
[37] Weiher 1991, Danielson 1976.

use-value from the land. Without the pressures of real estate developers, bedroom suburbs may have few issues on the municipal agenda that cause much controversy. The absence of social issues and the political consensus within residential suburbs may create an apathy toward public affairs that reduces participation. If a community has strict zoning ordinances that forbid commercial property development, or if all the land is already filled with homes, then the political pressures (and conflicts) generated by growth interests will be absent. If land is the center of local politics and land is, by municipal or county decree, removed from consideration for political negotiation, then there may be few focal points for the types of political conflicts that draw citizens into the public realm.[38]

Taken together, past research on suburbs in general, and thus bedroom suburbs in particular, offers three conflicting views about the contextual effects of homeownership and commuting on individual civic participation:

Bedroom suburbs as hotbeds of participation. Civic participation will be greater because higher percentages of homeowners instill cultures of participation, an organizational framework, and high participatory norms.

Bedroom suburbs as neutral sites. None of the characteristics of residentially predominant cities has any effect on civic participation once individual traits are considered.

Bedroom suburbs as anticivic. Civic participation will be lower in bedroom suburbs because the range of local concerns is constrained, and the community is deprived of the human capital needed to sustain a wide range of organizational choices.

EMPIRICAL TESTS

To sort through these completing claims, let us start again with some simple statistics. Figure 5.1 depicts the average rates of civic participation across three measures of residential predominance: the percentage of commuters in a city, the percentage of homeowners in a place, and a combined indicator based on both. Since almost all cities over 50,000 in size have very low rates of residential predominance, and because size is such a critical factor in shaping civic participation, the data in figure 5.1 are limited to places under 50,000 in size that are within metropolitan areas. As is clearly evident in the figure, among smaller places there are no clear differences in civic participation between residents of more or less residentially predominant cities. For example, people who live in cities with few commuters are, on average, slightly less likely than people in largely residential places to contact officials, attend organizational

---

[38] For more on this point, see Wood 1959.

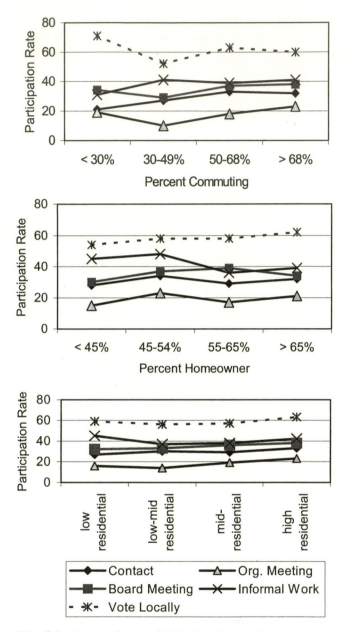

Fig. 5.1. Average Rates of Civic Participation by Percent Commuting and Homeowners and Residential Predominance (source: 1990 Citizen Participation / 1990 U.S. Census Dataset)

meetings, or work informally with neighbors; however, they are more likely to vote or attend board meetings. Moreover, there are few steady changes in any of the measures as the percentage of commuters in a city increases—the average rates of civic participation fluctuate rather haphazardly across the percent commuting scale. A city's level of homeownership is a similarly poor predictor of its average civic participation rate. Residents of cities with many renters average slightly lower rates of contacting and meeting attendance and higher rates of informal work than cities with mostly homeowners, but these are not linear or statistically significant differences. Not surprisingly, then, the measure of residential predominance (combined from the indicators of commuting and homeownership) also demonstrates little impact on average participation rates. Although people in the least residential cities exhibit slightly lower rates of contacting and meeting, they are just as likely to work informally and vote in local elections.

The absence of any significant differences between less and more residential places is actually somewhat surprising. Denizens of residentially predominant places are more likely to be homeowners, to be educated, and to have higher incomes—all traits associated with high civic participation. Similarly, bedroom suburbs are more likely to be smaller places, which we know foster civic activism. Considering these facts, we would expect to see steady increases in the average civic participation rates across the residential predominance scale. Instead, we find, at best, uneven results. Clearly, some other characteristics of either bedroom suburbs or their inhabitants are shaping these results.

To isolate the effects of residential land use from the individual characteristics of the survey respondents and from city size, I regressed the civic participation items on the measure of residential predominance, the city size measure, and the standard set of individual-level controls employed in previous chapters, for cities under 50,000 in population.[39] Figure 5.2 depicts the predicted differences across the residential predominance scale from the logistic regression coefficients.[40] The full equations are listed in Appendix B.

For four of the five civic activities, we find lower predicted rates of

[39] I selected for cities under 50,000 in size because when larger cities are included, the correlation between city size and residential predominance increases greatly and undermines the estimation with a high level of multicollinearity.

[40] I translated the coefficients from the logistic regressions into predicted probabilities using a technique similar to that employed in previous chapters. To calculate predicted differences, I divided the residential predominance scale into five increments. The bottom increment for the least residentially predominant cities had an average commuting rate of 38 percent and homeownership rate of 40 percent. The top increment of the scale had an average commuting rate of 71 percent and homeownership rate of 78 percent.

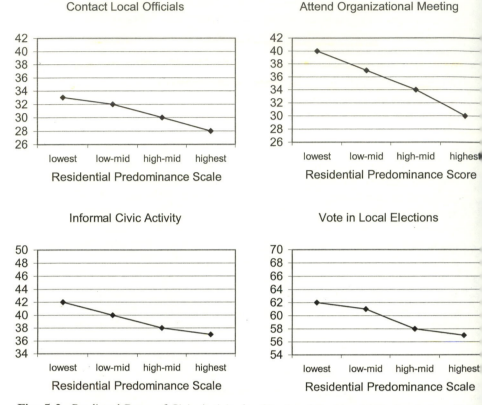

Fig. 5.2. Predicted Rates of Civic Activity by City-Level Residential Predominance (full equations in Appendix B)

participation in more residentially predominant cities. The models predict that compared to the least residentially predominant cities (i.e., places with fewer than 35 percent commuters and homeowners), residents of the most residentially predominant cities (i.e., places with more than 70 percent commuters and homeowners) are approximately 5 percent less likely to contact officials, work informally with their neighbors, and vote frequently in local elections. They are also 8 percent less likely to attend meetings of voluntary organizations, a difference that is statistically significant. There is no relationship between residential predominance and attendance of community board meetings.

On the whole, these findings are not large, but they are suggestive. While the civic differences between mixed-use and solely residential communities are much smaller than the effects from the other place-level traits (such as size, affluence, or race), they are relatively consistent.

Across most of the civic activities the results point in one direction: people in places composed largely of homes participate less than people in places with a greater variety of building sites. In terms of voting in local elections and working informally with neighbors, residents of bedroom suburbs are less civically engaged.

Growth machine models of urban politics would suggest that civic life is weak in bedroom suburbs because the singular land use of these places restricts the political conflicts or local issues that require public attention. With fewer compelling issues and less political controversy, presumably residents of bedroom suburbs will be less interested in local affairs. As with a place's size or affluence, residential predominance shapes civic participation not by directly influencing the acts of participation but by lowering the determinant of participation, citizen interest in local activities. Returning to the data, we find that this seems to be the case. Figure 5.3 depicts the predicted levels of citizen interest in local and national politics across the residential predominance scale (with the full equation listed in Appendix B).

Bedroom suburbanites are much less interested in local politics than residents of similar-size mixed-use places. The regression equations predict that people in the most residentially predominant cities score 0.25 points lower, on average, on the local political interest scale than those in the least residential places. There are no differences in the effects on national political interest. Nevertheless, local political and civic life in bedroom suburbs, by this measure, is less compelling for residents and presumably underlies their low civic engagement.

All of these results are consistent with general theories of local politics in the United States. Most scholars of local politics conclude that land-centered imperatives are the most important factor shaping municipal political outcomes. The three most influential books on local politics in the past two decades, Paul Peterson's *City Limits*, Clarence Stone's *Regime Politics*, and Logan and Molotch's *Urban Fortunes*, all concentrate on the ways that the competition for control over land use constrains local political leaders and determines policy outcomes. From these findings, it would appear that land use shapes mass behavior as well. As most political scientists would predict, places with mixed land use have more citizen interest and higher levels of citizen participation, probably because of the competition over zoning ordinances, development rights, and infrastructure improvements. Land, it would appear, is at the center of mass politics as well as elite politics.

But before proceeding further, we must take some other factors into consideration. Although the multivariate equations listed in Appendix B control for individual-level characteristics like age, income, and education, as well as the population size of a place, they do not take the eco-

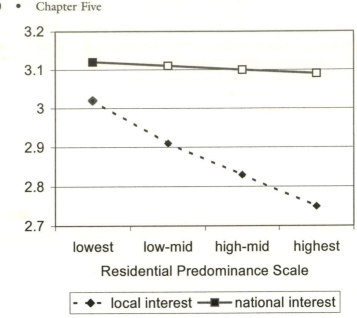

Fig. 5.3. Predicted Rates of Local and National Political Interest by City-Level Residential Predominance (full equations in Appendix B)

nomic and racial composition of the city into consideration. Bedroom suburbs tend to be more affluent and racially segregated than mixed-use places. Consequently, we do not know how much the small effects of residential predominance are attributable to the singular land use of the bedroom suburb and how much to its racial and economic makeup. To determine this, I reestimated the regression equations listed in Appendix B and included the measures of place-level income and racial composition (measured as the percent white). The new predicted probabilities are listed in figure 5.4 with the full equations in Appendix B.

When these other factors are taken into account, it is clear that the statistical effects arising from a place's residential predominance are really attributable to its race and class composition. As illustrated in figure 5.4, when the income and white racial percentage of a city are taken into account, there are virtually no predicted differences in civic participation between people in the least and most residentially predominant cities. Before the class and racial composition of their community was considered, bedroom suburbanites appeared to be participating at rates 5 to 10 percent lower than people in mixed cities; once their greater affluence and racial segregation is known, there are no longer such differences. The lower rates of political interest in bedroom suburbs also disappear

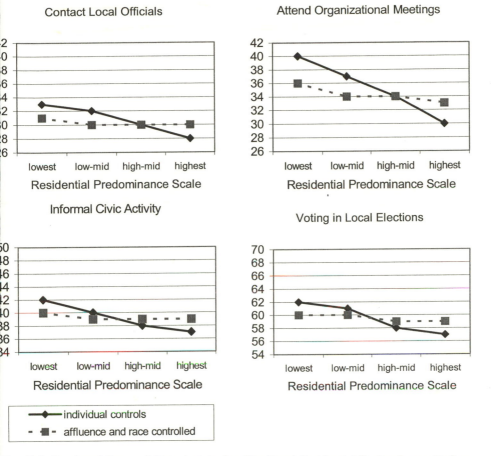

Fig. 5.4. Predicted Rates of Civic Activity by City-Level Residential Predominance Before and After Controlling for City-Level Affluence and Racial Composition (full equations in Appendix B)

when their economic and racial characteristics are controlled. If the regression predicting local political interest is reestimated with additional measures of place-level income and racial composition, bedroom suburbanites no longer demonstrate any sizable or statistically significant differences in their political engagement.

Thus despite the predictions of most works in local politics, there are few apparent differences in local political participation based upon a community's land usage. Although at first glance, places with high percentages of homeowners and commuters seem less likely to stimulate civic activism—as Robert Wood speculated—the politics of places with uniform land use are putatively banal.[41] This tranquillity, though, seems much more the consequence of their affluence and racial segregation. Once city-level income and racial composition are considered, bedroom suburbanites are just as civically involved as their neighbors in places with commercial and industrial land sites.

CONCLUSION

On May 15, 1998, two teenage boys entered Columbine High School in the Denver suburb of Littleton, Colorado, heavily armed with rifles, shotguns, and explosives. Over the course of several hours the boys killed twelve people and wounded several others before turning the guns on themselves and ending their own lives. The unexpected brutality of the killings shocked the nation. Littleton was a relatively affluent and quiet bedroom suburb. While Americans were accustomed to reports of violence in central cities, the occurrence of such mayhem in a seemingly "safe" place challenged many stereotypes. In fact, it made many begin to question what sort of communities were found in America's suburbs. Writing in the *New York Times*, sociologist Alan Wolfe described the reaction: "The moment the news broke about the massacre at Columbine High School, stories of suburban life were offered to make sense of what happened . . . Commentators implied that Littleton's residents were indifferent to moral principle . . . When you carve out new subdivisions, anomie spreads like strip shopping malls. In this view, the emptiness of Littleton's soul was caused by the emptiness of its landscape. No one can thrive in such artificial environments."[42] As indicated by Wolfe's observations, suburbs themselves, and specifically bedroom suburbs like Littleton, have now become derided as bad places. Their soulless, anticivic, and anticommunity designs are putatively fostering an alienation that threatens the fabric of American social life.

Yet these claims, insofar as they are directed at suburbs as residentially predominant places, are unwarranted. As demonstrated above, the negative civic effects of residential predominance largely arise from their economic and racial composition. When these aspects of suburban social composition are considered, there are few remaining social behaviors that vary systematically with a community's land use. All else being equal, people who live in municipalities composed solely of homes are no more or less likely to be civically involved than people in places composed of commercial, industrial, and other types of work spaces. If we use these measures of civic involvement as greater indicators of alienation and con-

[41] Wood 1959.
[42] Wolfe 1999.

nection to the community, we find little evidence that residents of a bedroom suburb like Littleton are any more alienated than residents of nearby Denver.

Of course, the measures employed here are rather crude and blunt. Census data on the percentage of commuters and homeowners in a community do not capture many of the architectural and street design elements of bedroom suburbs that draw so much critical fire. It may very well be that people who live in communities defined by garage-dominated home facades, nongrid street plans, and private backyards are less engaged than those in communities where the architecture promotes more public intercourse. And, as we will see in chapter 6, there is some evidence in support of this view.

Nevertheless, from the standpoint of urban democracy, what is most important about a bedroom suburb is not the type of home or street that the citizen inhabits but the overall pattern of land use. Most growth-oriented theories of local politics would presume that the level of home-ownership and the competition between commercial and residential real estate interests would significantly alter the dynamic of local politics. Presumably, communities with low percentages of homeowners will have low rates of civic engagement because local politics will be dominated by a handful of constituents with large financial stakes in local real estate. A community dominated by homeowners, while not having the enlivening conflicts that occur between pro- and antigrowth forces in mixed communities, still contains many residents with vested financial interests in local political outcomes. Presumably such people establish political organizations and participatory cultures to ensure that their investments are protected by municipal government. Yet the data give no indication of any systematic differences in mass citizen behavior based on land use.

Does this mean that growth-regime models of urban politics are incorrect? No, but what it does indicate is that the mechanisms of local democratic organization are not completely defined by land issues. Rather, economic class and race are more important for defining local political cultures and patterns of mass civic behavior than the distribution of property usage. The character of local politics is not as limited to land use concerns as some works might imply. Land questions may be at the center of city council meetings, but broad patterns of citizen involvement in local self-governance are much more affected by the size, affluence, and racial composition of a community than by how its land is allocated.

CHAPTER SIX

Boomtowns and the Civic Costs of Air-Conditioning

WILLINGBORO, NEW JERSEY, was a most unexpected boomtown. For most of its history this sleepy township contained mostly farms and fewer than a thousand people. Life was slow and characteristic of a quintessentially bucolic community. Yet within a few years of 1959 Willingboro had dramatically changed. Suddenly, it had miles of streets, acres of homes, and over 25,000 residents. Virtually overnight a sizable city had emerged from the farm land. Unlike similar boomtowns, however, Willingboro's instant growth did not come from the discovery of oil, gold, or other natural resources. People did not flock to Willingboro in search of instant wealth or fame. Rather, Willingboro's expansion was attributable to a relatively new factor driving community development in America: the affordability and availability of its homes.

Until the 1950s, most home construction, even in planned communities, was conducted on a piecemeal basis by small contractors. Most suburban communities were built incrementally and over the course of many years, if not decades.[1] Following World War II, however, pent-up housing demand from the depression and federal mortgage assistance to veterans generated a huge market of buyers that invited mass production. Developer Abraham Levitt took advantage of this market by building vast numbers of homes, assembly-line style, in large developments. Levitt bought a large parcel of land, carved out a plan of streets and thoroughfares, and, in a very short time, built thousands of homes at very affordable prices. For instance, a "Cape Cod" in Levittown could initially be had for under $15,000 and a down payment of $100.[2] Mortgage assistance to veterans made monthly costs less than most rents. With such a pricing scheme, the first "Levittown," begun on Long Island, New York, in 1947, was a fantastic success. It was soon followed by another in Bucks County, Pennsylvania, in 1951, and a third in 1959 in Willingboro.

American intellectuals were alternately intrigued and dismayed by Willingboro and the other Levittowns. Critics like Lewis Mumford derided their architectural blandness: "The ultimate outcome the suburb's aliena-

---

[1] For more on this point, see Jackson 1985, chaps. 2–4.
[2] Gans 1967, p. 14.

tion from the city became visible only in the twentieth century, with the extension of the democratic ideal through mass production . . . a new kind of community was produced: a multitude of uniform, unidentifiable houses, lined up inflexibly, at uniform distances, on uniform roads, in a treeless communal waste, inhabited by people of the same class, the same income, the same age group, witnessing the same television, eating the same tasteless pre-fabricated food."[3] Sociologists, however, were fascinated by the social and psychological consequences of community life in a place that was both so new and so large. What did it mean to live in an instant city where all the residents were equally new? How did social and political life differ in brand-new suburbs? Seeking answers to these questions, sociologist Herbert Gans moved to Willingboro and wrote what became the defining tract on suburban life, *The Levittowners*. According to Gans, residents of Willingboro viewed themselves as something akin to pioneers, making a fresh start and building a community from scratch.[4] Gans saw Levittowners as enjoying their new suburban environments, quickly making friends with neighbors, and building a cohesive network of relationships. Not surprisingly, he also found a very high rate of civic activism. Associations ranging from coffee klatches to voluntary organizations were highly common in Willingboro, and most residents reported increases in their civic activity as a consequence of their new place of residence. In its early days, Willingboro was teeming with associational life.

In the forty years since Willingboro was built, developers across the country have created hundreds of such instant communities. One recent suburban boomtown to gain a similar amount of attention is Celebration, Florida. Celebration is also a wildly popular, large-scale, planned suburb built by a famous developer (in this case, the Disney Corporation). But where Willingboro was noted as an archetype of suburban design, Celebration is famous partly for its antisuburb aspirations. Appalled by the conformity and isolation of suburbs like Willingboro, the planners of Celebration adopted "new urbanist" or neo-traditionalist ideas for their community. Celebration has a pedestrian-oriented design: its modest houses, with front porches, sit on small lots interconnected by bike paths and sidewalks, not far from a civic-oriented town center. It was designed specifically to combat the privatism and isolation that are so common in large-scale suburban developments.

Like the Levittowns, Celebration too has been the subject of many news articles and books including *Celebration, U.S.A: Living in Disney's Brave New Town* by Douglas Frantz and Cathy Collins, and *The Celebra-*

---

[3] Mumford 1961, p. 486.
[4] Gans 1967, p. 54.

tion Chronicles by Andrew Ross.[5] Interestingly these reports of social and civic life in Celebration do not differ much from Gans's descriptions of Willingboro. Similar to the Levittowners of a generation ago, Celebration residents are drawn to the prospects of starting fresh and making a new community, of getting involved in local affairs; they seem very civic-minded. As Frantz and Collins describe, "one of the most positive things was a vibrancy that we had not experienced anyplace else . . . Celebration has a striking level of neighborliness and social interaction."[6] Willingboro and Celebration, as new communities, both seem to encourage civic activity.

The experience of Willingboro and Celebration pose an interesting question in this exploration of suburban democracy: how does the newness or age of a community shape its residents' civic behaviors? Massive growth of new suburbs and metropolitan areas over the past thirty years has increasingly differentiated America's cities and towns by their age, yet previous speculations about whether the democracy in younger places differs from that in older ones are both contradictory and inconclusive. Some studies, like the ones mentioned above, suggest that the nascence of the suburban development is a catalyst for civic activity. Others wonder whether the lack of history and the physical design of many young cities undermine the abilities or inclinations of citizens to get involved. Both sets of reflections are without much empirical basis. As with other generalizations about suburbs, most assertions are derived from studies of particular communities or just pure speculation. While the creation of new places may be a quintessential aspect of suburbanization, the civic impact of community age is still unknown. This chapter takes up the question of how community age affects civic participation.

MEASURING CITY AGE

The United States has always been a country of visionary new communities that strive for some type of residential perfection. From John Winthrop's "city on a hill" to the latest Kaufman and Broade suburban development, American history is replete with examples of individuals and groups building new places, often in an endeavor to make a better community.[7] Over the past forty years, this development has accelerated at an even greater pace. With the expansion of the suburbs, thousands of new communities have been built in the past few decades. These range from gated communities of a few dozen homes to sprawling cities like Las

---

[5] Frantz and Collins 1999, Ross 1999.
[6] Frantz and Collins 1999, p. 56.
[7] See Mumford 1961.

Vegas, Nevada. This youth is evident in a very telling statistic—the median age of a home in the United States is just about thirty years. In other words, nearly half of America's homes were built in the last third of the twentieth century. The growth of these new metropolitan areas has followed three general trends.

First, since 1945 most older central cities in the Northeast and Midwest have either ceased to grow or lost residents.[8] As America's manufacturing sector declined, many older, industrial cities experienced massive population drops. Historic cities like Baltimore, Philadelphia, Detroit, and Rochester lost as much as 50 percent of their 1950s population. For instance, Cleveland contained nearly one million people in 1950, while today it has fewer than 500,000; Buffalo also shrank from nearly 600,000 inhabitants to just over 300,000. Although these cities are no longer hemorrhaging residents, few have gained much new housing stock or any significant new influx of migrants. Many large central cities have mostly old buildings, a very established infrastructure, and many longtime residents.

Not all suburbs, however, are necessarily young. Suburbs have been growing for over a century, and many, like their urban counterparts, have begun to age. For example, many suburbs like Greenwich, Connecticut, or Oak Park, Illinois, have existed for over a hundred years and have had several generations of families pass through. By American standards, these communities are venerable. The incorporation of older, rural towns into the ever expanding metropolis has also increased the age differentiation of suburban places. Historic towns like Concord, Massachusetts, Pennington, New Jersey, and Petaluma, California, were at one time self-sufficient rural communities; now they are just another municipality within a greater metropolitan mosaic. Meanwhile, new suburban communities like Celebration continue to be built and developed. Age is a trait that distinguishes not only cities from suburbs but suburbs from each other.

Finally, America's suburbanization has coincided with a much larger population migration to the "Sun Belt" areas of the South and West. Until the 1950s, the stifling summers of the South and Southwest inhibited much population growth. The climate in Galveston, Texas, was so severe, for example, that British counsel workers received hardship pay equal to that of those stationed in Singapore or New Guinea. But with the advent of air-conditioning, states like Texas, Florida, North Carolina, and Arizona suddenly became more hospitable. The construction of the interstate highway system and economic growth promoted by an antiunion labor environment also made southern and western metropolitan

[8] Frey 1993.

areas ripe for large-scale population development. At the same time that many northeastern cities were losing population, cities like Charlotte, Dallas, Houston, Atlanta, and Orlando were steadily increasing in size. For example, since 1950, Jacksonville, Florida, has tripled in size, and Phoenix, Arizona, has experienced a tenfold increase in population! As a result of this massive growth, both central and outlying cities in the South and West are much younger than their northern counterparts. Age signifies not just differences between places but differences between regions as well.

In light of these trends, it is important to clarify what is meant by a place's age. When most people think of a city's age, they typically refer to the date of municipal incorporation. Thus Boston and New York are old cities because they were founded long ago. Unfortunately, this indicator is not adequate for comparing contemporary metropolitan places because it does not take recent growth into account. For example, many cities, like Charlotte, North Carolina, and San Antonio, Texas, have older incorporation dates, but most of their buildings and population have been in these places for less than thirty years. In many ways, these cities are quite young. A good indicator of city age should reflect growth patterns; otherwise, cities that have not grown or changed in fifty years may be treated exactly like cities that were founded long ago but until recently contained nothing but a few buildings.

One might also think of a city's age in terms of its population's age. Just as suburbanization has differentiated the metropolitan population by income and race, it has also created new places that are distinguishable by their inhabitants' age. Not only are many bedroom suburbs composed largely of young families, many new retirement communities are made up entirely of the elderly.[9] While such communities may create distinctive types of civic environments, population age is still not high enough across all cities to represent a major characteristic that distinguishes metropolitan places the way income or race does. Nor does the age of a place's inhabitants necessarily indicate the age of the community. Some very old places, like Cambridge, Massachusetts, are teeming with young people, while new places, like Sun City, Arizona, are composed largely of the elderly.

With these considerations in mind, I measure city age by the median age of its housing stock. This measure provides an adequate indicator of a city's infrastructure with attention to recent growth patterns. As depicted in figure 6.1, most American cities are relatively "young," and a majority have a median building age under 30 years. For example, 34 percent of American cities have a median building age under 20 years

[9] Palen 1995.

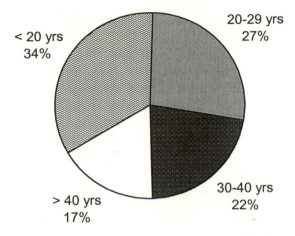

Fig. 6.1. Proportion of American Cities by Median
Building Age (source: 1990 U.S. Census [STF 3])

and 27 percent are between 20 and 29 years old; only 17 percent of
America's cities have a median building age over 40 years. This youthful-
ness reflects the tremendous growth of both the home-building industry
as a large-scale enterprise and the rapid expansion of the metropolitan
population.[10]

These patterns of age differentiation are not distributed uniformly
across the country as a whole but reflect larger migration patterns mentioned above. For instance, smaller cities (i.e., most suburbs) tend to be
younger than large cities. As illustrated in figure 6.2, the average median
building age is 27 years for a city under 50,000 in size and 25 years for a
city between 50,000 and 250,000 in population. For cities over 250,000
in size the average median building age is 33 years. There is, on average,
nearly a six-year age difference between cities by their size. This size differential in city age reflects both the high suburban growth rates and the
population decline of many large cities. Significant regional differences in
city age also occur. In the South and West, the proportion of younger
cities is much higher than in the North, where older cities dominate the
landscape.[11] The average median building age of a city in the South is
only 18 years, compared to 38 years in the Northeast and 27 years in the
Midwest. Other differences in size and region are also evident. For exam-

[10] See chapter 2 for comments on the growth of metropolitan population.
[11] The South is defined as the eleven states of the Confederacy. The West includes New
Mexico, Colorado, Wyoming, Montana, and all states west of these. The East includes all
states northeast of Virginia (including Pennsylvania). The Midwest includes all remaining
states.

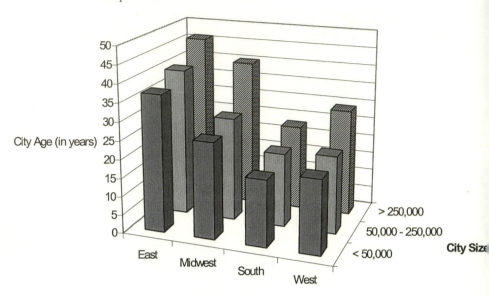

Fig. 6.2. Average Median Age of Cities (in years) by Size and Region (source: 1990 U.S. Census [STF 3])

ple, in the Midwest, places under 250,000 in size are at least 12 years younger, on average, than cities over 250,000 in population. In the South, cities over 250,000 in population are only 3 years older, on average, than cities between 50,000 and 250,000 and only 6 years older than those under 50,000.

New Frontiers versus Community Memory

As with the other characteristics of a city, understanding how a city's age influences political life depends upon first determining how age affects the pathways to participation. In other words, how does a place's age shape the costs of civic involvement, increase the likelihood that people will be mobilized, or shape people's interest in or attachment to their communities? Although previous research has not demonstrated an empirical relationship between city age and individual behavior, many studies contain suggestions about how civic life may be shaped by a community's history. As with the other factors examined thus far, once again these previous speculations are contradictory.

On the one hand, it is easy to imagine why civic participation would be higher in an older community than in a young one. Older places have had time and opportunities to establish an organizational infrastructure that can integrate citizens into public life. Places like Buffalo and New

Haven already have well-established Elks Clubs, Moose Lodges, and Masonic Temples. Many of these organizations have long histories and multigenerational ties and are well placed to integrate members of the community into their ranks. For example, many Irish Americans in Boston's Southside are affiliated with Democratic Party organizations that trace their roots back to the nineteenth century. Such an established civic infrastructure reduces the cost of civic involvement by providing easy avenues for participation. With buildings and phone lists they can also provide an easier mechanism for mobilizing citizens around community affairs. Conversely, the growth of many suburban cities and Sun Belt metropolitan areas may have outraced the creation of such organizations, particularly those which deal with local concerns. In other words, civic involvement may be lower in new cities because there are simply fewer organizations available to join. Residents of new places are less likely to have older relatives or friends as neighbors and are cut off from a vital source of organizational recruitment.[12]

Newer cities may also suffer civically from an absence of community history. This point is most clearly articulated by sociologist Robert Bellah and his colleagues in their 1985 study of individualism and commitment in American life. According to Bellah et al., "community is a group of people who are socially interdependent, who participate together in discussion and decision making, and who share certain practices . . . such a community is not quickly formed. It almost always has a history and is defined by its past and its memory of its past."[13] In their viewpoint, a community of memory is essential for American civic engagement. Without a shared past, Americans miss a crucial link to their neighbors and homes. A community's history is essential for giving its members a narrative tale with which to identify, one that engages them in local affairs. Plaques memorializing historic events, stately landmarks, and commemorative parades all signify a community's past that connects its citizens with their surroundings in a meaningful way. Most new suburban places lack this history and even seek to construct it in their names or architectural forms. For example, the Disney developers of Celebration, Florida, toyed with the idea of "imagineering" a history of the town as a phoenix that arose from the ashes of Sherman's march across the South. The plan was dropped following the discovery that Sherman never set foot in Florida.[14]

Some critics also believe that the architectural features of many new cities may limit spontaneous social contact and reduce the familiarity be-

---

[12] Babchuck and Booth 1969.
[13] Bellah et al. 1985, p. 333.
[14] Frantz and Collins 1999.

tween neighbors.[15] Most older towns were built before the advent of central air-conditioning or the heavy reliance upon automobile transportation. As result, homes tended to have front porches (to allow their residents to escape the summer heat) and to be close together to minimize walking distance. These architectural patterns promoted a front-porch or street-corner society whereby neighbors would congregate together in a shared public space.[16] New suburban homes typically are characterized by larger lots, fenced-in back yards, central air-conditioning, and facades dominated by garage doors. According to Kenneth Jackson, these architectural forms encourage the privatization of leisure time—instead of meeting on the front porch, new suburbanites spend evenings sequestered away in private yards or in air-conditioned television rooms.[17] "New urbanist" communities like Celebration, while gaining much notoriety, are nevertheless an exception; the vast majority of suburban developments continue to be constructed around automobile-oriented designs. As noted in chapter 1, architectural designs are notoriously difficult to quantify, and thus their effects on individual behavior are hard to measure. Nevertheless, the prevalence of standard suburban designs means that the age of a town's housing stock may be a good proxy for the form of its architecture. New places are more likely than older ones to have uncivic architecture.

Yet such negative expectations about civic life in new communities are not shared by all. As noted above, many ethnographies of new suburbs demonstrate strong linkages between the nascence of the suburban development and a high rate of civic involvement.[18] The unsettled quality of life in the new suburb often provides residents with opportunities to build community in new ways. Civic organizations and activities are places to make new acquaintances, find neighbors who share interests, and to remake oneself, that most American of activities. Gans observed organizational participation in new Willingboro in 1963 to be very high, but "people cared less about the nominal purpose and scope of the group than to be with fellow residents who had come at the same time."[19] Like pioneers in the American West, new suburbanites develop strong civic ties as a way of establishing community where none exists. Conversely, new residents of older places, lacking the opportunity to build a community from scratch, may have fewer incentives to get involved.

The problems of establishing a social organization and political infra-

[15] Calthorpe 1993, Jackson 1985, Duany and Plater-Zyberk 1991, Kunstler 1993.
[16] Warner 1962.
[17] Jackson 1985, p. 212.
[18] Franz and Collins 1999, Gans 1967, Berger 1960, Whyte 1956, Seeley, Sim, and Loosley 1956.
[19] Gans 1967, p. 63.

structure in a new community may also provide residents with more incentives for public action. New places also have new roads, sewers, water systems, schools, and other public services. The provision and administration of these services take time to work out, particularly in meeting citizen needs with system capabilities. Citizens of new towns may be forced to come together to solve problems ranging from the location of traffic stops to the schedule for garbage pickup. For example, the hyperplanned community of Celebration, Florida, appeared to have anticipated every public necessity, from the size of fences to the amount of green space. Community founders did not anticipate, however, the problems created by the unstructured character of the school. Troubled by the seeming failure of many education experiments (combining students of different ages, giving no grades, etc.), residents came together and fought over changing school policies.[20] Even the best-laid plans of men (or Disney mice) encounter problems that can stimulate citizen action and, interestingly, promote civic development.

EVIDENCE IN THE DATA

Previous commentators, once again, leave mixed expectations about the civic consequences of another important place characteristic. To sift through these possibilities, let us return again to the national data. Figure 6.3 depicts the average rates of civic participation across four categories of city age (as defined by the median building age) for places within metropolitan areas. Across the country as a whole, there are no consistent differences in civic activity between younger and older places. Respondents in younger cities report slightly lower levels of voting and working informally with neighbors, but for all other civic activities, there are few recognizable patterns across the city age scale. The average rates of meeting attendance for both community boards and voluntary organizations stay relatively constant for all categories of cities under forty years old and then drop slightly for the very oldest places. Rates of contacting are roughly the same in young and older cities. Even other civic activities not depicted in the figure, such as church attendance and organizational membership, stay relatively unchanged across the city age scale.

Thus it is difficult, from these results, to draw any conclusions about the civic consequences of city age. Low voting rates in new places may be less a reflection of their civic character than a consequence of lower registration rates and new polling places, or of their having a higher proportion of younger residents, who are less likely to vote. Similarly, lower rates of informal activity may result simply from the fact that new places

---

[20] Franz and Collins 1999, chap. 7.

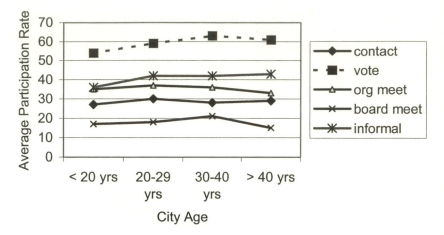

Fig. 6.3. Average Rates of Civic Participation by Place Age (source: 1990 Citizen Participation / 1990 U.S. Census Dataset)

have lots of residents who are unfamiliar with each other. While less-structured forms of civic participation may be inhibited, other types of civic engagement, such as working with voluntary organizations, are unaffected. In fact, when we take such individual-level factors into account using multivariate regression analyses, few consistent effects of city age emerge. The results of multivariate equations listed in Appendix B show no consistent relationships between a city's age and its residents' civic activities once other individual- and city-level factors are taken into account. None of the city age coefficients are large or statistically significant. It appears that city age has little if any effect on civic participation.

But before jumping to any conclusions, we must bear in mind regional differences and their effects. As noted earlier, much of the new growth in metropolitan areas has occurred in the South and West. In the Sun Belt, most large cities and their suburbs are relatively young, whereas in the Northeast and Midwest, only some suburbs are young; many other suburbs and most central cities are older. Consequently, age may have a different effect across different regions. In the Northeast, a new suburb may be surrounded by older communities. For example, Plainsboro, New Jersey, is a relatively young place (median building age of under ten years), but it is surrounded by other places, such as Princeton, Trenton, and Cranbury, that are much older (all with ages over forty years). For residents of Plainsboro, their young community is embedded in a region with much history and many established civic organizations. New suburbs outside of Orlando or Atlanta, on the other hand, are young places surrounded mostly by other young places. The civic impact of city age may be more profound in these Sun Belt metropolitan areas.

To examine these potential regional effects, I reestimated the average civic participation rates across the city age scale, comparing residents of the Sun Belt with the rest of the country's population.[21] The results are depicted in figure 6.4. Outside of the Sun Belt, the relationship between place age and civic participation resembles that for the entire country: residents of young places participate at rates roughly similar to that of people in older cities. People in the oldest cities are slightly less likely to attend meetings, but outside of this one activity, no other clear correlations occur with city age. In the Sun Belt, however, the effects of city age are very pronounced. Residents of young cities (under twenty years) participate at rates far below that of people in older Sun Belt cities (over thirty years). For example, the average rates of voting, informal civic activism, and board meeting attendance are all over twenty percentage points lower in younger Sun Belt cities than in older ones. Similarly, residents of younger Sun Belt cities have the lowest rates of organizational activity (25 percent compared to 35 percent in older cities) and contacting local officials (19 percent compared to 29 percent in older cities).

Clearly, then, a city's age does have some kind of effect on civic participation, but this effect is limited to places in the Sun Belt. In other regions, as in the country as a whole, place age does not have a significant relationship to civic involvement. Despite the expectation that an absence of community history or of a civic infrastructure may retard civic involvement, in most parts of the country residents of new places are just as active as their counterparts in older places. In Sun Belt cities, a strong correlation exists between city age and civic action. Residents of older Sun Belt cities are far more likely to be engaged with their communities than the people in new Sun Belt communities. Looking at the average rates of civic participation, one could easily conclude that young Sun Belt cities have some of the weakest civil societies of any place in the country. The question remains why this occurs.

CIVIC LIFE IN A NEW SUN BELT TOWN

The first approach to explaining why civic life in new Sun Belt communities is so different is to see what distinguishes them from their older counterparts. In the data two trends are evident. First, younger Sun Belt places are distinctive in the types of people who live there. Given the rapid growth of suburban areas in the Sun Belt, most new communities tend to be populated by people from other parts of the country, partic-

---

[21] Sun Belt here includes the eleven states of the South plus Arizona, Oklahoma, and Nevada. Although parts of California and Colorado, having large recent growth rates, might be included in this group, the distinct political history of these states distinguishes them from the other areas.

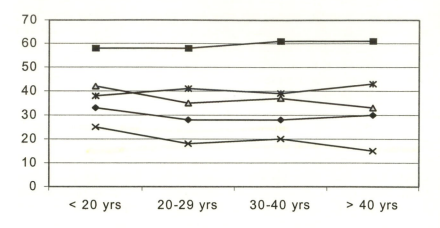

South

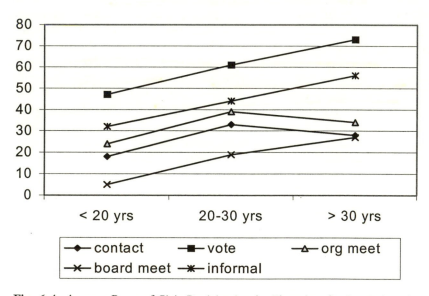

Fig. 6.4. Average Rates of Civic Participation by Place Age for Sun Belt and Non–Sun Belt (source: 1990 Citizen Participation / 1990 U.S. Census Dataset)

ularly from the Northeast and Midwest. For example, among metropolitan area residents as reported in the 1990 Census, only 12 percent of
Sun Belters had been living in the same house five years earlier, compared
to 16 percent for the rest of the country. Similarly, among those who had
moved into a different state in the past five years, 50 percent of transient
Sun Belters had relocated from areas outside of the Sun Belt, compared
to only 23 percent for residents of the Midwest or Northeast. Consequently, the inhabitants of such places are less likely to be long-term
residents of the region and may be more socially isolated. This could
reduce their familiarity with other residents or local civic customs. While
the individual-level CPS data do not have indicators of the respondent's
previous area of residence, they do have measures of other individual-
level characteristics that are related to civic action. Denizens of new Sun
Belt communities are younger and less likely to have lived at their address
for a long time, individual traits that correlate with lower civic
involvement.

Second, younger Sun Belt suburbs are much more racially and economically segregated, on average, than older Sun Belt communities. For
example, Sun Belt places under ten years old, on average, are under 5
percent black and have a median household income of $40,000; Sun Belt
places over twenty years old are, on average, over 15 percent black and
have a median household income of $26,000. Such economic differences
between young and older places are nowhere near as great outside of the
Sun Belt. Non–Sun Belt communities under twenty years old are only
slightly less populated by African Americans than older places (2 compared to 4 percent) and only slightly wealthier (average median income
of $42,000, compared to $36,000). As discussed in chapters 2 and 3,
high levels of racial and economic segregation are a detriment to many
types of civic participation. By limiting the diversity of their populations,
new Sun Belt communities may be inhibiting much of the conflict that
stimulates citizen interest and mobilization into local politics.

To determine the effects of these individual- and city-level differences,
I estimated the effects of city age among Sun Belt places for the three
civic activities listed in figure 6.4 that exhibited strong and consistent
differences across the city age scale (board meeting attendance, informal
civic activity, and voting in local elections), controlling first for city size
and individual-level traits, and then adding controls for city-level affluence and racial composition. The results of the logistic regression coefficients (listed in Appendix B) as translated into predicted probabilities are
depicted in figure 6.5.

On the whole, the low rates of civic participation in young Sun Belt
places are not attributable to other characteristics of their inhabitants.
Even though new Sun Belt communities are more likely to have younger,

Controlling for Individual Traits

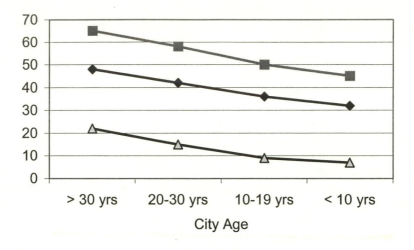

Controlling for Individual and City Traits

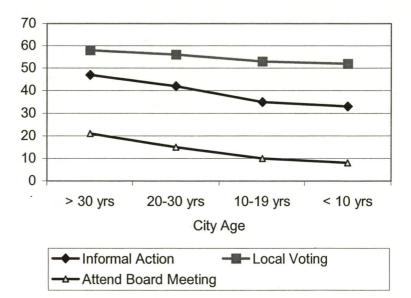

Fig. 6.5. Predicted Levels of Civic Activity by City Age in Sun Belt Places Controlling for Individual- and City-Level Characteristics (full equations in Appendix B)

more mobile residents, this does not explain why they are less civically active. When we control for individual-level factors such as age, income, education, and length of residence, the multivariate equations demonstrate patterns similar to those of the cross-tabulations: residents of younger Sun Belt towns are much less likely to attend board meetings, vote, or work informally with neighbors than their Sun Belt counterparts in older communities.[22] For example, the equations predicted a 50 percent average rate of informal civic activity in old Sun Belt places (over thirty years old) compared to 32 percent rate in the young Sun Belt places. Differences of twelve percentage points and twenty percentage points exist for board meeting attendance and voting, respectively, between older and younger places as well. Clearly, the effects of city age are not the result of the individual traits of the respondents in young Sun Belt places.

And, with the exception of voting, the civic differences are not caused by the fact that young Sun Belt communities are more economically and racially segregated. For both informal civic activity and board meeting attendance, the predicted gaps in participation between young and old places are not changed when their median household income and racial composition are controlled. The only civic activity that is altered is voting in local elections. Before the higher levels of economic and racial segregation are taken into account, a steep decline occurs in the predicted rates of voting between old and young Sun Belt places: the models predict that people in communities over thirty years old vote at rates twenty percentage points higher than those in places under ten years old. However, when the racially segregated character of new Sun Belt suburbs is accounted for, the decline attenuates by over half. The new model predicts that residents of older Sun Belt communities are only eight percentage points more likely to vote locally, a difference that is no longer statistically significant. Clearly, then, a significant portion of civic decline in young Sun Belt cities comes from their socially segregated character. As noted in previous chapters, economic heterogeneity helps stimulate political competition and brings citizens into the public arena, particularly with respect to civic acts like voting. Although we might expect voting to be boosted by racial segregation (see chapter 4), these results are only for the Sun Belt, a region noted for its high levels of interracial conflict.[23] Racial segregation in the Sun Belt may actually deter local voting while boosting it in the rest of the country. Nevertheless, for at least two types of civic activity, board meeting attendance and informal civic work, nei-

[22] The multivariate equations also predict that residents of younger Sun Belt places are less likely to contact officials or attend organizational meetings, but these differences are not statistically significant at a 0.05 level.

[23] See Key 1984 [1949], Glaser 1994.

ther the types of people who live in young Sun Belt places nor their social composition can explain the low participation rates. Something else about new Sun Belt communities must deter civic involvement.

Previous speculations postulate that civic participation is lower in new places because: (1) they have not developed an infrastructure of established civic institutions; (2) they lack a community history to draw residents into civic life; or (3) they are designed in ways that inhibit contact among residents. The first of these explanations does not really elucidate regional differences—a young community in New Jersey will face the same institutional shortcomings as a young community in North Carolina.[24] It is similarly unclear why the absence of community history would be any worse for a young place in the Sun Belt than for one the North. The only remaining explanation that might illuminate regional differences is the last one.

The design of new Sun Belt communities differs from younger places in the rest of the country in two respects. First, younger Sun Belt places are more likely than places in the North or Midwest to be designed around the automobile. It is important to remember that the median building age in the Sun Belt is only eighteen years, half of what it is in northern states. Most of these communities have been constructed around the demands of automobile transportation. This means that houses are more widely spread apart, businesses and commercial enterprises are less concentrated, and more public land is occupied by highways, parking lots, and wide streets.[25] While many suburbs in the Northeast and Midwest do not suffer from a lack of strip malls, planned developments, and automobile-dominated features, there are still a large number of pedestrian-oriented downtown areas and a greater reliance on mass transportation. Simply by virtue of the younger age of their surrounding infrastructure, new Sun Belt places are more likely to be designed around the needs of the automobile. According to many critics, the automobile-centered design is fundamentally alienating to citizens. Kenneth Jackson claims that "[a] major casualty of America's drive-in culture is the weakened 'sense of community' which prevails . . . a tendency for social life to become 'privatized' and a reduced feeling of concern and responsibility among families for their neighbors."[26] In civic

---

[24] Indeed, one might wonder whether Sun Belt places have any differences in their institutional arrangements that could account for these civic effects. In particular, one may wonder whether Sun Belt places have fewer special district or municipal governments than the North or Midwest. In Nancy Burns's analysis (1994), however, this does not appear to be the case. Sun Belt states have created new governments at a rate that is largely on par with other parts of the country.

[25] See Kunstler 1993 for details about automobile-dominated urban designs.

[26] Jackson 1985, p. 272.

terms, this could mean a lack of interest in local affairs, a reduced sense of civic capacity, or less social contact with neighbors.

Second, these anticivic tendencies may be exacerbated by another design element that is more common among new Sun Belt places than in the rest of the country—air-conditioning. In many parts of the country, particularly the Northeast and Midwest, summertime is when neighbors congregate and socialize in the coolness of long evenings. In his study of Willingboro, Gans observed that informal neighboring peaked in summer and was greatly reduced in the cold months of winter.[27] By contrast, air-conditioning has made summertime in the Sun Belt a time to withdraw indoors. Confronted with higher temperatures and humidity rates, newer Sun Belt homes are more likely to be built around privacy and air-conditioning and are less likely than older Sun Belt homes to have porches, terraces, or places to escape the trapped heat within the home. If Sun Belt places, particularly new ones, are designed to minimize exposure to summer climates, then an important source of community interaction may be limited. In an air-conditioned suburb, there is little of a "front-porch" society in the summertime, when days are longest and neighboring behavior is at its peak. Once again, these design elements may promote a privatization of life and may reduce neighborly interaction.

Although the data do not allow for these speculations about the design of new Sun Belt communities to be tested directly, they do provide indications that residents of these communities are less psychologically and socially engaged in their communities than are their counterparts in older, Sun Belt places. Figure 6.6 depicts the average scores on the three primary determinants of participation as identified by the civic voluntarism model (interest in politics, feelings of political efficacy, and patterns of mobilization).[28] In all three cases, average indicators of civic engagement decline from older to younger Sun Belt communities. For example, only 30 percent of residents of younger Sun Belt places (under twenty years old) reported being mobilized for political action, compared to 40 percent in older Sun Belt communities. Similarly, residents of new towns also score 15 percent lower on the political efficacy scale and 10 percent lower on the political interest scale than their counterparts in older places.

As we have seen in the previous chapters, all of these items are important indicators of the nature of politics and social life among members of a community. Mobilization is a good proxy for the contact between

[27] Gans 1967, p. 85.

[28] For purposes of easy comparison, I rescaled the four-point political interest scale and seven-point political efficacy scale from 0 to 1. The score for mobilization is the average percent reporting being mobilized for political activity.

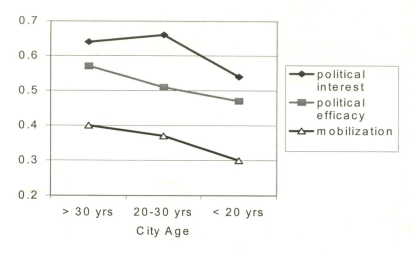

Fig. 6.6. Average Scores on Local Interest, Efficacy, and Mobilization Scales by City Age for Sun Belt Places (source: 1990 Citizen Participation / 1990 U.S. Census Dataset)

neighbors; in places where people are less familiar with their neighbors, they are less likely to be mobilized. Similarly, the fact that residents are less interested in politics or feel they have less control over local decisions may reflect their greater removal from the public realm in general. People who are isolated in the air-conditioned confines of their homes and cars may have, as many critics suggest, less affinity and connection with their neighbors and may see themselves as divorced from the affairs of their community. If low civic activism in new Sun Belt places arises from less familiarity or contact between residents and less public-regarding attitudes, then it should decline once the low rates of political interest, efficacy, and mobilization are considered.

And, indeed, this is exactly what occurs. Figure 6.7 depicts the predicted rate of informal activism and board meeting attendance before and after the civic voluntarism indicators listed above are controlled for. As with the earlier figure, when holding just individual- and city-level characteristics constant, the model predicts a steep drop of twelve percentage points in rates of informal civic activism and board meeting attendance between old and young Sun Belt cities. However, when the civic voluntarism items are controlled, the participation differences between young and old places is considerably less. While residents of older places are still more likely to work informally with neighbors or attend board meetings, the model predicts that they now do so at a rate only seven, rather than twelve, percentage points higher.

In short, residents of young Sun Belt places are less likely to engage in

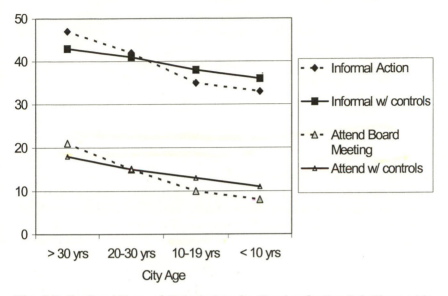

Fig. 6.7. Predicted Rates of Civic Activity by City Age for Sun Belt Places with Controls for Political Interest, Efficacy, and Mobilization (full equations in Appendix B)

civic activities like working informally with neighbors because they have less contact with the people they live around than do their counterparts in older communities. When these low levels of neighbor familiarity and political interest are considered, the differences between old and young Sun Belt places are much less great. Although the data do not allow for further tests of why people in new Sun Belt communities are less familiar, the architectural form of their cities seems the most likely suspect. Homes and neighborhoods designed around cars and shielding residents from overbearing summers are not good formulas for furthering connections between residents. While the indicators of political interest and mobilization may be crude measures of this "privatization," they are supportive of previous speculations.

CONCLUSION

One feature that epitomizes the massive growth of suburbs over the past four decades is the creation of new communities. From the Levittowns of the 1950s to the Town and Country subdivisions of today, contemporary suburbs are partly distinguished by the development of instant cities, large places of several thousand residents that are created within a few years. These new developments reflect a greater trend in the differentiation of American places by age. While many places, particularly in the

North, have added few new buildings and stand as old and stable communities, others, particularly in the suburbs and the Sun Belt, have materialized quite recently.

For the most part, the civic consequences of place age are negligible. When we compare places across the country as a whole, new communities have rates of civic participation that are roughly on a par with that of older places. If previous research is correct, we might speculate that whatever disadvantages arise from the newness of a place (the lack of history or of a civic infrastructure) are offset by the incentives of people in new places to make a new community. In other words, a new place like Plainsboro, New Jersey, may not have the same set of civic institutions already established or an interesting history with which residents can connect, but it does provide residents with an opportunity to make a "fresh start" and with the incentives to build new social networks.

The exception to this trend is in the Sun Belt. Young Sun Belt communities have the lowest rates of civic participation in the country; these rates are particularly low compared to those of older Sun Belt places. Partly this is a consequence of their social composition. Unlike older Sun Belt cities, new Sun Belt places are much more racially and economically segregated. As discussed in earlier chapters, this social differentiation is a great deterrent to many types of civic activity, particularly voting. The civic problems of new Sun Belt places arise also from a low level in neighborly interaction, political interest, and efficacy. According to several indicators, such as informal activism and patterns of mobilization, residents of younger Sun Belt communities demonstrate much less contact and familiarity with their neighbors than do residents of older places. The lower rates of political interest and efficacy may also indicate greater "privatization" of orientation among residents.

While the reasons for the greater social isolation of young Sun Belt communities are not entirely clear, a plausible explanation lies in their architecture and design. Unlike the older Sun Belt communities built around porches and shady sidewalks, many new Sun Belt suburbs are designed around air-conditioned spaces and the automobile. In communities where residents go from air-conditioned homes to air-conditioned cars (in air-conditioned garages), and on to shop in air-conditioned malls, the likelihood of spontaneous social contact with neighbors is limited, particularly in the glory months of summer when neighborly interactions in other parts of the country are so predominant. While this assertion cannot be directly tested with the data, it seems the most likely explanation. In the Sun Belt, places designed to promote social interaction, like Celebration, are the exception. The technologies of automobiles, interstate highways, and air-conditioning that precipitated the growth of Sun Belt metropolitan areas also have an adverse effect on their civic life.

CHAPTER SEVEN

Reform Governments and Their Aftermath

ALTHOUGH RON DRAKE and Anthony Russo are mayors of similarly populated suburbs, their jobs are hardly similar. Russo is the center of political life in Hoboken, New Jersey. As mayor, he enjoys an enormous amount of political power and responsibility. He selects the heads of all major departments, approves all city contracts, sets the agenda of city council meetings, and can veto any decision made by the council. Drake, mayor of Avondale, Arizona, has little such power. Although he was elected as mayor, his jurisdiction differs minimally from that of the other six council members, and he has no authority to veto any of their decisions. Avondale is ostensibly run by Scott Schrader, a newly hired and Harvard-trained professional city manager. Schrader, not Mayor Drake, is primarily responsible for overseeing Avondale's municipal departments. And Schrader, not Drake, drafts the city budget and selects the contracts. In these matters Drake has the same role as any other member of the city council.

The comparison of Drake and Russo highlights an important distinction in the governance of cities and suburbs—the incredible variety in the structure and form of America's municipal institutions. America's local governments are distinguishable by a wide range of governing structures (mayor-council, council-manager, commission, and town meeting government), electoral selection procedures (at-large versus by-district), ballots (partisan versus nonpartisan), municipal services offered, taxation structures, number of elected representatives, and methods of referendum and recall. To complicate matters further, all of these traits come in varying combinations: some mayor-council cities have small city councils elected at large with nonpartisan ballots, while others elect all their council members from districts in partisan elections. If one were to identify the governing arrangements of America's municipalities, scores of different categories would be necessary.

Much of this variation reflects the historical development of urban and suburban life in the United States. Early local government in the United States was often centered on town meetings that were run primarily by white men of property. With most of America living in rural areas and with such a limited franchise, local government could be effectively run as a direct democracy. But as urban areas began to grow and the franchise was expanded, representative-type governments began to emerge, and with them urban political parties and machine politics. From roughly the 1840s to the 1930s, urban areas in the East and Midwest greatly expanded in population with incoming migrant populations. These immigrant groups, often economically dispossessed, were organized into powerful political constituencies guided by patronage politics. The structure of city government was crafted to reflect the needs of these political machines. City representatives were elected from wards or other small districts, within which they could maintain the loyalty of immigrant groups and control the distribution of government benefits.

By the end of the nineteenth century, Anglo, middle-class reformers began to challenge the control and corruption of the urban machines, and one of their favorite targets was the structure of municipal institutions. Reformers advocated the election of council members at large rather than from wards, the strengthening of mayoral power (or the elimination of mayors in favor of professional managers), and the general professionalization of city services. Many of these same reformers were also part of the middle class that was the vanguard of suburbanization in the 1890s and the early twentieth century. These groups often resisted the annexation efforts of the machine-controlled central cities by incorporating their new areas as separate municipalities. In line with this political independence and the spirit of reform, these same groups often instituted new types of governing arrangements that ran counter to the imperatives of machine politics. These included smaller councils whose members were elected at large and with nonpartisan ballots.

The differences between the governing arrangements of central cities and suburbs are apparent today. As illustrated in table 7.1, among metropolitan places most large municipalities function under what is called a mayor-council arrangement—the city elects a mayor separate from the governing council. Often, but not always, these mayors have some independent powers over government decisions and the ability to veto council decisions. The other most common form of governing arrangement is termed a council-manager government: here citizens elect a council, one of whom sometimes serves as a "mayor"; council members effectively leave the administration of the city to a professional city manager whom they oversee. This type of arrangement is much more common among medium-size places, typically those that are not the central or nodal city within a metropolitan area. Most suburbs over 25,000 in population have a council-manager system. The smallest places are more likely to be mayor-council, partly because they do not have the tax base or infrastructure to hire a professional city manager. Smaller places are also more likely to have town meeting or commission forms of government, which also discourage patronage-type politics. In addition to having different forms of government, larger cities also elect their representatives in a

TABLE 7.1
Forms of Government by Population Size among Metropolitan Area Municipalities

	Population Size					
	Under 10,000	10,000– 25,000	25,000– <50,000	50,000– <100,000	100,000– 250,000	Over 250,000
Form of govt.						
Mayor-council	79%	54%	42%	38%	43%	62%
Council-manager	12%	40%	56%	59%	54%	35%
Commission	2%	4%	2%	2%	3%	3%
Town meeting	3%	1%	—	—	—	—
Other	4%	1%	—	1%	—	—
Electoral districts						
At large	85%	69%	65%	55%	49%	30%
By district	11%	12%	14%	14%	18%	34%
Both	4%	19%	22%	31%	33%	36%

Source: 1987 Census of Governments, number of cases = 5,714.

different way. Most small cities elect their council members at large. In other words, the entire municipality votes on all the candidates for city council. A majority of places under 50,000 in size elect all of their representatives in this way. Among larger places, smaller electoral districts or a mix of at-large and council wards is present. For example, roughly a third of all cities over 50,000 in size have a mixture of at-large and by-district candidates.

As these figures demonstrate, smaller suburban municipalities differ in their governing structures not only from central cities but from each other as well. If we were to list the other ways in which city institutions differ, such as whether they have partisan ballots, weak or strong mayors, or powers of referendum and recall, we would find further differentiation. It is important to note that not all large central cities have unreformed governments, nor do all suburbs have "reform" type structures. For example, Tulsa, Oklahoma, and Portland, Oregon, both function under commission governments, which are very inhospitable to machine politics. Meanwhile, Nassau County on Long Island, New York, the quintessential suburban community, is firmly under the control of a Republican political machine, and many of its cities operate with machine-friendly political institutions. Thus, in our inquiry into suburban democracy, we must consider how these institutional arrangements might structure the opportunities for participation.

Within political science, it is commonly assumed that reform-type institutions deter civic participation. In their classic study of turnout in municipal elections, Robert Alford and Eugene Lee find that turnout is significantly lower in cities with "unreformed" political structures but also lower in places with fewer class or racial cleavages.[1] Albert Karnig and Oliver Walter attribute much of the decline in municipal-level electoral turnout over the past sixty years to the adoption of nonpartisan ballots and council-manager governments.[2] Timothy Bledsoe and Susan Welch, in their study of 186 cities, argue that local party activity is much less in cities with nonpartisan elections, which further depresses turnout.[3] From these findings, one might naturally assume that suburban civic disengagement is the consequence of suburban municipal institutions.

There are several reasons, however, why such a conclusion would be premature. Most research on local civic affairs has focused only on voting in local elections; most is based solely on aggregate-level data or employs relatively simple statistical analyses that do not permit control for the other ways that cities can be differentiated. Other aspects of civic participation have not been examined, and the statistical limitations of earlier research leave many questions unanswered. Quite simply, we do not have a clear picture of what effect institutional arrangements may have, particularly on nonelectoral types of participation. This chapter presents such a picture. As we will see, reform institutions have far fewer effects on local civic behavior than one might suspect. In other words, Hobokenites and Avondalers may be governed by radically different types of institutions, but this does not generally differentiate their patterns of civic participation.

THE CIVIC COSTS OF MUNICIPAL REFORMS

One of Anthony Russo's predecessors was a legendary figure named Bernard McFeeley. While mayor of Hoboken, McFeeley steered all city garbage collection contracts to a company he owned, which not only enriched him personally but also helped fund his party's electoral activities.[4] On election day, ward captains in Hoboken, like their counterparts in Kansas City, Boston, New Haven, and scores of other northeastern cities, would use promises of assistance, offers of jobs, or even cash payments to persuade citizens to vote for McFeeley and his partisan cronies. Such machine politics—the use of the powers of public office to "induce partisan participation," as Raymond Wolfinger puts it—is still a vital part of political life in many places.[5] Although the *political machines* that once

[1] Alford and Lee 1968, p. 809.
[2] Karnig and Walter 1983.
[3] Welch and Bledsoe 1988, p. 249.
[4] Harrigan 1993.
[5] Wolfinger 1974.

dominated many American cities no longer enjoy such prominence, a casual observation of elections in many parts of Chicago, New York, and Washington, D.C., reveals the ongoing presence of *machine politics*.

The effective working of machine politics requires institutional arrangements that are sympathetic to the distribution of such benefits and the coordination of mass behavior. One crucial factor is having a large number of council members who represent small, geographically bounded districts or wards. Representing small geographic areas, council members can more effectively tailor services and distribute jobs and rewards to particular neighborhoods. Their precinct officers can coordinate voter mobilization more easily as well. According to Bledsoe and Welch, the adoption of at-large council elections "depersonalizes community politics, shifting the role of the representative from that of ombudsman or personal servant of constituents to one of a legislator or issue-oriented rule-maker."[6]

Mayor-council governments are also important for distribution of patronage. When mayors appoint the heads of city departments or are responsible for the disbursement of most city contracts, the opportunities for rewarding friends and supporters are high. When such decisions are made by a professional city manager, as with most council-manager governments, the ability of elected officials to manipulate public resources in reward of their supporters is significantly limited. In other words, the ability to manipulate public resources to induce partisan participation, the very definition of machine politics, is greatly restricted when elected officials have only indirect control over such resources.

The question for our purposes, therefore, is whether or how these differing institutional arrangements shape the civic life of these places. Do "unreformed" political structures encourage civic participation and community involvement? Does the presence of machine politics induce or discourage citizen involvement in public affairs? How might these effects vary not only between cities and suburbs but among suburbs themselves? Once again, the answers to such questions depend on how municipal governmental arrangements shape the determinants of civic engagement. In other words, the real question is whether mayor-council governments make citizens more interested in local affairs, make voting or attending council meetings easier, or increase the likelihood that citizens will be mobilized into public life.

Previous studies in political science, while not conclusive, generally suggest that reform-style institutions narrow many of these pathways to civic participation. Take, for example, citizen interest in local politics. Local political life is easy to grapple with in a place like Hoboken, be-

[6] Welch and Bledsoe 1988, p. 255.

cause it revolves so much around the figure of the mayor. In a mayor-council government, the mayor is the human face of the local institution. The struggles and public appearances of this person provide a focal point for local conflicts and give citizens a person with whom to identify their concerns. Moreover, if city leaders engage in patronage-style politics, then the outcomes of elections or city council meetings will have a direct influence on the livelihood and well-being of a larger number of residents. When each municipal decision is directly tied to patterns of civic participation, then the participants have a greater incentive to follow city affairs. However, if hiring, spending, and contracting decisions are made by a professional who is largely removed from city politics, then elections and city council meetings will have less meaning for the average city resident.

Another factor that may stimulate citizen participation in unreformed places is the level of local party activity. Where political structures provide opportunities for patronage, they also provide a compelling logic for party organization. By linking together under one political party, local leaders can coordinate the distribution of government benefits more efficiently and maintain their electoral control. Strong local parties, in turn, can facilitate citizen participation.[7] Parties will seek to mobilize their supporters on election day, establish the local field offices that make contacting officials easier, provide a nexus of information about local political events, and foster social connections between citizens that can encourage more informal types of public activities.[8]

Finally, many have argued that reform-style governments are unrepresentative of the class and racial concerns within a community, which might also deter citizen involvement. Previous research has demonstrated that reform institutions, particularly at-large electoral districts and council-manager forms of government, often lead to the neglect of minority groups and Democratic voters.[9] By not providing authentic representation or voice for much of the citizenry, these types of structures may also dampen citizen interest in local affairs and deter the likelihood of their mobilization for civic activities. As we saw in chapters 2 and 4, when citizens feel less efficacious about politics or feel that their concerns may go unrepresented, then they will be less inclined to get involved in civic affairs. The poor and minorities who live under reform regimes may feel precluded from any kind of meaningful input in local affairs. In sum, there are several motives to suspect that reform governments are quite powerful in discouraging civic involvement.

[7] Crotty 1977.

[8] For examples of such activities, see Wolfinger 1974, Welch and Bledsoe 1988, Erie 1988.

[9] Judd and Swanstrom 1994, Welch and Bledsoe 1988.

Although this view is the conventional wisdom, there are many reasons for doubting the strength of the effects. As noted above, most past research on the civic consequences of municipal reform has focused solely on voting. Since patronage politics often revolves around aggregating votes to maintain public offices, it is clear that voting should be affected. What remains unclear, however, is whether these same types of incentives hold for other civic activities. It is not intuitively obvious that a city with city council wards and an elected mayor is going to generate more attendance at meetings of voluntary organizations or informal civic activism among residents.

We may question the validity of previous research, as most of these studies are based on data over thirty years old; further, they did not control for the other characteristics of cities, such as affluence and racial composition, which, as we have seen, are important determinants of civic participation. But beyond this, we may also doubt many of the claims regarding the impact of reform institutions, particularly on nonelectoral types of activities. For example, it is often asserted that nonpartisan ballots significantly reduce party activity within a municipality. In many instances, however, cities that have nonpartisan elections still have active local party organizations and candidates have party affiliations. Take the recent mayoral election in Los Angeles. Although it was ostensibly a nonpartisan election, most voters could recognize Richard Riordan, the eventual winner of the election, as a Republican. As a result of ties between local candidates and state and national party organizations, parties often have a larger a role than supposed. As Fred Greenstein observed, "numerous styles of politics seem to take place beneath the facade of nonpartisanship."[10]

Finally, reform-style governments may inhibit the representation of minority interests, but it is unclear whether this effect occurs on an individual level and which groups are most adversely affected. As we found in chapter 4, whites are more active in racially mixed cities because of the social problems in such places, not because of the nature of their representation, whereas African Americans living in predominantly white places are less active, possibly because of such reform-style institutions. To sort through these competing hypotheses, we must examine the data from the country as a whole.

THE ABSENCE OF INSTITUTIONAL EFFECTS

Table 7.2 lists the average rates of civic participation among residents of metropolitan places by the type of governing structure and electoral dis-

[10] Greenstein 1964.

TABLE 7.2

Average Rates of Civic Participation by Government Form among Metropolitan Area Municipalities

	Contacting Officials	Attend Brd. Meeting	Attend Org. Meeting	Informal Activity	Vote Locally
Form of government					
Mayor-council	30%	16%	35%	42%	64%
Council-manager	27%	17%	35%	37%	52%
Other	30%	23%	36%	43%	61%
Electoral districts					
At-large only	30%	17%	34%	43%	59%
By-district only	26%	17%	36%	41%	62%
Mixed	30%	19%	38%	40%	59%

Source: 1990 Citizen Participation / 1987 Census of U.S. Governments Dataset.

tricts they live under. The information on local political structures comes from the 1987 Census of Governments. Data on each of the cities was appended to the 1990 CPS/Census dataset so that we can determine the average rates of individual civic activity by these different arrangements. Unfortunately, the Census of Governments does not have any information on whether the city has partisan elections, so this important aspect of reform governance must remain unmeasured. Nevertheless, government structures and electoral districts are two of the most important reform-style measures that differentiate most places and can provide some good indications about the effects of municipal institutional arrangements.

Outside of voting in local elections, there are few differences in average levels of civic participation between residents of "unreformed" and "reformed" municipalities. For example, residents of council-manager governments contact their local officials at rates only three percentage points below those under mayor-council governments and all other types of government, a difference that is not statistically significant. Indeed, the only civic activities that seem to differ among the different forms of government are voting and informal civic activity. Residents of municipalities with mayor-council and other governments report voting at rates over nine percentage points higher and working informally at rates at least five percentage points higher than people in council-manager forms of government. Interestingly, there are no noteworthy differences in civic participation between residents of cities with at-large electoral procedures and those of cities with by-district or mixed procedures. In no instances were the average rates of civic participation above a four-percentage-point differential.

As with other simple measures, we might wonder, however, whether these results are influenced by unrepresented individual- or place-level characteristics. Larger, more racially diverse places, particularly in the Northeast, are more likely to have mayor-council governments and mixed or by-district council representation. Residents of suburbs with council-manager governments are more likely to be educated, white, and affluent. To control for these factors, I employed a multivariate logistic regression analysis. Each of the five civic acts was regressed on a set of variables that included two dummy variables each measuring governmental structure (mayor-council and other government; council-manager was the excluded category) and electoral district type (at-large and by-district only; mixed arrangements was the excluded group) and measures of city population size, percent white, and median household income, as well as the standard set of individual-level controls. The results are listed in table 7.3.

Once again, the only type of civic act to vary with changes in a place's municipal structure is voting in local elections. When all the other factors for both a city and the individual respondents are held constant, there are virtually no differences in nonelectoral civic participation that can be attributed to a municipality's governing structure. Residents of municipalities with mayors and council members elected by district are no more likely to contact officials, attend board meetings, or work informally with the neighbors than people who live in cities with other types of arrangements. Indeed, we might conclude that municipal institutions have little civic impact except for the fact that people who live in cities with mayor-council governments report voting more frequently than residents of cities with council-manager governments. Based on these self-reported measures, unreformed governmental structure enhances turnout, a finding similar to those discovered by Alford and Lee (1968) and Karnig and Walter (1983).

Subsequent analysis shows that residents of mayor-council municipalities report greater interest in local politics, which accounts for much of their higher electoral activity. If a measure of interest in local politics is regressed on the same variables listed above, the equations predict that residents of cities with mayors are more engaged by local politics than are residents of cities without. This heightened level of political interest is responsible for much of the variation in turnout between residents of reformed and unreformed cities; when political interest is included in the equations listed in table 7.3, the coefficient predicting differences in voting among residents of places with mayors diminishes. Electoral politics is more compelling, it seems, when mayors are running for office, a fact that contributes to higher voter turnout. Nevertheless, across all other

TABLE 7.3

The Effects of Municipal Government Forms on Civic Participation

	Contacting Officials	Attend Brd. Meeting	Attend Org. Meeting	Informal Activity	Vote Locally
Mayor-council	.204 (.125)	−.087 (.156)	.046 (.121)	.154 (.117)	.513 (.128
Other government	.039 (.391)	.106 (.463)	.048 (.389)	.016 (.384)	.621 (.460
At-large only	.057 (.141)	−.145 (.174)	−.092 (.137)	.153 (.132)	.138 (.143
By-district only	−.189 (.168)	.028 (.205)	.105 (.158)	.172 (.153)	.175 (.169
Population size	−.083 (.307)	−.178 (.037)	.021 (.029)	−.056 (.023)	−.021 (.032
Med. hse. inc.	−.000 (.000)	−.000 (.000)	−.000 (.000)	−.000 (.000)	−.000 (.000
Percent white	−.242 (.401)	−1.34 (.485)	1.20 (.392)	−.426 (.373)	.057 (.408
Education	.385 (.053)	.404 (.067)	.384 (.051)	.386 (.049)	.509 (.056
Income	.132 (.041)	.188 (.052)	.224 (.039)	.185 (.038)	.152 (.042
Age	.009 (.004)	.009 (.005)	.010 (.004)	.009 (.004)	.061 (.005
Female	−.192 (.119)	−.205 (.148)	−.191 (.115)	.029 (.117)	.132 (.122
Homeowner	.405 (.146)	.665 (.192)	.258 (.137)	.164 (.132)	.504 (.139
Black	−.157 (.171)	−.182 (.217)	.409 (.158)	.599 (.151)	.171 (.164
South	−.202 (.151)	−.299 (.187)	−.101 (.144)	.029 (.138)	−.091 (.151
ncases	1,538	1,462	1,543	1,539	1,532

Source: 1990 Citizen Participation / 1987 Census of U.S. Governments Dataset, selecting from metropolitan areas only.

Note: Cell entries are coefficients from logistic regression equations. Council-manager and mixed electoral districts are excluded categories.

civic acts, there are few differences between the civic activities of people in reformed municipalities and those in unreformed ones.

CONCLUSION

A century ago, America's cities were the focal point of major political struggle. Progressive, middle-class reformers contested with political machines over the control of city offices and the distribution of public resources. In many ways, these fights reflected cleavages dividing American society at the time: cultural differences between Protestants and Catholic immigrants, class battles between rich and poor, ethnic differences between Anglo-Saxons and Irish, Polish, Italians, and Jews. The legacy of this struggle is to be found not only in the ongoing political organizations and municipal institutions in many northeastern cities but in the political structure of the suburbs and other parts of the country. As both suburbs and many places in the South and West were founded by the Protestant, middle-class portion of the population, they also imparted their progressive ideas about how city institutions were to be constructed. Rather than make governments that were responsive to geographically situated minority groups, reformers used council-manager arrangements, nonpartisan ballots and open primaries, and representatives elected at large to prevent the establishment of partisan political organizations. These arrangements varied not just by state but often across individual places. Although suburban places are more likely than not to have reform-style governments, a great variety of institutional arrangements occurs across all places in the American metropolis.

The results of this chapter suggest, however, that these institutional variations, particularly the presence of reform-style governments, are not a source of suburban civic ennui. Across all civic acts except voting, there are no significant differences in participation rates between residents of reformed municipalities and those of unreformed ones. People living under council-manager governments and represented by council members elected at large are just as likely to contact public officials, attend community board meetings, or work informally with neighbors to solve social problems as people who live in cities with mayors and council members elected by small districts. The one civic act that is adversely affected by reform institutions is voting in local elections: residents of cities with mayor-council forms of government report voting more frequently than those in cities with council-managers or other forms of government. Having the figure of a mayor seems to make local politics more interesting, increases the stakes of local elections, and gets citizens more interested in voting. Outside of this one instance, institutional arrangements have little impact on suburban civil society.

Consequently, for those seeking to address the decline of community and civic life in suburbs, a change in the structure of government does not seem to be the answer. Altering how leaders are elected or how administrative power is concentrated will do very little for changing most patterns of community involvement for the average citizen. Partly this is the consequence of local institutions' having such limited powers. Most discretionary power of elected officials involves appointing the heads of departments, awarding city contracts, or setting budget and tax rates. Given protections to civil servants, federal and state requirements on the distribution of city contracts, and the incremental character of budget change, old-style machine politics is becoming increasingly difficult to pursue. With fewer resources available to induce partisan participation, particularly outside of voting, the impact of local institutional arrangements is simply less relevant for shaping how citizens get involved in civic life. Political machines and unreformed local governments may have been useful for integrating large immigrant populations into the community life of American cities a century ago, but today such institutions are less important.

As I will discuss in the next chapter, local institutions matter, not in terms of whether they elect mayors, council members, or commission heads, but rather in terms of how their borders are determined and how their powers over zoning and land use influence the composition of their populations. By shaping the economic and racial diversity of a population or keeping a municipality smaller in size, city policies influence the agenda of local politics, the extent of intramunicipal conflict, and the patterns of citizen involvement. The key institutional changes that shape the civic life of suburbs must come in the way their populations are constituted and their borders are drawn rather than in the manner in which they elect or empower their representatives.

CHAPTER EIGHT

Remaking the Democratic Metropolis

"*CIVIC LIFE IN SUBURBIA! Is there any?*" More often than not, this is the response I hear when I tell people about the book I've been writing. Most folks, even if they like their own suburb, seem to have a pretty dim view of suburbs in general. In many ways, these negative views are understandable. After all, the term itself, *sub-* (beneath or inferior to) and *urb* (city), is pretty inauspicious. From intellectual circles, a deafening chorus of academics and journalists, including Lewis Mumford, Jane Jacobs, Kenneth Jackson, Alan Ehrenhalt, Ray Suarez, Thomas Geogehan, Witold Rybczynski, and James Kunstler, decry the isolating, banal, and overly privatized quality of suburban areas. Images in popular culture are equally unfavorable. In films like *Happiness*, *The Ice Storm*, and *American Beauty*, suburbs are portrayed as conformist, alienating, and meaningless. Even Martha Stewart, a quintessential celebrant of suburban living, has moved to the city. Thus, when it comes to thinking about democracy, community, and civic life in suburbs, most people, not surprisingly, are quick to draw on negative clichés.

Yet we must be wary of such knee-jerk reactions to suburbs or their civic vitality. Given the variety of places that fall under the suburban heading, any single generalization can be easily contradicted. Simply by virtue of size and demographic composition, civic and community life in a place like Spring Valley is going to be far different from that in Avondale, Cherry Hill, Sterling Heights, Celebration, Hoboken, or any of the other "suburban" communities mentioned in the previous chapters. It is also worth remembering that, not too long ago, many of the same complaints lodged against suburbs today, depicting them as alienating and isolating places, were directed at large cities. According to early sociologists such as Max Weber, Ferdinand Tonnies, and Louis Wirth, the predatory and rational-situated relationships found in large cities were fundamentally contrary to the organic and interdependent relations in rural areas.[1] In fact, suburbs were initially lauded as a corrective to the dense and unhealthy conditions of urban life.[2] Considering these facts, it is hard not to question whether the denigration of suburbs reflects a contempo-

---

[1] And, of course, those who romanticize preurban communities might reflect on Karl Marx's observations about the "idiocy of rural life." For extensive comments on early urban sociological thought, see Sennett 1969.

[2] See Jackson 1985, chap. 2, Mumford 1961, chap. 16.

rary cultural elitism. By virtue of their residential choice, most Americans seem to think suburbs are a good place to live, and most negative stereotypes about suburban life are still based on speculation rather than on any firm evidence about distinctive suburban behavior or attitudes.

As we have seen in the previous chapters, suburbanization *is* shaping civic life in America, but in ways that are more complicated than the stereotypes or popular images suggest. By creating smaller political entities, suburbanization fosters community, involves citizens in local affairs, and promotes civic engagement. "The suburb superficially restores the dream of Jeffersonian democracy," as Lewis Mumford observed, by providing "the conditions essential for its success: the small face-to-face community of identifiable people, participating in the common life as equals."[3] As the size of a municipality increases, its residents grow even less likely to take part in a wide assortment of activities ranging from informal work with neighbors to contacting local officials. These effects are attributable to the greater costs of participation, declines in feelings of efficacy and interest, and diminished social contact between residents in larger cities.

Yet when municipal zoning authority and other advantages of small size are used to create pockets of economic homogeneity and affluence, the civic benefits of smaller size are undermined. The racial bifurcation of cities and suburbs also has civic costs, partly through concentrating the problems of urban areas in racially mixed settings. By taking much of the competition for resources and much of the political conflict that naturally exists among members of an interdependent metropolitan community and separating them with municipal boundaries, suburbanization also eliminates many of the incentives that draw citizens into the public realm. By shielding residents from political contests over resources or the problems of urban centers, suburbanization demobilizes much of the American citizenry from local politics.

Meanwhile, many of the other distinguishing characteristics of suburbs that are often believed to stifle civic activity, such as the structure of their political institutions and the nature of their land use, actually have little influence on their residents' civic behavior. Suburbanites who live in bedroom communities and under reform-style governments are no less civically engaged than people in other types of places. The only possible evidence that the design of suburbs may inhibit civic activity comes from the political disengagement of residents of young southern communities, which are more likely to be automobile and air-conditioning oriented in their designs than older southern places. And even this last point, like much written about the design of suburban communities, is still largely speculative.

[3] Mumford 1961, p. 500.

Nevertheless, taken as a whole, these findings have a number of significant implications. Most important, the findings highlight the often overlooked role of social contexts and institutions in civic life. Most research on citizen participation in civic affairs focuses on individuals in isolation. From the authoritative studies of Campbell et al.'s *The American Voter* and Verba, Schlozman, and Brady's *Voice and Equality* to Anthony Downs's economic models of democratic life, scholars have typically analyzed citizen participation in terms of individual questions of "who participates?" But as valuable as national survey samples and mathematical models of "rational actors" may be, these styles of research inadvertently promote a distorted picture of isolated citizens making choices completely independent of their surroundings. Citizens do not float about in civic ether but live in distinctive social and institutional contexts, contexts that are important determinants of their behavior. The differences in participation between residents of the largest and smallest, most and least affluent, and most and least racially segregated places are larger than the differences for many of the individual characteristics long identified as important for civic engagement, such as age, homeownership, race, and sex. Outside of individual education and income, the combined effects of contextual measures are some of the greatest predictors of civic participation. To fully understand the mechanisms of democratic governance, we must consider both individuals and their environments.[4]

By viewing social contexts, we also come to understand the role of local political institutions as influences on civic life. The factors that make suburbs distinctive as places are largely the result of their political origins and autonomy. Municipalities are the children of state governments, created largely to administer state functions that pertain to smaller geographic areas. Over time, states have granted local governments powers

---

[4] Some might argue that these findings are not the result of contextual forces but represent selection biases on the part of individual respondents. For example, civic participation may be lower in larger cities not because living in a large city deters participation but because the types of people who choose to live in large cities or affluent suburbs are also the types who are less interested and less likely to be civically active. Although such self-selection may be present, there are several reasons why, in this study, it does not seem to be a factor. First, the multivariate equations used to predict organizational participation include individual-level measures of education, income, age, and homeownership that should control for many of problems of self-selection. Indeed, the full relationship between civic participation and many of the contextual measures is revealed only after these individual traits are considered. Second, selection biases should not be problematic considering that such a wide range of civic behaviors was examined. In other words, it seems highly improbable that people are moving to certain cities simply because they wish to avoid voting, attending organizational meetings, and working informally with neighbors. Third, there is nothing in past research to suggest that people with certain civic propensities are likely to move to particular types of suburbs. It is recognized that people move to suburbs for schools, public safety, home prices, or quiet, not because the obligations of citizenship are too onerous.

of home rule, allowing them to set their own laws, raise their own taxes, and, perhaps most important, determine their own land-use policies. As America's metropolitan population has grown, this political autonomy has allowed certain groups to create distinctive types of communities that are highly singular in their economic and racial composition and their types of land use. Indeed, if there is any single way to characterize America's suburbanization, it is as the political fragmentation and institutionalizing of social differences among residents of a common metropolitan area.

This segregating role of local institutions has important civic consequences. As illustrated in figure 8.1, local institutions influence civic participation by defining the *content* of political life. By determining who can afford to live in a community, how many people it will contain, and what types of public policies it will pursue, local governments set the political conflicts, patterns of social interaction, and salient issues of a municipality. These factors exert a tremendous influence on citizen interest in local affairs and their patterns of political organization and mobilization. If a community is structured in such a way that it generates little internal conflict or seeks nothing more than to maintain a set of policies that most residents agree with, then it provides little motivation for citizens to become civically active. Therefore, if we want to understand how and why citizens involve themselves in civic affairs, then we need to focus on how their local political institutions define and shape the character of local politics.

But while it is evident that suburbs have a major influence on their residents' civic behaviors, it is not clear whether these influences are necessarily harmful for American democracy. Many writers who assert that suburban civic ennui is undermining the strength and vitality of American society assume that higher participation levels are an unquestioned benefit for a democracy because they correspond to more authentic, representative, and fair governing processes. Many thinkers naively assert that more citizen participation is equivalent to more democracy.[5] But this view, while intuitively compelling, oversimplifies the relationship among citizen participation, democratic institutions, and policy outcomes. The importance of citizen participation depends largely on whether and how citizen preferences are being articulated and represented to the governing process; this, in turn, depends on the distribution of such preferences, the size and diversity of the polity, and the way its governing structures are constructed. For example, one fundamental dilemma of democracy is that the extent to which citizens can directly participate in controlling government decisions changes as the size of their polity grows. When a

---

[5] See, for example, Verba and Nie 1972, pp. 1–8.

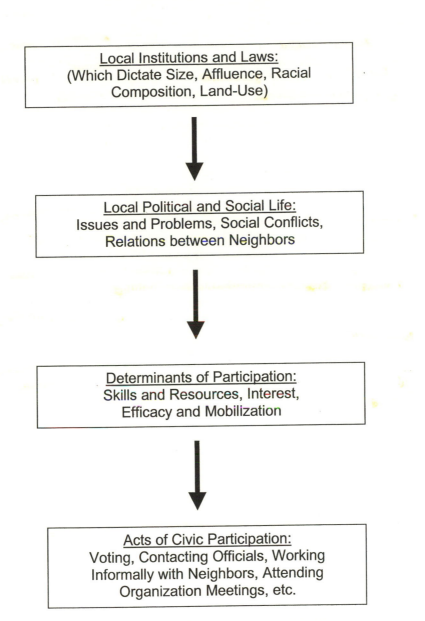

Fig. 8.1. How Suburban Political Institutions and Social Environments Shape Civic Participation

polity reaches a certain size (and not too big, at that), direct democracy becomes impossible and representative democracy a necessity. Citizenship thus goes from a "town-hall" model of direct participation to a republican model of elections, lobbying, and interest group mobilization. If representatives are adequately representing the aggregate of citizen interests, then the level of citizen participation either necessary or possible in the governing process is fairly low. Similarly, if a person shares a polity with people who have an identical set of preferences, then the necessity of mass participation is quite low, as any one voter can articulate the views of many. Given these complexities, the role and importance of citizen participation in suburbia depends on how one views the relationship among the state, the individual, and society.

In this final chapter, I investigate whether suburbs are "bad" for American democracy. I start by considering two different perspectives on citizen participation and self-governance: classical liberal and public choice theory and civil society and social capital arguments. Finding problems inherent to both of these, I then offer a third perspective for understanding participation and the goals of democracy, what I call the civic capacity argument. Then, taking insights from all these views, I offer some guidelines for restructuring local municipal arrangements in the United States. The civic problems of suburbs are correctable, but only if a radically new way of understanding the role and function of local government is employed.

Classical Liberal and Public Choice Assessments of Suburban Civic Life

From the standpoint of a classical liberal, low civic participation in suburbs is not necessarily problematic for the ends of democratic governance.[6] Most liberal democratic thinkers, such as John Locke, conceptualize citizens as basically autonomous, egoistic, and rational beings who submit to state control only to safeguard their collective well-being. Political states function primarily to create a protected sphere enabling individuals to pursue their own goals in relative isolation. The good life, in this view, is pursued outside of the public realm of citizens and in the private domain of individuals. The liberal critic is thus somewhat ambivalent, if not skeptical, about the importance of civic participation. In most conceptions, political action is primarily a mechanism for maintaining the social compact or keeping the potential tyranny of state power in check;

---

[6] Here I use "liberal" in the classical sense—someone who advocates the utmost limitations on government interference in social and economic affairs—as opposed to the contemporary use of the term to mean someone to the left on the political spectrum.

if public leaders behave in egregious ways, the theory goes, citizens will be quick to "throw the bums out."[7] A more sophisticated, Madisonian liberal view might add that citizen participation also varies with the diversity of opinion in a polity. When citizens greatly diverge in their political preferences, the only way leaders can actively represent the interests of all is by hearing from the largest selection of citizens. But in communities with a limited range of interests, the preferences of citizens can be easily represented by a few voices. If all people in a society think alike, then any one member can speak for the group.

Thus liberals might argue that low civic participation in small, homogeneous suburbs is even appropriate relative to the similarity of opinions and political interests within the community. Despite their meager levels of citizen participation and interest, many suburbs function well as democracies because their residents' preferences are effectively represented in the small, homogeneous context. Low rates of civic engagement in suburbia merely reflect citizen satisfaction with their local institutions. According to the liberal perspective, the best course for local democracy in America would be to create more small, homogeneous polities—that is, to foster suburbanization.

This celebration of political fragmentation is echoed in a contemporary variant of the liberal argument mentioned in chapter 3, the public choice and "rational actor" models derived from economics. These models start with the Hobbesian-like premise that individuals in a political system are isolated and autonomous, with the added condition that all individuals are motivated to act in ways that maximize the utility of their actions. Under this framework, participation is seen merely as a function of individuals' calculating the costs and benefits of their actions: if the rewards outweigh the costs, the thinking goes, citizens will participate.[8] A more sophisticated version of this argument, public choice theory, postulates that quasi-market mechanisms have emerged as effective replacements for civic participation, particularly in local democracies. In this view, low levels of local civic participation are untroubling because, in a fragmented

---

[7] Fiorina 1981.

[8] The difficulty with this perspective, of course, is that it is in few citizens' interest to participate in politics, particularly in low-benefit activities such as voting. Some rational choice theorists might argue that citizen participation occurs at the equilibrium point between citizen desires and state actions. As long as states and leaders behave in a way that is acceptable to the citizenry, they will not participate. At some point, when states or leaders behave egregiously, citizens will find it in their interests to get mobilized and act politically. Indeed, according to many models, it is simply the threat of mass participation that prompts leaders to behave appropriately. Once again, low participation is symptomatic of citizen gratification with the direction of local policy. See, for example, Riker and Ordeshook 1968, Aldrich 1995, Downs 1957.

political environment, citizens have replaced old-fashioned political action with modern consumer behavior. According to public choice models, citizens dissatisfied with local policies or leaders need not protest, undertake campaign work, or lobby officials; rather, they can simply "vote with their feet" and move to another jurisdiction.[9] Fearful of losing taxable sources of revenue, such as businesses or middle-class residents, leaders craft policies to retain such valued constituencies. Responsive democratic government comes, in this view, not from democratic action but from the potential mobility of revenue-producing citizens. Suburban homogeneity is thus beneficial for democracy because it relieves citizens of the costly and time-consuming burdens of political participation. By acting as consumers of government services, citizens force local leaders to respond to market pressures—low participation in homogeneous suburbs may reflect the substitution of consumer pressure for citizen action.

But while the liberal and public choice arguments offer compelling logic, they are deficient as frameworks for evaluating the importance of local civic participation. To begin with, both models suffer from an unrealistically narrow characterization of human life as unidimensionally isolated and autonomous. Humans may sometimes hold an atomistic understanding of self and may often seek to maximize the rewards from their actions, but reducing all social connections to calculated and bargained market exchanges between estranged, selfish actors belies the multifaceted and inherently social condition of human existence. The pure liberal vision of the autonomous citizen abjures the reality of inherited and socialized preferences acquired from family, friends, neighbors, and fellow citizens. As a characterization of human motivation, rational choice theory is both intuitively and demonstrably false. If citizens were solely utility maximizers, then it would be in no one's interest to participate at all, a supposition that entirely fails to account for mass political behavior.[10]

In addition, the public choice model of citizen-consumers violates the basic precepts of democratic governance. The root premise of democracy is that all citizens have equal voice in representing their political preferences. By substituting the threat of mobility for the power of civic action, public choice theory inadvertently eliminates conditions of political

---

[9] Tiebout 1956, Keating 1995.

[10] Some rational choice theorists have tried to salvage their theories by saying that participation often provides expressive benefits to citizens—that is, people vote because it feels good. By admitting this, however, rational choice theory loses its explanatory power and quickly dissolves into a tautology: any action, no matter how illogical or self-destructive, must be "rational," else why would the actor pursue it? But if all behavior is rational, then the theory loses much ability to explain differences in behavior. For evidence against the rational choice theory, see Green and Shapiro 1994, Oliver and Wolfinger 1999.

equality because not all citizens are equally mobile, particularly in a competitive housing market. Those with greater resources not only have more residential choice but, in the competitive municipal world of public choice theory, are more desirable to local leaders and have disproportionate influence over local policy. By positing that all municipal services reflect the preferences of residents, public choice theory also rationalizes the discrepancies in public services that exist between rich and poor areas. In other words, to assume that residential choice simply reflects one's preferences for services and taxes implies that people who live in areas with high crime and poor schools do so from market choice; in reality, residents of these places live in these conditions because they have limited options for leaving.

Moreover, setting up local institutions to be in competition with each other distorts their function as providers of public services. Municipalities are not voluntary organizations or private corporations (although cities did at one time have such a character) but rather are administrative creations of states to facilitate the delivery of goods and the well-being of citizens. When local institutions are in a position of competing for citizens, this mission can become distorted as priorities shift from the public good to the demands of particular groups. Bewitched by the putative efficiencies that arise from a vision of municipal market competition and citizens as consumers, public choice theory loses sight of the democratic principles of political equality and inadvertently justifies gross disparities in public services.[11]

Given the problems with its root assumptions, classical liberal or public choice theory offers poor rationalizations for the variations in civic participation across cities and suburbs. Economically homogeneous suburbs may require less citizen input to represent the narrow range of political preferences within their boundaries, but in this instance, low participation serves only to highlight the antidemocratic character of suburban institutional arrangements. By allowing certain economic groups to politically incorporate and set exclusionary zoning rules that effectively bar lower income groups or businesses, states also enable citizens with economic power to divorce themselves from the greater community with which they interact. Most residents of affluent bedroom suburbs derive their income and other services from the remainder of the metropolis. In ob-

---

[11] Moreover, it is not evident that conditions of political fragmentation actually do generate greater efficiencies in public service provision. In his analysis of the public choice literature, Keating (1995) notes the inherent difficulties in measuring and testing claims of allocative efficiency in fragmented political states. "Assessing the evidence about the costs and services we face the old problems about measuring service outputs and controlling for other factors which may be present at the same time. Merely because smaller jurisdictions have lower costs does not mean that they are more efficient" (p. 126).

taining economic well-being from a neighboring city without sharing in the responsibility for its social and political maintenance, the disengaged suburbanite is a civic parasite on the metropolitan community. Social segregation cannot relieve citizens of their civic obligations, even if it means that within their homogeneous municipality, their preferences can be articulated with a minimal gesture.

Finally, at a deeper level, liberal-based political theory has a more fundamental problem in describing local political organization: the understanding of self in a context of collective self-governance. Liberal and rational choice theory all too easily portrays a presocial self, "a solitary and sometimes heroic individual confronting society, who is fully formed before the confrontation begins."[12] Yet self-conception is a dynamic and continually adjusted phenomenon that is highly dependent upon social context.[13] Seeing myself as an isolated individual, I may want to pay lower taxes, but seeing myself as a member of a community, I may also want to ensure that my neighbors have adequate shelter and enough to eat. The ordering of these competing preferences depends upon how I realize myself at any particular moment, an understanding that is profoundly shaped by my institutional and social circumstances.

Many worry that the social and economic segregation of suburban municipalities reinforces an isolated and class-based conception of self in relationship to the greater metropolitan community. If people can erect class-specific municipal institutions or if intermunicipal competition allows them to "buy out" of civic engagement, they understand politics from the perspective of isolated consumers rather than engaged citizens and members of an interdependent collective. Such a puerile self-conception can destabilize a democratic polity. As Gerald Frug notes, "values commonly associated with democracy—notions of equality, of the importance of collective deliberation and compromise, of the existence of a public interest not reducible to personal economic concerns—are of secondary concern, or no concern at all, to consumers."[14] The history and structure of local government law celebrated by public choice scholars is also one that creates, in Frug's terms, a "centered" subject (i.e., narrowly self-interested citizen). By curtailing the necessity of public engagement

---

[12] Walzer 1995, p. 68.

[13] For example, social psychologists have long noted that people are likely to favor others randomly assigned to an in-group and to discriminate against others in equally arbitrary out-groups, and that this bias can heightened or attenuated if the parameters of the group interaction are altered (see Tajfel and Turner 1979, Brown 1985). In his famous Robber's Cave experiments, Sherif (1966) found that antagonisms between groups of boys randomly assigned to one of two "gangs" were exacerbated when the gangs competed for prizes, and were lowered when they worked cooperatively on a project with shared benefits.

[14] Frug 1999, p. 172.

and replacing a notion of civic obligation with consumer choice, the public choice ideal reifies an ego-centered understanding of self, an infantile perception that is ultimately destabilizing for democratic governance. One may seek to justify the paucity of civic participation by claiming it to be the rational response of utility-maximizing citizens, but doing so also glorifies an egoistic and elitist conception of democracy.

THE CIVIL SOCIETY PERSPECTIVE

In sharp contrast to the liberal and public choice theory, the civil society perspective views citizen participation as not simply important for democratic organization but essential for realizing one's humanity. Aristotle argued that the "good life," the ultimate goal of human existence, was possible only through participation within a self-governing community. According to his conception, the optimal life is directed by each individual's *phronesis*, and the optimal *phronesis* is one that advances the betterment of the *polis*, or political community. Civic action is not just a mechanism for advancing public policy but an end in itself. In the Aristotelian conception, a person can be fully human only by ultimately equating his personal needs with the needs of the *polis*, and by acting democratically within the *polis*.[15] More contemporary democratic philosophers have resurrected the Aristotelian notion of civic action. Writers such as Jean-Jacques Rousseau, Hannah Arendt, Benjamin Barber, Carole Pateman, and Jane Mansbridge argue that self-interest and civic participation ultimately are more interrelated: citizen participation is not simply a mechanism for influencing leaders or policy ends but an existential activity with transcendent potentiality.[16] By working in the public sphere, citizens not only learn the practice of self-governance but create a "meaning for their lives beyond their own individual identity and accomplishments."[17]

This "civil society" view is most famously articulated in Alexis de Tocqueville's *Democracy in America*. According to Tocqueville, participation in local civic activities and associations is essential for democratic governance not simply because it helps citizens aggregate their preferences but because it alters their conceptions of themselves and their relationship to society. Tocqueville attributed France's early failure with democratic governance to the narrow, self-interested motives of mobs and the inability of individuals, in a condition of social equality, to identify with the needs of the collective. Associational activity, in Tocque-

[15] Aristotle 1958.
[16] Barber 1984, Mansbridge 1983, Pateman 1970, Rousseau 1988 [1761]. For other writings on this, see Arendt 1958, Sandel 1998, Bellah et al. 1985, Dewey 1927, Rosenblum 1998, Schwartz 1988.
[17] Berry, Portney, and Thomson 1993, p. 6.

ville's estimation, was the key element in sustaining democratic government. By participating in civic associations and local democratic processes, Tocqueville observed, Americans gained a "self-interest rightly understood." In other words, participation in local civic activities putatively changed what citizens consider to be in their "interest." Rather than simply acting on narrow or parochial concerns, citizens come to equate the needs of the collective with their own. As Tocqueville explains,

> Though private interest, in the United States as elsewhere, is the driving force behind most men's actions, it does not regulate them all. I have often seen Americans make really great sacrifices for the common good, and I have noticed a hundred cases in which, when help was needed, they hardly failed to give each other trusty support. The free institutions of the United States and the political rights enjoyed there provide a thousand continual reminders to every citizen that he lives in society. At every moment they bring his mind back to this idea, that it is the duty as well as the interest of men to be useful to their fellows. What had been calculation becomes instinct. By dint of working for the good of his fellow citizens, he in the end acquires a habit and taste for serving them.[18]

The stability of a democratic society, in this view, ultimately lies in the perceptual shift of citizens away from narrow, private concerns to public, collective ends, a shift that comes from local civic and associational activity. Civic participation does not necessarily make altruists out of egoists, but it can change what citizens see as in their interest; rather than simply wanting to maximize their own private rewards, citizens come to value the well-being of their communities.[19]

The transforming potential of civic behavior underlies the recent scholarly interest in civil society. In the past five years, scores of books and articles have been written on civic engagement in the United States and

---

[18] Tocqueville 1969 [1835], pp. 512–13.

[19] This Tocquevillian perspective has gained new life in the recent debates over Robert Putnam's (1993) characterization of "social capital." For instance, compared to noncivic Sicilians, the civically rich Tuscans are less egoistic in their political concerns and work for the betterment of the collective. In later work, Putnam (1995) has argued that declines in associational membership in the United States threaten the social norms and networks that have sustained American democracy. Putnam's sentiments are not shared by all, however. Many question the relative importance of a civic association for sustaining democracy. For instance, Berman (1997) argues that a strong civic sector in Weimar Germany was not sufficient for preventing the ascendance of the National Socialist Party prior to World War II. See also Jackman and Miller 1996. Although Putnam's arguments have not lacked their critics, most current writing on social capital and civic engagement accepts the Tocquevillian appreciation of civic participation as a qualitative good (e.g., Skocpol and Fiorina 1999, Eberly 1994, Box 1998, Janoski 1998, Dionne 1998).

the role of civil society in sustaining American democracy.[20] Perhaps the most notable of these has been the interest in "social capital," particularly as characterized by Robert Putnam. As I noted in chapter 1, social capital is the social resources and links to other people that facilitate the achievement of goals.[21] Putnam has argued that social capital is vital for effective democratic performance, and that strong horizontal bonds of trust and reciprocity are promulgated by participation in voluntary civic organizations. By volunteering and working in civic clubs, leagues, and organizations, citizens come to appreciate collective concerns and acquire trust of other people, just as Tocqueville noted. As citizens build social linkages with neighbors and acquire more social capital, they learn democratic skills of compromise and consensus building and gain a pro-social self-conception.[22]

Thus, from the civil society perspective, the patterns of suburban civic participation are quite suggestive. Smaller municipal units bring citizens together and promote local civic and social engagement. The political fragmentation of metropolitan areas into small suburbs can be an important mechanism for cultivating a citizenry that values social concerns. However, the social and racial segregation that comes as a by-product of this fragmentation undermines this community-building potential. When economically and racially segregated suburbs provide few incentives for citizen action, their residents cease to gain benefits from civic engagement. Divorced from the public realm, Tocqueville may argue, these citizens no longer value the well-being of their neighbors and become hostile to the collective aspects of democratic governance. By separating citizens from the metropolitan community and stifling civic activity, segregation prevents suburbanites from realizing their "self-interest rightly understood." The social segregation of suburbs is not only harmful to democratic practice but impoverishing of the human spirit.

But once again, we are faced with an intuitively compelling claim that, upon further inspection, is somewhat problematic. Despite the popularity and appeal of Tocqueville's and Putnam's arguments, the notion that civic participation holds all sorts of benefits arises largely from the observation and speculations of political theorists. Given the eminence of these

---

[20] See, for example, Skocpol and Fiorina 1999, Eberly 1994, Janoski 1998, Dionne 1998, Berry, Portney, and Thomson 1993, Barber 1984, Box 1998.

[21] See Coleman 1990, pp. 300–317.

[22] Some have criticized Putnam's arguments for ignoring the dangers of deinstitutionalized civic engagement. A strong civil society in the absence of equally responsive and flexible political institutions can, as Sheri Berman (1997) has persuasively argued, lead to political instability and totalitarian political orders. While the threat of fascism or political instability is relatively low in the United States, the value of civic participation by itself for sustaining democratic practice is not entirely self-evident.

theorists, including Aristotle, Rousseau, Mill, Dewey, and Tocqueville, we would be ill-advised to pay them no heed. Nevertheless, for much of human history, many smart people also thought the earth was flat—any speculations about our world, no matter how worthy the source, should be subjected to empirical verification. Unfortunately, the evidence on the beneficial effects of civic activity is more suggestive than conclusive. The best empirical study of the social capital argument has come from John Brehm and Wendy Rahn, who find a reciprocal relationship between activity in political campaigns and interpersonal trust: political participation corresponds to higher trust, but more trusting people are also more likely to be politically active, although campaign work seems to increase levels of trust more than vice versa.[23] As intriguing as such findings are, they are limited to issues of interpersonal trust and political campaigns and say little about people's general orientation toward collective ends. Research in psychology is similarly evocative and inconclusive. In repeated experiments, psychologists have found strong linkages between cooperative activity and more "pro-social" dispositions, but it is difficult to know whether the conclusions drawn from the laboratory are applicable to the real world.[24]

In Appendix C, I analyze evidence from the 1996 American National Election Studies (NES) to determine whether participation in local civic activities makes citizens more public-regarding in their orientations. The evidence from the data indicates that participation in local civic activities is highly *correlated* with attitudes that epitomize Tocqueville's conception of "self-interest rightly understood." People who work with others in their community also value helping others and cooperation. Further, they are more trusting of people in general. The NES survey data do not indicate, however, that organization participation is *causal* to these pro-social attitudes. Equations that take the reciprocal nature of the civic

---

[23] Brehm and Rahn 1997. See also Uslaner 1998, Shah 1998.

[24] Voluminous research in psychology on the determinants of pro-social or altruistic orientations is also supportive of Tocqueville's hypothesis. Psychologists have tried to account for altruistic or self-sacrificing behavior through perspectives of evolutionary biology (Wilson 1975, Trivers 1971), personality theory (Staub 1975), cognition and aversive arousal reduction (Hoffman 1981), empathic rewards (Batson 1991), and social contexts (Latane and Darley 1970). While strong debates continue on the definitions of altruism and its sources, some clear evidence has emerged from the experimental data. In particular, researchers have found that altruistic or "pro-social" behavior is a learned capacity that seems to increase with age and to represent higher levels of moral reasoning. As Monroe (1996) found in her interviews with rescuers of Holocaust victims, altruistic and pro-social behavior reflects a perception of shared humanity, a perception that comes from a variety of sources, including learned behaviors or influences from social surroundings. Most research on pro-social behavior, however, is based on findings from laboratory experiments or individual case studies, and it is unclear whether pro-social behavior can be learned through civic action.

activism / pro-social attitude relationship into account find that neither is antecedent to the other. Civic activism, as demonstrated in the survey data, seems no better at predicting pro-social attitudes than vice versa. While civic activism may be strongly related to a pro-social self-conception, there is no indication from these data that it comes prior to such attitudes.

The civil society perspective thus provides a hazardously tempting critique of suburban civic life. One might easily assume that suburban social segregation, by deterring citizen participation, is denying suburbanites even the possibility of benefiting from civic action. Civic withdrawal in segregated suburbs may not only lead to a narrow vision of self among citizens; it may also preempt the opportunity for learning essential democratic skills and a broader understanding of community. Such claims have a strong intuitive resonance and are familiar to those who have participated in civic life. As Jane Mansbridge notes, "Participating in democratic decisions makes many participants better citizens. I believe this claim because it fits my experience. But I cannot prove it."[25]

Unfortunately for advocates of this perspective, neither can we. And this is a significant problem. It may simply be, as Mansbridge claims, that the kinds of interpersonal transformation that come from civic activity "cannot be easily measured with the blunt instruments of social science."[26] Nevertheless, until these claims can be validated, they remain in the realm of conjecture. Suburbanization may be inhibiting the schooling of citizens on "self-interest rightly understood," but we have no way of proving this. We cannot justly condemn suburbs for their failure to provide opportunities for personal transformation of their inhabitants if we are not even certain that such transformations take place. Suburban democracy may have problems, but we cannot lay the blame on its failure to promote the civic enlightenment of their residents.

• • •

In short, the two major perspectives for evaluating suburban civic participation are both limited. The liberal / public choice perspective correctly notes that high levels of participation may not be necessary for citizens who have their preferences represented in small, homogeneous suburbs, but it stumbles on the problem of intramunicipal discrepancies in the distribution of public resources, and in its conceptions of democratic citizens. Advocates of a civil society perspective may point out that suburban civic withdrawal inhibits the promotion of collective orientations among

[25] Mansbridge 1999, p. 291.
[26] Mansbridge 1999, p. 291.

the citizenry, but such claims are heavily dependent upon individual-level transformations that may not actually occur. Given these limitations, a new way of understanding local democracy, civic participation, and suburbs is necessary. One way to develop such an understanding is to reconsider the relationship among social conflict, political institutions, and civic participation in metropolitan areas.[27]

THE CIVIC CAPACITY PERSPECTIVE

Conflict is at the heart of politics and the raison d'être of government. The inevitable conflict that arises from social interaction generates the need for regularized channels and vested authority for resolving differences. In a democratic system, civic participation is the primary mechanism for translating potentially anarchic social conflict into peaceful and workable systems of social organization. Through voting or participating in civic organizations, citizens express dissatisfactions, contentions, and grievances and learn nonviolent ways of formulating and resolving their differences. Although political scholars have noted the importance of civic participation for resolving conflict, they generally have not recognized that social conflict is itself an important factor motivating civic action, particularly nonpartisan types of civic engagement such as working with neighbors or joining organizations.[28] Most political theorists portray civil society, the associational realm between individuals and the state, as existing in an apolitical vacuum—patterns of civic association are thought to exist irrespective of any social cleavages, divisions, or conflicts within a society.[29] Yet in a community without social conflict there is little need for the civil, as society itself is self-contained and harmonious. Social conflict and civic engagement actually have a symbiotic relationship in a well-functioning democracy: civic engagement is more essential in places with more conflict, and in places with more conflict, social tensions need to be directed into civic channels.[30]

One might take this view to justify low levels of suburban civic participation: economically and racially homogeneous suburbs, having populations with similar interests, may simply contain less conflict and require less civic participation. But this view overlooks the importance of suburban municipal structures as instruments in the conflict between social groups. In his landmark work, *The Semi-Sovereign People*, E. E. Schatt-

---

[27] Although this "conflict perspective" is not formally articulated as a body of thought, it is a way of evaluating civic participation and democratic politics distinct from both liberal and civil society perspectives.

[28] For a notable exception, see Foley and Edwards 1997.

[29] See, for example, Hall 1995, Seligman 1992, Putnam 1993.

[30] For a similar argument, see Berman 1997.

schneider observed that the outcome of any political conflict was determined by the scope of its contagion, that is, the extent to which outsiders are drawn into the struggle. Any change in the number of participants, Schattschneider argues, changes the results. Political struggle is often centered on the efforts of participants to enlarge or reduce the scope of political conflict. Weaker parties to conflict, Schattschneider reasoned, seek to bring others into the fray, while stronger parties will seek to limit its expansion. In other words, "conflicts are frequently won or lost by the success that the contestants have in getting the audience involved in the fight or excluding as the case may be."[31]

Suburban social segregation, and the low level of civic participation that results, is the consequence of certain groups' using local institutions to limit the scope of conflict in metropolitan areas. Metropolitan areas contain a wide assortment of social cleavages defined by race, class, and land tenure. These divisions reflect in many ways the natural geographic community of the metropolis. Linked together by employment, services, culture, and history, as well as common air, water, and space, people in a metropolis constitute a single interdependent community. Political fragmentation and social segregation sharply limit the role of local government as a socializing agent for the conflicts that come from its internal social divisions. Through exclusionary zoning and tax policies, many suburban municipalities effectively curtail the types of conflicts that arise and the agenda of local politics.[32] High levels of racial and economic segregation also prevent many class and racial issues from being contested within municipal boundaries and force their resolution at the state or federal level. And with less internal political conflict, as was evident in chapters 3 and 4, civic participation in segregated suburbs declines.

Some may argue that this situation is appropriate, if not natural, because class and racial conflicts, by their very nature, are not suitable for local resolution. Cities, unable to control the flow of capital, people, or labor, are quite limited in the types of disputes they can resolve, particularly those that involve the redistribution of wealth from the rich to the poor.[33] This is particularly the case in fragmented metropolitan areas where municipal leaders are in brisk competition for tax ratables. Thus if the poor are able to get a city to spend more on public shelter, affluent residents, whose increased taxes are subsidizing a policy from which they derive no benefit, may be prompted to move to a nearby suburb where zoning laws prohibit low-income housing. Similarly, if a city promotes affirmative action hiring practices, whites seeking government jobs may

---

[31] Schattschneider 1960, p. 4.
[32] See Danielson 1976, Teaford 1979.
[33] Peterson 1981, p. 8.

be likely to move to other cities where race-based hiring is not in place. That social and racial conflict cannot be resolved within most municipalities, some may argue, is simply a natural outcome of the inherently limited ability of local governments to adjudicate many types of social disagreements in a politically fragmented metropolis.

There are two problems, however, with this rationalization. First, relegating certain types of class and racial conflict to venues with a larger scope of conflict (i.e., state or national government) also limits effective citizen participation in the decision-making process. As more and more parties become involved in a conflict, the capacity of any one citizen to affect its outcome is reduced—that is, the average citizen is typically less effectual and less capable of acting in larger political arenas than in small ones.[34] And, as we saw in chapter 2, citizens in larger polities are less engaged and feel less efficacious than those in smaller ones. Indeed, many on both the political left and the right often argue for devolving federal power and decision making down to localities and even neighborhoods as a means for empowering citizens to have more control over government policies.[35] Yet if metropolitan political fragmentation means that certain types of policies, particularly redistributive ones, must always be contested in larger venues, then the structure of local government reflects a class bias—any issue involving the redistribution of wealth to groups with less revenue-producing capability will not be advanced by a locality. This highlights the disjunction between the putative role of local government as the most accessible unit of government for solving community problems and the difficulties facing American urban and suburban areas today. Citizens may face poverty as a community issue, experiencing it in crime rates, the physical state of their surroundings, and the well-being of their neighbors, but may be precluded from developing community-based solutions because the competitive structure of their political institutions makes poverty a national or state issue rather than a local one. By preventing municipal institutions from addressing such conflicts, political fragmentation undermines the much-lauded role of America's localities as arenas for democratic governance. Local institutions are not fundamentally incapable of addressing or resolving many issues of class and race; they are only ill-suited because of the divisions and competition between cities and suburbs. If institutional arrangements were restructured to eliminate this competition, then local government could resume its function as an optimal venue for adjudicating important social conflicts and addressing social needs.

---

[34] Given this situation, it is not surprising that citizens feel more trust, confidence, and efficacy with regard to local political institutions than with regard to national ones.

[35] For summary, see Berry, Portney, and Thomson 1993.

Second, by externalizing conflict and limiting citizen involvement in local politics, suburban political fragmentation and social segregation have the unintended consequence of depriving localities of *civic capacity*. Civic capacity is the extent to which a community's residents are voluntarily engaged and connected with the public realm.[36] This engagement can manifest itself in a variety of forms ranging from local voluntary organizations to working on campaigns to voting. Civic capacity, as the aggregated indicator of civic participation, is important for democratic governance. Through citizens' attendance at town meetings or their working with neighbors, community issues can be more easily transmitted, norms of civic involvement can be inculcated, and collective solutions can be formulated. If Tocqueville and others are correct, by taking part in these activities, citizens will also begin to prioritize the well-being of the community and become motivated to work toward that end. Further, civic capacity can make local political institutions more responsive to citizen concerns. As Clarence Stone has noted, city governance is typically biased in favor of business interests because these groups can organize more easily to form governing coalitions with local elected officials.[37] However, in communities with greater civic capacity, citizens can be more easily organized and mobilized. Governing regimes in such places, I would suggest, are more responsive to the concerns of average citizens and less dominated by commercial property interests.

But perhaps the biggest, and least recognized, benefit of a greater civic capacity is that it helps communities solve social problems. Local governments are limited in their ability to deal with many difficulties facing their communities. Constrained by limited revenue, and by the inability to control "the productive resources" of an economy,[38] cities and towns must look, as they always have, to the private efforts of citizens to meet social concerns. From early almshouses to the settlement movements to contemporary community-based organizations, the history of American urban life is replete with examples of private citizens coming together in civic organizations to fill social needs unmet by local governments. These nongovernmental, voluntary contributions of citizens to their locality are invaluable for maintaining its well-being and the stability of its democratic institutions. In the same way that an economy benefits from its

---

[36] The term "civic capacity" is similar to "social capital" as used by Robert Putnam, in that both arise from the associational activities of citizens and both are important for democratic governance. However, civic capacity is different in what it entails. Social capital, as defined by Putnam (1995), comprises "the norms and networks of reciprocity" that citizens cultivate through organizational participation. It relates primarily to the social behavior and attitudes of citizens toward each other.

[37] Stone 1989, p. 214.

[38] Elkin 1987.

unpaid working sector (child rearing, housekeeping, voluntary elderly care), so a social order benefits from its unpaid civic sector.

Localities with greater civic capacity have greater resources available to identify social problems, develop governmental solutions if possible, and craft alternatives if public efforts cannot be mustered. In places where citizens are active in the public realm, they will be aware of existing social problems and will be available for efforts to generate both political and nongovernmental solutions. Localities with a weak civic capacity have less capability of making local government responsive and fewer options for addressing social problems; consequently, they will be subject to greater social tension. When citizens provide for the public good and satisfy the needs of the deprived, they also ensure that social order and civility among residents are maintained, that the economy continues to operate, and that democracy persists.

America's current arrangement of local political institutions is not conducive to maximizing the civic capacity of its communities or promoting the benefits of civic engagement for its citizens. To begin with, too many people are living in municipalities that are too large. Contrary to commentators like David Rusk who advocate central cities' further annexing their suburbs, I would argue that such moves are harmful from the perspective of democratic government.[39] Municipalities with larger populations lose vital civic capacity as residents tune out local politics; the smaller the local unit, the more citizens are involved in community affairs. Although neighborhood-based political organizations can provide some benefits in larger cities, they are not sufficient as representative organizations.[40] Local institutions can create a sense of community that residents identify with, even if that community is contiguous with a large metropolis.[41]

But simply dividing the metropolis into a patchwork of tiny municipalities is not an optimal solution either. Too many suburbs are situated as homogeneous and segregated places, and this depresses civic capacity. By separating citizens along class and racial lines with municipal boundaries, suburbs too often shield residents from the conflicts and problems that exist within their greater metropolitan community. Rather than be-

[39] Rusk 1993.

[40] Berry, Portney, and Thomson (1993) find that neighborhood organizations in five medium-size cities correspond to increased confidence in government and a greater sense of community, although they admit that such institutions are not effective at representing all citizen interests.

[41] David Rusk (1993), former mayor of Albuquerque, has argued that metropolitan areas with "elastic" central cities—that is, those that allow central cities to annex surrounding areas—are better suited for governing with less racial segregation and fewer fiscal disparities between cities and suburbs.

ing instruments for bringing diverse elements of a community to work together toward collective solutions to community problems, suburban governments function as barriers keeping citizens apart. Suburban segregation, by demobilizing the citizenry, is depriving localities of their civic capacity and possibly keeps citizens from valuing the well-being of the polity, a situation that, as Tocqueville noted, is dangerous for a democracy.

Consider, for example, the communities of Mamaroneck and New Rochelle, New York, mentioned in chapter 5. The affluent residents of Mamaroneck live within a few hundred yards of New Rochelle's poorer neighborhoods. Yet these communities do not see themselves as bound together; rather, the municipal separation of Mamaroneck and New Rochelle promotes a false distinction in a sense of community between the two locales. Mamaroneck residents have used the powers of their municipality in opposition to the entire community of New Rochelle—political conflict is now between the neighboring towns rather than among citizens. This separation of communities not only undermines cooperation between the two political institutions, it also means that many of Mamaroneck's affluent citizens use their resources and skills in opposition to their neighbors who live in close proximity, rather than seeing themselves as part of the same community. As a result, residents of the two places see themselves as antagonists based on their place of residence—Mamaroneckers withdraw behind their municipal boundaries, and the well-being of the overall metropolitan community remains undermined. Mamaroneckers exist in a civic oblivion where, as Mumford notes, "domesticity can flourish, forgetful of the exploitation on which so much of it was based . . . not merely a child-centered environment, but a childish view of the world, in which reality is sacrificed to the pleasure principle."[42]

RECONSTITUTING THE DEMOCRATIC METROPOLIS

In light of both the civil society and civic capacity perspectives, the political organization of America's metropolitan areas is having adverse effects on the process of democratic governance. More than any other source, local political institutions are a key factor in defining the civic life of a community. By demarcating borders, determining citizenship, and ensuring rights of speech and association, political institutions create a space for civic engagement. And, in determining what types of people, buildings, or activities take place within a particular region, local governments also shape the agenda of local politics and the dynamic of citizen partici-

[42] Mumford 1961, p. 494.

pation. The zoning and housing policies of an affluent suburb like Cherry Hill, New Jersey, prevent the construction of low-income housing, which affects the character of local politics, the nature of local social relations, and the extent of civic participation. Political institutions, by defining the composition of a community, also determine the nature of its social, civic, and associational life. If we want to address the problems of democracy in suburbia, we need to rearrange the configuration of local governments in metropolitan areas.

As with so many things, however, such changes are easier said than done. The current arrangements of class and racial segregation in suburban areas did not happen by accident, nor did they stem from the natural sorting of citizens by political preferences; suburban segregation is itself a by-product of larger class and racial struggles, particularly among whites and the affluent seeking to protect their racial and economic privileges. These groups remain the most vocal and influential participants in America's democratic process. Reorganizing metropolitan governance in the name of civic capacity is not likely to be a political idea that attracts a natural or large political constituency. Any proposal to change the current system of suburban governance is likely to meet with fierce, if not overwhelming, resistance. Moreover, structuring government with an eye to optimizing local government finance and service delivery is itself an important consideration, and it is unclear what costs alternative plans might have. Nevertheless, from the standpoint of democracy, simple acquiescence in a civically dysfunctional and discriminatory system of local government is not satisfactory. In light of these considerations, I propose the following set of recommendations. How such proposals can be enacted I will leave for others to determine; rather, I simply offer a new set of guidelines for structuring local government and some possible ideas as to how they could be institutionalized.

To best meet the requirements of democracy, metropolitan political arrangements should be structured along what I call the *authentic governance principle*. There are three key components to this principle:

1. Local government should be as accessible as possible to the control of the maximum number of citizens (i.e., local governments need to be small);
2. Local government jurisdictions should be drawn to encompass the predominant social conflicts that occur within a given geographic area; or, conversely, local government jurisdictions should not be configured so as to give any particular economic, racial, or ethnic group monopolistic control over municipal institutions (i.e., local governments need to be *representatively* diverse);
3. Given the competitive demands among municipalities for tax ratables, and to inhibit the creation of homogeneous municipalities, certain types of poli-

cies that involve the entire metropolitan area, such as growth management, transportation, water, and waste disposal, should be administered by political units constituted at the metropolitan level (i.e., local governments need to be forced to work in concert rather than in opposition).

These ideas echo the writings of Robert Dahl.[43] As Dahl noted, the ideal local democracy needs to balance smaller size with the need to accomplish necessary public endeavors. This can be achieved in a number of ways. One strategy is to simply redraw municipal boundaries so that *all* cities are between 50,000 and 100,000 in size, and so that the population of each is representative of the economic and racial composition of the metropolis. In other words, break up larger cities and consolidate smaller suburbs with each other or with other parts of the city. Reflecting on the findings in chapter 2, we may wonder why cities should be 50,000 in size; after all, isn't civic participation even higher in smaller places? Although small towns promote even more civic capacity, it is unreasonable to expect that in today's metropolitan areas, economic and racial diversity could be maintained in communities under 50,000 in size. The small amount of civic capacity that is lost with the elimination of the smallest cities would be more than compensated for by the division of larger cities and the abolition of racial and class segregation. In fact, the advantages of small size can be created through small neighborhood organizations, which are quite effective in medium-size places.[44]

Moreover, it is important to remember that the greatest civic effects among comparably sized municipalities come from their economic characteristics. More than size or land usage, affluence and economic homogeneity have the largest and most negative civic impact of any social characteristic. This economic exclusion also underlies the negative effects of racial segregation, where citizens of all-white communities are demobilized from certain types of public activities because the social problems of urban areas are disproportionately concentrated in racially mixed settings. If suburbs seem to suffer from overprivatization and a lack of community, it is not simply because of their architectural design or the prevalence of the automobile but because of the municipal practices that segregate the metropolitan population along class lines. The best way to revitalize suburban civic life is to promote greater racial and economic integration.

In today's metropolitan areas, there are dozens of communities that exemplify this optimal balance between small size and economic and racial diversity. Places like Cleveland Heights, Ohio, Alameda and San Mateo, California, Southfield, Michigan, Oak Park, Illinois, Montclair, New

---

[43] Dahl 1967.
[44] Berry, Portney, and Thomson 1993.

Jersey, and Asheville, North Carolina, have an optimal combination of size and diversity. Although it is unclear whether such places have more civic capacity than other types of communities (such questions await exploration in future research), some limited anecdotal evidence suggests that they might.

Take, for example, New Rochelle, New York. New Rochelle is probably most famous as the affluent, white suburb featured in E. L. Doctorow's novel *Ragtime*. Today, however, it is much different from the segregated hamlet it was in the early twentieth century. With a population of under 69,000, New Rochelle is not dominated by any single racial or economic group. In 1990, 28 percent of its households had an annual income below $25,000, 20 percent were above $75,000, and the rest were in between. New Rochelle has also maintained a relatively equitable racial balance, being 68 percent white, 18 percent black, and 10 percent Latino. This diversity has helped fuel a large number of local civic organizations. The Coalition of Mutual Respect is an organization composed of black and Jewish residents who visit each other's places of worship and hold forums on race relations. Neighborhood associations have formed to maintain the racial balance of communities and prevent white flight. Whereas nearby Mount Vernon, with a similar size, was unable to maintain its racial diversity and is predominantly black, New Rochelle continues to maintain a broad mix of racial and economic groups. Consequently, in a region of the country with some of the most racially segregated schools, New Rochelle's public education system is a model of racial coexistence. New Rochelle High School is 44 percent white, 30 percent black, and 21 percent Latino, far more diverse than the racially segregated schools in Yonkers or Mount Vernon. New Rochelle is, as Doctorow describes, a "small enough community where people [can] recognize each other's humanity," and diverse enough to sustain an active civic culture.

Another option is to simply get rid of municipal government as we currently know it. America's present system of municipalities, counties, and townships is largely the product of an older, agrarian society. Most local municipal institutions were created to provide road, postal, and judicial services for a dispersed, rural population.[45] With time, these localities gained greater home rule and autonomy over zoning and their social composition. The political organization of America's metropolitan areas into counties, municipalities, and special districts may be an archaic relic of a time past. Moreover, the problem with simply reconfiguring a

---

[45] See Burns 1994 for an excellent discussion about how new governments, specifically special district governments, have been formed over the past fifty years in response to the pressures of certain developers and other concentrated interests.

metropolitan area into a set of equal-size and diverse municipalities (beyond issues of political feasibility) is that they will not be sufficient for addressing many social problems. The difficulty with small cities, as Robert Dahl recognized, is their limited capacity to achieve major public works. Municipalities of under 100,000 in size do not have the revenue capacity to create major airports, convention centers, mass transit systems, and other institutions of metropolitan living. Furthermore, current arrangements and legal standing give almost supreme power to municipalities and set them in dysfunctional competition with each other. The structure of local government law basically treats municipalities as isolated actors and gives them few incentives to cooperate with each other.[46] These institutional arrangements allow the wealthy to benefit from this political fragmentation and prevent collective solutions from being formulated. In an era when metropolitan areas are being increasingly plagued by the consequences of unplanned growth and development, inter-municipal cooperation is especially vital.

Such problems could be met through a reorganization of local government into a two-level system based on service provision and geography; at one level, the metropolitan area is one jurisdiction to be governed; at a smaller level, the region could be divided into a collection of small to medium-size microunits with populations representative of the entire metropolis. These localities would retain many of the functions enjoyed today, including education, police and fire protection, limited zoning powers, libraries, and community services. They could elect council members and administrators, but their boundaries would be subject to periodic reconfiguration. They would also send representatives to a metropolitan area government that could take on many powers, such as coordinating transportation (highways, airports, mass transit, etc.), growth management (setting guidelines and enforcing local growth plans), and providing services that benefit from economies of scale, such as water and sewage provision. Not only would this metropolitan government provide the advantage of coordinating growth management and services for the entire region; it would also help foster a greater sense of civic connection among all the metropolitan area residents. Such a system could displace the current arrangement of separate counties and municipalities, designating the metropolitan area as the more logical unit of geography that needs political administration.

Metropolitan area governments, while rare, have been successful at ministering to the needs of a metropolis. Portland, Oregon, for the past twenty years, has had a metropolitan area government responsible for growth management. Despite high growth rates, Portland's Metro has

[46] See Frug 1999.

kept sprawl in check, fostering higher housing density, greater mass transit use, and the fiscal health of the central city. While comparable cities like Baltimore, Cleveland, and St. Louis have struggled to maintain the commercial viability of their downtowns, Portland's central business district is vibrant and bustling. But what is remarkable about Portland is not simply that it continues to preserve open space in the face of tremendous economic and political pressure; it is that Metro goes on enjoying the support of citizens. Growth management has meant higher population densities, higher home prices, and other costs for residents. Despite efforts to dismantle Metro and occasional setbacks to its public efforts, Metro continues to maintain a high level of public support.[47] That so many Portlanders have been willing to make sacrifices for a collective and long-term good is testament to the power of community-spiritedness and a willingness to identify with the entire region. Oregon has one of the most vibrant civic cultures in the United States. That Portland is one of the country's most "livable" cities is due in part to its residents' engagement in community affairs.

Of course, calls for metropolitan area governments are not a new idea. Many political scientists since the time of Woodrow Wilson have long argued that the best way to administer services such as transportation, water and sewage, and waste, as well as to coordinate growth, is to create some type of superordinate regional political institution to induce cooperation among local units. Although these plans range from complete metropolitan consolidation to planning mandates from states, they all share an understanding that in most American metropolitan areas, current institutional arrangements are failing to provide either efficient or well-coordinated government services.[48] However, like many such plans, they lack a natural political constituency that has short-term and quantifiable interests in seeing them come to fruition. Like the calls for political reformation in times past, calling for a complete reconfiguration of local government in the United States is likely to garner attention only if necessitated by some political crisis.

Such crises, however, may not be so far away. In Atlanta, Georgia, traffic and pollution that have accompanied the uncontrolled and massive growth of the past twenty years have become so perilous that the gov-

---

[47] Metro has had a number of setbacks, including difficulty in getting public approval to finance light rail transit systems. Much of Metro's weakness, however, comes from its peculiar institutional composition. Its governing board, which has all the power, is elected from district representatives. It has no executive with substantial power that represents the whole region. If Metro were a federation of similar-size municipalities, many of these deficiencies might be overcome.

[48] For an excellent review of the history and various proposals for metropolitan government, see Stephens and Wikstrom 2000.

ernor has recently appointed a "growth czar" to tackle the situation. This administrator, not elected by residents of the Atlanta area, has great powers to determine the future of their communities. The current system of local government in Atlanta, as in many other fast growing metropolitan areas, is simply not well suited for solving the problems of contemporary society in a democratic fashion. The current arrangement of political fragmentation, social segregation, and local zoning autonomy creates large dysfunctions in the provision of public services, the concentration of poverty, and the inability to coordinate growth. Local democratic institutions need to be reshaped so that citizens are brought into the decision-making process and linked with all members of their geographic community. While the details of such reforms are open to debate, the findings above suggest that the combination of some system of micro and macro governmental units is the ideal democratic solution.

Irrespective of the political feasibility of these suggestions, it is clear that the study of suburban civic life offers some important lessons on the importance of local government. In an era of mass communication and unprecedented mobility, our traditional notions of community are often called into question. For many Americans, their spaces of daily interaction go beyond their neighborhood or central business district—they may shop in one place, play golf in another, volunteer somewhere else, and have their home in another town altogether. Insofar as all of these activities take place in a metropolitan area, we need to recognize these large settlements as interdependent communities that have governing requirements. Yet, despite their far-flung engagements, people also need to have governing units that are immediate and workable in scale. When people have some bounded notion of place that is small and recognizable, they will involve themselves in local affairs. The challenge for enhancing democracy in suburbia is find new ways of governing that optimize the virtues of towns, the diversity of cities, and the necessities of metropolitan living.

The Citizen Participation / Census Dataset

THE DATA FOR THIS STUDY come from two primary sources. The first is the 1990 Citizen Participation Study (CPS). The CPS was a two-stage survey of Americans' voluntary activities. As described by Verba, Schlozman, and Brady (1995):

> The first stage consisted of 15,053 telephone interviews of adult (18 years or older) Americans conducted by the Public Opinion Laboratory of Northern Illinois University and the National Opinion Research Center (NORC) during the last six months of 1989. These short telephone interviews were between 15 and 20 minutes in length . . . respondents were selected randomly from phone exchanges matched to the primary sampling units of the NORC national, in-person sampling frame. This clustered phone sample was designed to be representative of the American population. Within each household, adults were chosen at random using a Kish table.

It was from these interviews that the basic demographic information and primary measures of organizational membership used in most of the figures and tables are derived. For most of the information about what types of organizations members belong to, the questions on political mobilization, or what their attitudes were, the follow-up portion of the CPS was used. Verba, Schlozman, and Brady (1995) describe the construction of the follow-up portion:

> To select respondents for a second stage of in-person interviews, the sample of 15,053 was first reweighted to adjust for the fact that the screener had yielded a slightly disproportionate share of women. The sample was then stratified by race and ethnicity and by level and type of political participation. Blacks, Latinos, and political activists were oversampled, with weights ranging from 1 for the inactive Anglo-Whites to 16 for highly active Latinos. In the spring of 1990, NORC conducted in-person interviews of an average length of almost two hours each with 2,517 of the original 15,053 respondents.

The next step in the construction of the CPC came in identifying the place of residence of the respondents. Part of this information was provided to me by Sidney Verba, Kay Schlozman, Henry Brady, and Nancy Burns. Along with some research assistants, Burns had identified the city of residence for 14,950 respondents in the original sample, using their mailing address, zip codes, and business directories. I then used these city names to acquire the "FIPS" codes (the five-digit identification code used by the Census Bureau to uniquely identify every place) for 14,019 of the respondents using the *Geographic Identification Code Scheme, 1980* from the Bureau of the Census. After manually entering all of the FIPS codes for each case in the original CPS study, I then used these codes to extract data on the "place" level for each respondent.

At this point I was ready to merge the CPS data with the 1990 Census, the second source of the CPC data. Using retrieval programs in DBASE and the STF3C Census Data for 1990 on CD-ROM, I was able to extract census information on 1,973 of the places identified by Burns. From the census I pulled off 183 different items for the place level, ranging from the size of the population to the number of homeowners. Using the place-level information, I then identified the county of each place and, using the county information, extracted data on the metropolitan area, pulling off the same items used on the place level. This produced a file with census data on the place level for 13,071 of the respondents, and on place and metropolitan level for 9,605 who lived in identifiable metropolitan areas. For this study, the respondents who lived in identifiable metropolitan areas were selected. All other respondents were considered to live in rural areas and were not used in the analysis. Most of the missing cases arose because of cities whose FIPS code could not be identified, errors in coding and data extraction, or cities for which there was no information provided in the STF3C files. Because of the randomized nature of this missing values problem, I do not believe the missing cases significantly alter the results.

The data in Appendix C come from the 1996 American National Election Studies, a large-scale national survey conducted every election year by the Institute for Social Research at the University of Michigan, Ann Arbor.

CODING OF THE VARIABLES

Dependent Variables

CONTACTING LOCAL OFFICIALS. "In the past 12 months . . . have you initiated any contacts with an elected official on the state or local level—a governor or mayor or a member of a city or town council—or someone on the staff of such an elected official?" (31 percent responded yes).

ATTENDING COMMUNITY BOARD MEETINGS. ". . . have you attended a meeting of (any official local governmental board or council that deals with community problems and issues such as a town council, a school board, a zoning board, a planning board, or the like) in the past 12 months?" (18 percent responded yes).

ATTENDING MEETING OF VOLUNTARY ORGANIZATIONS. (Respondent had previously identified being a member of a voluntary organization.) "Here is a list of things that people sometimes have to do as part of the involvement with organizations. After I read each one, please tell me whether or not you have engaged in that activity as part of your involvement with this organization. Have you (gone to a meeting)?" All other respondents coded as zero (35 percent responded yes).

WORK INFORMALLY WITH NEIGHBORS. "I'd also like to ask about informal activity in your community or neighborhood. In the past twelve months, have you gotten together informally with or worked with others in your community or neighborhood to try to deal with some community issue or problem?" (41 percent responded yes).

VOTING. The five-point, voting-in-local-elections scale was based on response to the following query: "In the past five years, how often have you voted in elections for local or city officials?" (1—never, 2—rarely, 3—sometimes, 4—often, 5—always). This variable was recoded into a two-point scale with those voting "often" or "always" counted as one, and all others counted as zero (59 percent scored 1).

MOBILIZATION. A positive response to either of the following questions was scored as positive: "In the past 12 months, have you received any request directed to you personally asking you to contact a government official—asking you to write to or talk to a government official?" and "serve on community board or council"? (41 percent had been mobilized).

POLITICAL INTEREST. The political interest variables were drawn from the following questions: "Thinking about your local community, how interested are you in local community politics and local community affairs? Are you . . ." and "How interested in national politics and national affairs? Are you . . ." (1—not at all interested, 2—slightly interested, 3—somewhat interested, 4—very interested) (average score on local interest: 2.86).

POLITICAL EFFICACY. This variable was drawn from two questions added together and rescaled from 1 to 4: "If you had a complaint about a local government activity and took that complaint to a member of the local government, do you think that he or she would pay a lot of attention to what you say, some attention, very little attention, or none at all?" and "How much influence do you think someone like you can have over local government decisions—a lot, some, very little, or none at all?" (average score on combined scale of 2 to 8: 5.19).

Individual-Level Independent Variables

EDUCATION. 1—less than 8 years, 2—8 to 12 years, 3—high school diploma, 4—some college, 5—college degree, 6—advanced degree (average score 3.7).

INCOME. 1—< $7,500, 2—$7,500 to < $15,000, 3—$15,000 to < $25,000, 4—$25,000 to < $35,000, 5—$35,000 to < $50,000, 6—$50,000 to < $75,000, 7—$75,000 to $125,000, 8—> $125,000 (average score 4.2)

AGE. Coded directly 18–90 (average age 41).

LENGTH OF RESIDENCE. 0—reside in town less than two years, 1—reside in town two or more years (90 percent lived in town for more than two years).

SOUTH. 0—live outside South; 1—live in Arkansas, Alabama, Florida, Georgia, Louisiana, Mississippi, North Carolina, South Carolina, Tennessee, Texas, or Virginia (28 percent in South).

FEMALE. Coded as 1, male as 0 (53 percent female).

BLACK. Coded as 1, all other races as 0 (18 percent black).

NONWHITE. Coded as 1, self-reported whites (excluding Latinos) as 0 (36 percent nonwhite).

MARITAL STATUS. Married coded as 1, all other as 0 (59 percent married).

HOMEOWNERSHIP. Own home coded as 1, all other as 0 (64 percent homeowners).

Contextual Variables

CITY SIZE. 0—< 2,500, 1—2,500 to < 5,000, 2—5,000 to < 10,000, 3—10,000 to < 25,000, 4—25,000 to < 50,000, 5—50,000 to < 100,000, 6—100,000 to < 250,000, 7—250,000 to < 500,000, 8—500,000 to 1 million, 9—> 1 million (distribution of variables [including rural areas]: 0—11 percent, 1—7 percent, 2—11 percent, 3—10 percent, 4—14 percent, 5—11 percent, 6—12 percent, 7—9 percent, 8—4 percent, 9—11 percent).

RURAL. Thirty-three percent of sample drawn from rural areas.

LOG OF MEDIAN HOUSEHOLD INCOME. The median household income for the place of residence was taken from the census. Because of the skewed distribution, the log of this measure was substituted. It ranges in value from 3.98 to 5.07.

PERCENT WHITE (FROM METROPOLITAN AREAS ONLY). Coded directly from 0.04 to 1 (average score 73 percent).

PERCENT HOMEOWNER (FROM METROPOLITAN AREAS ONLY). Coded directly from 0.10 to 0.98 (average score 65 percent).

PERCENT COMMUTING (FROM METROPOLITAN AREAS ONLY). Coded directly from 0.11 to 95 (average score 66 percent).

CITY AGE (FROM METROPOLITAN AREAS ONLY). Coded from 0 to 50 (all places over 50 coded as 50) (average age 28 years).

Logistic and OLS Regression Equations for the Figures

(Cox & Snell r-squared indicates logistic regression, r-squared indicates OLS regression)

TABLE B.1

The Effects of City and Metropolitan Area Size on Local Civic Participation with Controls for Individual and Contextual Population Characteristics (fig. 2.3)

	Contact Officials		Attend Board Meeting		Attend Org. Meeting		Informal Civic Activity		Vote Local Elections	
City-level variables										
City size	−.133**	(.037)	−.165**	(.045)	−.047	(.038)	−.091**	(.035)	−.086*	(.015)
Med. hsehld. inc.	−.013*	(.007)	−.021*	(.009)	−.019**	(.007)	−.016**	(.007)	−.011	(.007)
Percent white	−.419	(.366)	−1.00*	(.426)	.886**	(.374)	−.267	(.433)	−.253	(.363)
Large metro area	−.669*	(.317)	.337	(.369)	−.395	(.318)	−.235	(.298)	−1.13**	(.322)
Rural	.039	(.236)	−.518	(.303)	−.189	(.247)	−.153	(.230)	−.216	(.247)
Large metro × city size	.102*	(.051)	−.032	(.062)	.069	(.051)	.078	(.047)	.168**	(.051)
Rural × city size	−.002	(.078)	.146	(.101)	−.005	(.082)	−.008	(.075)	−.075	(.081)
Other variables										
Education	.431**	(.047)	.394**	(.058)	.431**	(.049)	.430**	(.043)	.525**	(.048)
Income	.155**	(.035)	.199**	(.044)	.204**	(.054)	.183**	(.033)	.154**	(.036)
Age	.008**	(.004)	.008	(.005)	.007	(.003)	.006*	(.003)	.056**	(.004)
Homeowner	.354**	(.126)	.585**	(.174)	.419**	(.134)	.233*	(.115)	.452**	(.118)
Black	−.168	(.157)	−.299	(.199)	.321*	(.147)	.471**	(.135)	.083	(.143)
Female	−.230*	(.104)	−.188	(.128)	−.103	(.101)	−.011	(.097)	.097	(.105)
Length of residence	.368**	(.135)	.171	(.170)	.179	(.199)	.288	(.124)	−.089	(.128)
South	−.146	(.122)	−.285	(.153)	−.103	(.121)	−.021	(.115)	−.211	(.122)
Cox & Snell r-sq.	.12		.10		.13		.13		.22	
ncases	2,032		1,914		2,038		2,034		2,022	

Source: 1990 Citizen Participation Study / 1990 Census, standard error in parentheses.

Note: Excluded category is metropolitan area under 2.5 million in size.

TABLE B.2
Interest in Local and National Politics by City Size (fig. 2.6)

	Local Politics	*National Politics*
City-level variables		
City size	−.021** (.010)	.001 (.010)
Med. hsehld. inc.	−.007** (.000)	.003 (.002)
Percent white	−.199 (.130)	.007 (.123)
Rural	−.002 (.060)	.007 (.057)
Other variables		
Education	.196** (.017)	.224** (.016)
Income	.058** (.014)	.054** (.013)
Age	.012** (.001)	.008** (.001)
Homeowner	.170** (.046)	.053 (.046)
Black	.133** (.054)	.000 (.052)
Female	−.014 (.040)	−.116** (.038)
Length of residence	.055 (.049)	.077 (.046)
South	−.004 (.046)	−.021 (.043)
r-squared	.17	.19
ncases	2,028	2,028

Source: 1990 Citizen Participation Study / 1990 Census, standard error in parentheses.
**$p < .05$.

TABLE B.3

The Effects of City Size on Nonelectoral Civic Participation with Controls for Individual and Contextual Population Characteristics and Local Political Interest, Efficacy, and Mobilization (fig. 2.10)

	Standard Controls	Interest, Efficacy, and Mobilization Controlled
Variables		
City size	−.012** (.003)	−.009** (.003)
Med. hsehld. inc.	−.006** (.000)	−.003** (.000)
Percent white	−.021 (.044)	−.012 (.039)
Large metro area	.011 (.018)	.031* (.017)
Rural area	−.212 (.020)	−.005 (.015)
Political interest		.064** (.007)
Political efficacy		.031** (.004)
Mobilization		.205** (.013)
Education	.075** (.006)	.033** (.005)
Income	.032** (.004)	.016** (.004)
Age	.001** (.001)	.000 (.000)
Homeowner	.058** (.015)	.026** (.013)
Black	.022 (.018)	.022 (.016)
Female	−.014 (.013)	−.006 (.011)
Length of residence	.051** (.016)	.043** (.014)
South	−.024 (.015)	−.012 (.013)
r-squared	.21	.40
ncases	1,904	1,883

Source: 1990 Citizen Participation Study / 1990 Census, standard error in parentheses.
**p < .05.

TABLE B.4
The Effects of City Income Levels on Participation in Local Civic Activities among Residents of Metropolitan Areas (fig. 3.3)

	Contact Officials		Attend Board Meeting		Attend Org. Meeting		Informal Civic Activity		Vote in Local Elections	
City-level variables										
Log med. hsehld. inc.	-1.19**	(.504)	46.58*	(25.6)	59.6**	(20.1)	33.5*	(18.1)	37.7**	(18.3)
Log med. hsehld. inc. sq.	N.S.		-5.28*	(2.85)	-6.78**	(2.25)	-3.82*(	2.02)	-4.33**	(2.04)
City size	-.089**	(.028)	-.167**	(.031)	-.063**	(.027)	-.055**	(.026)	-.040	(.028)
Percent black	.660	(.400)	1.598**	(.435)	-.489	(.391)	.348	(.375)	.726	(.415)
Other variables										
Education	.486**	(.069)	.501**	(.035)	.401**	(.051)	.312**	(.049)	.641**	(.069)
Income	.175**	(.059)	.269**	(.075)	.297**	(.057)	.182**	(.037)	.206**	(.061)
Age	.009**	(.004)	.009**	(.005)	.009**	(.003)	.009**	(.004)	.059**	(.005)
Homeowner	.406**	(.151)	.660**	(.200)	.258	(.146)	.111	(.135)	.413**	(.142)
Black	-.239	(.175)	-.291	(.223)	.333*	(.162)	.614**	(.154)	.065	(.167)
Female	-.200	(.119)	-.213	(.148)	-.178	(.125)	.035	(1.18)	.136	(.122)
Length of residence	.126	(.219)	.318	(.253)	.208	(.208)	.344	(.203)	.386	(.205)
South	-.255	(.148)	-.321*	(.154)	-.084	(.141)	.067	(.136)	-.181	(.415)
Cox & Snell r-sq.	.10		.11		.13		.12		.24	
ncases	1,538		1,462		1,543		1,539		1,531	

Source: 1990 Citizen Participation Study / 1990 Census, standard error in parentheses (selecting only residents in census-designated metropolitan areas).

*$p < .1$. **$p < .05$.

TABLE B.5
The Effects of City Income Levels and Economic Diversity on Participation in Local Civic Activities among Residents of Metropolitan Areas (fig. 3.4)

	Contact Officials		Attend Brd. Meeting		Attend Org. Meeting		Informal Civic Activity		Vote Local Elections	
City-level variables										
Log med. hsehld. inc.	-1.23**	(.513)	-1.02*	(.645)	-1.39**	(.513)	-1.64**	(.641)	-1.23**	(.525)
IQV (econ. diversity)	.964	(1.33)	3.32*	(1.81)	4.01**	(1.42)	3.52***	(.178)	2.74**	(1.34)
City size	-.095**	(.028)	-.174**	(.035)	-.069**	(.027)	-.069**	(.029)	-.045	(.029)
Percent black	.680	(.400)	1.61**	(.485)	-.478	(.391)	.354	(.374)	.742	(.415)
Other variables										
Education	.486**	(.069)	.499**	(.035)	.400**	(.051)	.385**	(.049)	.640**	(.069)
Income	.174**	(.059)	.267**	(.075)	.295**	(.057)	.182**	(.038)	.205**	(.061)
Age	.009**	(.004)	.009	(.005)	.009**	(.003)	.009**	(.004)	.059**	(.005)
Homeowner	.407**	(.151)	.661**	(.200)	.260	(.146)	.174	(.132)	.415**	(.142)
Black	-.239	(.175)	-.290	(.223)	.337*	(.162)	.622**	(.150)	.067	(.167)
Female	-.201	(.119)	-.215	(.148)	-.181	(.125)	.033	(.112)	.134	(.122)
Length of residence	.126	(.219)	.318	(.295)	.206	(.208)	.334	(.203)	.385	(.206)
South	-.262	(.148)	-.344	(.183)	-.114	(.141)	.054	(.135)	-.199	(.146)
Cox & Snell r-sq.	.10		.11		.13		.12		.24	
ncases	1,538		1,462		1,543		1,539		1,531	

Source: 1990 Citizen Participation Study/1990 Census, standard error in parentheses (selecting only residents in census-designated metropolitan areas).

*p < .1. **p < .05.

TABLE B.6

The Effects of City Affluence and Economic Diversity on Interest in Local and National Politics (fig. 3.5)

	Local Politics	National Politics
City-level variables		
Log med. hsehld. inc. (50 pt.)	−.575** (.194)	.096 (.183)
Economic heterogeneity (IQV)	1.287** (.496)	−.015 (.469)
City size (10 pt.)	−.023** (.011)	−.034 (.010)
Percent black	.129 (.150)	.041 (.142)
Other variables		
Education (6 pt.)	.189** (.019)	.227** (.018)
Income (8 pt.)	.065** (.015)	.063** (.015)
Age (18–90)	.014** (.002)	.008** (.001)
Homeowner	.132** (.055)	.064 (.052)
Black	.141 (.057)	−.001 (.059)
Female	−.012 (.040)	−.118** (.038)
Length of residence	.116 (.078)	−.092 (.074)
South	−.078 (.054)	−.118** (.052)
r-squared	.19	.21
ncases	1,536	1,536

Source: 1990 Citizen Participation Study / 1990 Census, standard error in parentheses (selecting only residents in census-designated metropolitan areas).

$*p < .1.$ $**p < .05.$

TABLE B.7
The Effects of City Income Levels and Economic Diversity on Participation in Local Civic Activities among Residents of Metropolitan Areas with Controls for Interest in Local Politics (fig. 3.6)

	Contact Officials		Attend Brd. Meeting		Attend Org. Meeting		Informal Civic Activity		Vote Local Elections	
City-level variables										
Log med. hsehld. inc.	-.889	(.531)	-.428	(.667)	-1.12*	(.522)	-.993	(.385)	-.853	(.542)
IQV (econ. diversity)	-.087	(.711)	1.06	(.935)	1.70**	(.746)	2.30	(1.79)	1.85	(1.34)
City size	-.085**	(.030)	-.175**	(.037)	-.059	(.028)	-.061**	(.030)	-.032	(.031)
Percent black	.637	(.420)	1.79**	(.515)	-.582	(.401)	.359	(.385)	.751	(.434)
Other variables										
Interest in local pol.	.832**	(.083)	1.049**	(.115)	.567**	(.073)	.590**	(.069)	.679**	(.072)
Education	.354**	(.072)	.363**	(.093)	.322**	(.053)	.299**	(.052)	.503**	(.073)
Income	.130**	(.062)	.225**	(.078)	.265**	(.058)	.152**	(.038)	.139**	(.064)
Age	-.002	(.005)	-.005	(.006)	.001	(.004)	.001	(.004)	.053**	(.005)
Homeowner	.335*	(.158)	.625**	(.201)	.199	(.146)	.095	(.135)	.365**	(.148)
Black	-.373*	(.183)	-.517**	(.236)	.283	(.167)	.544**	(.155)	-.049	(.176)
Female	-.214	(.124)	-.236	(.148)	-.194	(.125)	.048	(.114)	.140	(.126)
Length of residence	.019	(.227)	.199	(.307)	.132	(.211)	.142	(.214)	.297	(.212)
South	-.211	(.148)	-.315	(.193)	-.067	(.143)	.096	(.138)	-.131	(.153)
Cox & Snell r-sq.	.16		.17		.17		.16		.29	
ncases	1,532		1,456		1,537		1,533		1,525	

Source: 1990 Citizen Participation Study / 1990 Census, standard error in parentheses (selecting only residents in census-designated metropolitan areas).

*p < .1. **p < .05.

TABLE B.8
The Effects of Percent White in a City on Civic Activity by Three Racial Groups (figs. 4.3 and 4.4)

Variables	Contact Officials		Attend Brd. Meeting		Attend Org. Meeting		Informal Civic Activity		Vote in Local Elections	
Percent white	-.537	(.497)	-1.41**	(.594)	1.46**	(.496)	-.379	(.478)	-7.08**	(2.53)
Percent white squared									5.67**	(1.79)
City size	-.081**	(.031)	-.165**	(.038)	-1.51**	(.490)	-.042	(.029)	.067*	(.034)
Log med. hsehld. inc.	-1.43**	(.507)	-1.12*	(.609)	.013	(.030)	-.842*	(.475)	-1.65**	(.527)
Black * per. white	.243	(.805)	-.187	(.999)	-1.32*	(.7629)	-.334	(.728)	-1.07	(.934)
Latino * per. white	.275	(1.11)	-.773	(1.42)	.575	(1.07)	-.125	(.927)	.601	(.525)
Black	-.496	(.522)	-.248	(.631)	1.067**	(.502)	.736	(.480)	.631	(.621)
Latino	-.944	(.817)	-.187	(1.02)	-.983	(.809)	-.213	(.683)	-.833	(.699)
Education	.348**	(.054)	.378**	(.067)	.362**	(.052)	.373**	(.050)	.492**	(.057)
Income	.115**	(.042)	.173**	(.053)	.205**	(.040)	.166**	(.038)	.123**	(.043)
Age	.007	(.004)	.008	(.005)	.008*	(.004)	.008*	(.004)	.058**	(.005)
Homeowner	.362**	(.148)	.658**	(.195)	.227	(.139)	.142	(.134)	.441**	(.141)
Female	-.192	(.119)	-.029	(.148)	-.198*	(.115)	.0268	(.112)	.149	(.227)
South	-.209	(.148)	-.291	(.184)	-.087	(.142)	.0526	(.136)	-.017	(.152)
Cox & Snell r-sq.	.11		.11		.14		.12		.25	
ncases	1,538		1,462		1,543		1,539		1,532	

Source: 1990 Citizen Participation Study / 1990 Census, standard error in parentheses (selecting only residents in census-designated metropolitan areas).

$*p < .1.$ $**p < .05.$

TABLE B.9

The Effects of Percent White in a City on Political Interest, Efficacy, and Mobilization for Three Racial Groups (fig. 4.5)

	Local Interest		Local Efficacy		Mobilization	
Variables						
Percent white	.208	(.195)	.208	(.296)	.179	(.490)
Log med. hsehld. inc.	−.591**	(.191)	.096	(.183)	−.746	(.495)
City size (10 pt.)	.003	(.011)	−.042**	(.018)	−.041	(.030)
Black * percent white	−.568*	(.299)	−1.35**	(.454)	.392	(.773)
Latino * percent white	.096	(.343)	−.127	(.522)	.009	(1.01)
Black	.450**	(.196)	.702**	(.298)	−.647	(.507)
Latino	−.266	(.254)	−.177	(.386)	−.908	(.752)
Education	.176**	(.020)	.247**	(.030)	.399**	(.053)
Income	.065**	(.015)	.104**	(.023)	.204**	(.039)
Age	.012**	(.002)	.002	(.002)	.014**	(.004)
Homeowner	.144**	(.055)	.183**	(.080)	.403**	(.141)
Female	−.015	(.040)	−.176**	(.068)	−.162	(.116)
South	−.067	(.054)	−.081**	(.084)	−.229	(.143)
r-squared	.19		.16		(Cox & Snell) .19	
ncases	1,536		1,524		1,543	

Source: 1990 Citizen Participation Study / 1990 Census, standard error in parentheses (selecting only residents in census-designated metropolitan areas).

**$p < .05$.

TABLE B.10
Predicted Average Number of Civic Acts for African Americans by Percent
White in City with Controls for Political Interest and Efficacy (fig. 4.6)

	Civic Acts		Controlling for Interest & Efficacy	
Variables				
Percent white	−.716*	(.383)	−.380	(.359)
Log med. hsehld. inc.	−1.75**	(.698)	−1.23*	(.647)
City size (10 pt.)	−.032	(.032)	−.031	(.030)
Local political interest			.425**	(.077)
Local political efficacy			.180**	(.051)
Education	.415**	(.067)	.262**	(.065)
Income	.128**	(.048)	.119**	(.045)
Age	.021**	(.005)	.016**	(.005)
Homeowner	.203	(.155)	.038	(.147)
Female	.020	(.147)	.073	(.136)
South	−.136	(.169)	−.108	(.157)
r-squared	.27		.39	
ncases	307		304	

Source: 1990 Citizen Participation Study / 1990 Census, standard error in parentheses
(selecting only African American residents in census-designated metropolitan areas).
  *$p < .1$. **$p < .05$.

TABLE B.11

Predicted Rates of Voting for Whites by Percent White in City for Racially
Mixed and Predominantly White Metropolitan Areas (fig. 4.7)

	Predominantly White Metropolitan Areas		Racially Mixed Metropolitan Areas	
Variables				
Percent white	1.45	(1.05)	1.38	(1.03)
Log med. hsehld. inc.	.253	(1.17)	−3.41**	(1.10)
City size	−.017	(.062)	.122*	(.069)
Education	.502**	(.106)	.506**	(.110)
Income	.116	(.077)	.182**	(.078)
Age	.065**	(.009)	.055**	(.009)
Homeowner	.490*	(.282)	.278	(.281)
Female	.343	(.225)	.031	(.230)
South	.117	(.357)	−.344	(.265)
Cox & Snell r-sq.	.21		.20	
ncases	496		426	

Source: 1990 Citizen Participation Study / 1990 Census, standard error in parentheses
(selecting only white residents in census-designated metropolitan areas).
$*p < .1. **p < .05.$

TABLE B.12
The Effects of Residential Predominance on Civic Activity (fig. 5.2)

Variables	Contact Officials		Attend Brd. Meeting		Attend Org. Meeting		Informal Civic Activity		Vote Local Elections	
Residential predominance	−.285	(.331)	−.027	(.410)	−.517	(.320)	−.237	(.316)	−.278	(.351)
City size	−.155**	(.057)	−.186**	(.069)	−.165**	(.056)	−.101*	(.055)	−.084	(.060)
Education	.399**	(.074)	.389**	(.089)	.394**	(.073)	.473**	(.072)	.539**	(.081)
Income	.080	(.056)	.108**	(.071)	.146**	(.054)	.121**	(.053)	.130**	(.057)
Age	.011*	(.006)	.019**	(.007)	.004	(.006)	.014**	(.006)	.059**	(.007)
Homeowner	.333*	(.226)	.778**	(.315)	.528**	(.215)	.116	(.207)	.303	(.211)
Black	−.006	(.252)	.362	(.304)	.129	(.240)	.688**	(.231)	.254	(.251)
Female	−.243	(.162)	−.339*	(.198)	−.144	(.157)	.000	(.155)	−.074	(.171)
Length of residence	.143	(.291)	.591	(.413)	.354	(.286)	.497*	(.280)	.738**	(.291)
South	−.254	(.198)	−.371	(.251)	−.287	(.191)	.145	(.185)	−.058	(.198)
Cox & Snell r-sq.	.11		.12		.13		.13		.25	
ncases	798		748		802		801		797	

Source: 1990 Citizen Participation Study / 1990 Census, standard error in parentheses (selecting only residents in census-designated metropolitan areas and places under 50,000 in population).

$*p < .1. **p < .05.$

TABLE B.13

The Effects of Residential Predominance on Local and National Political
Interest (fig. 5.3)

	Local Politics	National Politics
City-level variables		
Residential predominance	−.257** (.124)	−.002 (.345)
City size (10 pt.)	−.066** (.022)	−.031 (.043)
Education (6 pt.)	.127** (.028)	.213** (.015)
Income (8 pt.)	.065** (.021)	.064** (.014)
Age (18–90)	.015** (.002)	.012** (.001)
Homeowner	.140 (.081)	.035 (.049)
Black	.144 (.093)	−.003 (.055)
Female	−.058 (.062)	−.124** (.045)
Length of residence	.129 (.106)	−.049 (.086)
South	−.257** (.127)	−.105** (.057)
r-squared	.18	.20
ncases	788	788

Source: 1990 Citizen Participation Study / 1990 Census, standard error in parentheses
(selecting only residents in census-designated metropolitan areas).

*$p < .1$. **$p < .05$.

TABLE B.14
The Effects of Residential Predominance on Civic Activity with Controls for City-Level Affluence and Percent White (fig. 5.4)

	Contact Officials	Attend Board Meeting	Attend Org. Meeting	Informal Civic Activity	Vote Local Elections
Variables					
Residential predominance	−.041 (.425)	−.044 (.534)	−.403 (.414)	−.025 (.401)	−.040 (.438)
City size	−.108* (.064)	−.182** (.077)	−.082 (.062)	−.068 (.061)	.022 (.067)
Log med. hshld. inc.	−1.78** (.755)	−.848 (.912)	−1.10 (.737)	−1.31* (.717)	−2.45** (.789)
Percent white	−.379 (.541)	−1.07* (.644)	1.99** (.556)	−.447 (.519)	.933* (.562)
Education	.430** (.075)	.393** (.091)	.398** (.073)	.489** (.072)	.560** (.083)
Income	.114* (.058)	.124* (.071)	.173** (.056)	.142* (.054)	.177** (.057)
Age	.012* (.006)	.022** (.007)	.004 (.006)	.016** (.006)	.062** (.007)
Homeowner	.296 (.215)	.882** (.302)	.621** (.209)	.179 (.199)	.397** (.202)
Black	−.090 (.298)	.097 (.354)	.648 (.279)	.619** (.263)	.534* (.288)
Female	−.234 (.162)	−.337* (.198)	−.152 (.157)	.001 (.156)	−.088 (.170)
Length of residence	.143 (.291)	.567 (.443)	.354 (.286)	.484* (.278)	.735** (.290)
South	−.425** (.210)	−.484 (.263)	−.288 (.201)	.024 (.193)	−.221 (.209)
Cox & Snell r-sq.	.12	.12	.13	.14	.25
ncases	798	748	802	801	797

Source: 1990 Citizen Participation Study / 1990 Census, standard error in parentheses (selecting only residents in census-designated metropolitan areas and places under 50,000 in population).

*p < .1. **p < .05.

TABLE B.15
The Effects of City Age on Civic Activity with Controls for Individual- and City-Level Traits (fig. 6.5)

Variables	Attend Board Meeting		Informal Civic Action		Vote in Local Elections	
Place age	.045** (.017)	.041** (.019)	.028** (.013)	.031** (.015)	.034** (.012)	.014 (.015)
City size	−.045 (.049)	−.036 (.054)	−.034 (.035)	−.068* (.039)	−.043 (.037)	−.046 (.041)
Log md. hschld. inc.		−.012 (.021)		.025* (.015)		−.022 (.015)
Percent white		.041 (.834)		−.764 (.620)		−1.30** (.662)
Education	.311** (.105)	.311** (.106)	.402** (.078)	.402** (.078)	.566** (.086)	.571** (.086)
Income	.241** (.076)	.249** (.078)	.175** (.006)	.158** (.057)	.130** (.059)	.156** (.062)
Age	.009 (.008)	.009 (.008)	.005 (.006)	.005 (.006)	.049** (.007)	.050** (.007)
Homeowner	.692** (.307)	.704** (.307)	.415** (.199)	.412** (.201)	.492** (.197)	.533** (.199)
Black	−.292 (.338)	−.295 (.327)	.113 (.202)	.027 (.216)	.068 (.208)	−.086 (.223)
Female	−.226 (.235)	−.230 (.236)	−.086 (.172)	−.087 (.173)	.015 (.181)	.021 (.182)
Res. length	−.166 (.278)	−.179 (.280)	.289 (.161)	.313 (.208)	−.121 (.210)	−.132 (.212)
Cox & Snell r-sq.	.10	.11	.14	.15	.22	.23
ncases	623	623	664	664	659	659

Source: 1990 Citizen Participation Study / 1990 Census, standard error in parentheses (selecting only residents in census-designated metropolitan areas and in South).

$*p < .1$. $**p < .05$.

TABLE B.16

The Effects of City Age on Informal Civic Action and Attending Board Meetings with Controls for Interest, Efficacy, and Mobilization for Southerners (fig. 6.7)

	Attend Board Meeting				Informal Civic Action			
Variables								
Place age	.041**	(.019)	.035	(.023)	.031**	(.015)	.021	(.016)
City size	−.036	(.054)	−.007	(.061)	−.068*	(.039)	−.048	(.043)
Log md. hsehld. inc.	−.012	(.021)	−.003	(.002)	.025*	(.015)	.002	(.002)
Percent white	.041	(.834)	.206	(.948)	−.764	(.620)	−.732	(.670)
Political interest			.598**	(.185)			.437**	(.115)
Political efficacy			.484**	(.122)			.204**	(.074)
Mobilized			1.65**	(.308)			1.14**	(.212)
Education	.311**	(.106)	.074**	(.125)	.402**	(.078)	.176**	(.086)
Income	.249**	(.078)	.105	(.089)	.158**	(.057)	.070	(.063)
Age	.009	(.008)	−.006	(.009)	.005	(.006)	−.007	(.006)
Homeowner	.704**	(.307)	.573*	(.338)	.412**	(.201)	.303	(.215)
Black	−.295	(.327)	−.164	(.368)	.027	(.216)	.017	(.234)
Female	−.230	(.236)	−.287	(.269)	−.087	(.173)	−.059	(.187)
Res. length	−.179	(.280)	−.200	(.327)	.313	(.208)	.224	(.223)
Cox & Sn. r-sq.	.11		.23		.15		.24	
ncases	623		616		664		654	

Source: 1990 Citizen Participation Study / 1990 Census, standard error in parentheses (selecting only residents in census-designated metropolitan areas and in South).

$*p < .1.$ $**p < .05.$

Testing the Relationship between Civic Participation and "Self-Interest Rightly Understood"

GIVEN THE DEARTH of evidence for the civil society critique, it is worthwhile to detour slightly and examine these claims with survey data. The 1996 American National Election Studies (NES), a large-scale survey of the American population taken both before and after the 1996 presidential election, provides an excellent opportunity for just this. Using the survey, I constructed a six-point scale of local, face-to-face civic activity from several self-reported items measuring whether the person had (1) volunteered in the past twelve months; (2) "worked with others or joined an organization" to solve some community problem; or attended a meeting or an activity of a (3) church group, (4) civic group, (5) neighborhood or community group, or (6) fraternal-type organization such as the Elks Club or Junior League. Each of these activities was scored on a (0, 1) scale and then combined into a seven-point scale. Thirty-four percent of the respondents participated in none of these acts, 29 percent participated in only one, 33 percent in two or three, and only 4 percent in four or more. Regressing the six-point civic activity scale on a number of demographic items, I find that the people who are active in local civic life are the same types of people who are active in national political affairs (Verba, Schlozman, and Brady 1995). Consistent with past research, the best predictors of local civic involvement are education, homeownership, length of residence, sex, and political interest. In particular, the model predicts that educated, homeowning women who have lived at their address for more than two years and are interested in politics are the most likely to be active in local civic associations. Interestingly, age and income are not very good predictors of civic engagement—while older respondents are slightly more likely to volunteer, this difference is not statistically significant. Also, political ideology seems unrelated to civic activity. Self-identified liberals and conservatives were no more likely than their "middle-of-the-road" counterparts to volunteer.

Capturing the ephemeral notion of "self-interest rightly understood" with a survey instrument is a more difficult matter. After all, when asking people about how they value their neighbors and community relative to themselves, most survey respondents would probably feel an enormous pressure not to sound explicitly selfish. With the caveat of response bias in mind, I did locate three indicators of how much people might have the sense of "shared humanity" that Tocqueville noted as so important for stable democracy. These were measures of how much respondents' (1) valued cooperation, (2) sought to help others, and (3) trusted people. The first item is how much the respondents believe it is "more important" to be either self-reliant or cooperative with others. This variable is called COOPERATE. The second item was combined from four five-point scales that asked the respondents to rate the importance of several statements including whether one should always help the less fortunate, whether one should be concerned with others, whether it is best *not* to get involved in helping others, and whether people pay too much attention to others' well-being. I call this summary item HELP OTHERS. Finally, as indicated by past research (Brehm and Rahn 1997, Monroe 1996), interpersonal trust can be a great indicator of whether one is pro-social in orientation. I measure TRUST with a three-point measure based on combining the response to two dichotomous items on whether respondents agree that "people can be trusted most of the time" and whether "most people would try to take advantage of [the respondent] given the chance." All three items have relatively normal distributions; for instance, the respondents fall roughly into thirds on the trust item and are almost split in half on the distinction between cooperating and being self-reliant.

At first glance, civic activity seems a powerful indicator of more pro-social attitudes or "self-interest rightly understood." When the three pro-social attitudinal items are regressed on the civic activity scale with controls for demographic traits, political interest, and ideology, there are consistent and strong effects of civic activity. Political interest is measured on a four-point scale of how closely the respondent follows politics. For comparability, all variables in table C.1 were rescaled from 0 to 1.

As illustrated in table C.1, all three equations demonstrate statistically significant increases in pro-social attitudes with increases in the civic activity scale. In fact, civic activity is the greatest predictor of one's attitudes toward helping others, outpacing the effects of education, gender, and political ideology. People who are civically active are also more likely to value cooperation and, in accordance with past research, are more likely to be trusting of others. Thus even when we take a person's age, education, or political orientation into account, civic activity seems to have a large and independent effect on people's attitudes toward others.

The problem with this perspective, however, is that the items measuring civic activity may not be exogenous to those predicting "self-interest rightly understood." Some may argue that the very act of volunteering, an activity with higher costs and largely indivisible benefits, itself already reflects a pro-social orientation. The fact that anyone would take the time

TABLE C.1
The Effects of Civic Activity on Pro-Social Attitudes

	COOPERATE	*HELP OTHERS*	*TRUST*
Local civic activity	.023* (.012)	.042** (.007)	.033** (.009)
Age	−.065 (.062)	−.037 (.038)	.204** (.050)
Married	.053 (.029)	.037* (.018)	.015 (.024)
Education	−.002 (.055)	.126** (.034)	.357** (.044)
Homeowner	−.011 (.032)	−.008 (.020)	.055* (.025)
Income	−.084* (.043)	.011 (.027)	.120** (.035)
Length of residence	.045 (.052)	−.033 (.032)	−.088* (.042)
Female	−.010 (.027)	.080** (.017)	.005 (.022)
Liberal	.103* (.044)	.056* (.027)	.159** (.035)
Conservative	.007 (.041)	.001 (.025)	.088** (.033)
Follow politics	−.067 (.044)	.070** (.027)	.072* (.036)
adjusted r-sq.	.01	.08	.15
ncases	1,500	1,519	1,492

Source: 1996 American National Election Studies, standard error of the coefficients in parentheses.
*$p < .05$. **$p < .01$.

to volunteer or attend the meeting of a civic organization, instead of engaging in some private, personal activity, is an indicator of preexisting values. The early results may simply be capturing the prior orientations of the activists—the priority these activists give to helping others and cooperating comes not from their experiences within the organization but from other sources, such as personality traits or earlier learned behaviors. One might even argue that the civic scale items should be the activity to be explained, with the pro-social attitudinal measures as explanatory variables. In fact, when a civic activity is regressed on the attitudinal items with the same set of controls, this is exactly what happens: people who express higher levels of trust and who value cooperation and helping others are much more likely to be civically active.

Consequently, testing Tocqueville's propositions with survey data presents a problem of causality. Civic activity may correspond with pro-social attitudes, but those with pro-social attitudes are also much more likely to be civically engaged. The experience of participating in civic activities may simply reflect prior orientations. To sort through this simultaneity, I employed a two-stage least squares (2SLS) estimation procedure, which takes into account the potential reciprocal relationship between civic activity and pro-social attitudes and allows the effect of each to be separated. The key to this procedure is identifying variables that can predict local civic activity but are not related to the three types of pro-social attitudes. A person's length of residence, trust in local government, and likelihood of being mobilized to vote are all good predictors of whether he or she is civically active, yet these factors have no relationship to the value placed on cooperation or helping others. Therefore, I used these items (residential length, local government trust, and mobilization) to identify the unique effects of civic activity on attitudes toward cooperation and helping behavior in the 2SLS equation. For measures of interpersonal trust, different identifying variables were used. Specifically, marital status, frequency of religious attendance, and attention to local politics are also related to civic activity but are unrelated to how much people trust others. (Interestingly, married people do value cooperation more than self-reliance, begging the question of whether people who value cooperation are more likely to be married or if the experience of marriage makes someone value cooperation.) The results, listed in table C.2, predict what distinct effects, if any, can be found of civic activity on pro-social attitudes.

When we take the endogenous character of the civic activity and prosocial attitudinal variables into account, the positive linkage between participation and the indicators of "self-interest rightly understood" disappears. In all three simultaneous equations, the coefficients for civic activity as a predictor are small and not statistically significant. While education and political ideology still retain their explanatory power over

TABLE C.2
2SLS Analysis of the Relationship of Civic Activity on Pro-Social Attitudes

	COOPERATE		HELP OTHERS		TRUST	
Local civic activity	.119	(.082)	.009	(.048)	.012	(.024)
Age	−.077	(.067)	−.033	(.041)	.176**	(.054)
Married	.015	(.034)	.046*	(.019)	−	
Education	−.144	(.100)	.167**	(.058)	.417**	(.051)
Homeowner	−.042	(.037)	−.003	(.021)	.107*	(.025)
Length of residence	−		−		−.067	(.048)
Female	−.030	(.034)	.089**	(.020)	.008	(.024)
Liberal	.103*	(.044)	.053*	(.027)	.169**	(.038)
Conservative	−.009	(.043)	.006	(.026)	.100**	(.036)
Follow politics	−.116	(.063)	.089*	(.039)	.078*	(.041)
ncases	1,500		1,519		1,275	

Source: 1996 American National Election Studies, standard error of the coefficients in parentheses.
$*p < .05.$ $**p < .01.$

pro-social attitudes, civic activity does not. Interestingly though, pro-social attitudes do not appear to be exogenous to civic activism. If the equations are run with variables identifying the attitudinal indicators (income and liberal political orientation), with civic activity set as the dependent variable, the robust and positive relationships between community-oriented dispositions and civic activism also lose size and statistical significance. As with the findings in table C.1, pro-social attitudes do not seem to influence civic engagement any more than vice versa.

References

Abramson, John, and John Aldrich. 1982. "The Decline of Electoral Participation in the United States." *American Political Science Review* 76:502–21.

Achen, Christopher, and W. Phillips Shively. 1993. *Cross-Level Inference*. Chicago: University of Chicago Press.

Adams, John S. 1989. *Housing America in the 1980s*. New York: Russell Sage Foundation.

Aldrich, John H. 1995. *Why Parties?* Chicago: University of Chicago Press.

Aldrich, John H., and Forrest D. Nelson. 1984. *Linear Probability, Logit and Probit Models*. Beverly Hills: Sage Publications.

Alford, Robert. 1972. "Critical Evaluation of the Principles of City Classification." In *City Classification Handbook: Methods of Applications*, edited by Brian Berry and Katherine Smith. New York: Wiley-Interscience.

Alford, Robert, and Eugene C. Lee. 1968. "Voting Turnout in American Cities." *American Political Science Review* 62:796–813.

Arendt, Hannah. 1958. *The Human Condition*. Chicago: University of Chicago Press.

Aristotle. 1958. *The Politics of Aristotle*. Translated by Ernest Barker. New York: Oxford University Press.

Babchuck, Nicholas, and Andrew Booth. 1969. "Voluntary Association Membership: A Longitudinal Analysis." *American Sociological Review* 34:31–45.

Baldassare, Mark. 1986. *Trouble in Paradise: The Suburban Transformation in America*. New York: Columbia University Press.

———. 1992. "Suburban Communities." *Annual Review of Sociology* 18:475–94.

Barber, Benjamin. 1984. *Strong Democracy*. Berkeley and Los Angeles: University of California Press.

Batson, Daniel. 1991. *The Altruism Question*. Hillsdale, NJ: Lawrence Erlbaum Associates.

Baumgartner, M. P. 1988. *The Moral Order of a Surburb*. New York: Oxford University Press.

Bellah, Robert N., Richard Madsen, William M. Sullivan, Ann Swidler, and Steven Tipton. 1985. *Habits of the Heart: Individualism and Commitment in American Life*. New York: Harper & Row.

Berger, Bennet. 1960. *Working Class Suburb*. Berkeley and Los Angeles: University of California Press.

Berman, Sheri. 1997. "Civil Society and the Collapse of the Weimar Republic." *World Politics* 49:401–29.

Berry, Brian. 1972. "Latent Structure of the American Urban System." In *City Classification Handbook: Methods of Applications*, edited by Brian Berry and Katherine Smith. New York: Wiley-Interscience.

Berry, Jeffrey M., Kent E. Portney, and Ken Thomson. 1993. *The Rebirth of Urban Democracy*. Washington, DC: Brookings Institution Press.

Bianchi, Suzanne. 1999. "Feminization and Juvenilization of Poverty: Trends, Relative Risks, Causes, and Consequences." *Annual Review of Sociology* 25:307–33.

Blalock, Hubert M. 1967. *Toward a Theory of Minority-Group Relations.* New York: Wiley.

Bledsoe, Timothy, Susan Welch, Lee Sigelman, and Michael Combs. 1995. "Residential Context and Racial Solidarity among African Americans." *American Journal of Political Science* 39:434–58.

Bobo, Lawrence, and Franklin Gilliam. 1990. "Race, Sociopolitical Participation, and Black Empowerment." *American Political Science Review* 84:377–93.

Boger, John Charles. 1997. "Race and the American City: The Kerner Commission Report in Retrospect." In *Race, Poverty, and American Cities,* edited by John Charles Boger and Judith Welch. Chapel Hill: University of North Carolina Press.

Books, John, and Charles Prysby. 1991. *Political Behavior and the Local Context.* New York: Praeger.

Bott, Elizabeth. 1971. *Family and Social Networks.* New York: Free Press.

Box, Richard C. 1998. *Citizen Governance.* Thousand Oaks, CA: Sage Publications.

Brehm, John, and Wendy Rahn. 1997. "Individual-Level Evidence for the Causes and Consequences of Social Capital." *American Journal of Political Science* 41:999–1023.

Brooks-Gunn, Jeanne, Greg J. Duncan, and J. Lawrence Aber, eds. 1997. *Neighborhood Poverty: Context and Consequences for Children.* New York: Russell Sage Foundation.

Brown, Roger. 1985. *Social Psychology.* 2d ed. New York: Free Press.

Browning, Rufus P., Dale R. Marshall, and David Tabb, eds. 1997. *Racial Politics in American Cities.* 2d ed. New York: Longman.

Bryk, Anthony, and Stephen W. Raudenbush. 1992. *Hierarchical Linear Models: Applications and Data Analysis Methods.* Newbury Park, CA: Sage Publications.

Burnham, Walter Dean. 1982. *The Current Crisis in American Politics.* New York: Oxford University Press.

Burns, Nancy. 1994. *The Formation of American Local Governments.* New York: Oxford University Press.

Burrows, Edwin, and Mike Wallace. 1998. *Gotham: A History of New York City to 1898.* New York: Oxford University Press.

Cain, Bruce, Roderick Kiewiet, and Carole Uhlaner. 1991. "The Acquisition of Partisanship by Latinos and Asian Americans." *American Journal of Political Science* 35:390–422.

Calthorpe, Peter. 1993. *The Next American Metropolis.* New York: Princeton Architectural Press.

Campbell, Angus, Philip E. Converse, Warren E. Miller, and Donald E. Stokes. 1960. *The American Voter.* New York: John Wiley and Sons.

Campbell, Lori, Ingrid Connidis, and Lorraine Davies. 1999. "Sibling Ties in Later Life: A Social Network Analysis." *Journal of Family Issues* 20:114–48.

Cannon, David. 1999. *Race, Redistricting, and Representation: The Unintended Consequences of Black Majority Districts.* Chicago: University of Chicago Press.

Chan, Suchang. 1991. *Asian Americans: An Interpretive History*. Boston: Twayne.

Citrin, Jack, Beth Reingold, and Donald Green. 1990. "American Identity and the Politics of Ethnic Change." *Journal of Politics* 52:1124–54.

Cloward, Richard, and Francis Fox Piven. 1974. *The Politics of Turmoil: Essays on Poverty, Race, and the Urban Crisis*. New York: Pantheon Books.

Cohen, Cathy, and Michael Dawson. 1993. "Neighborhood Poverty and African American Politics." *American Political Science Review* 87:286–302.

Coleman, James S. 1990. *Foundations of Social Theory*. Cambridge: Harvard University Press, Belknap Press.

Conover, Pamela. 1988. "The Role of Social Groups in Political Thinking." *British Journal of Political Science* 18:51–76.

Couto, Richard A. 1999. *Making Democracy Work Better*. Chapel Hill: University of North Carolina Press.

Crotty, William J. 1977. *Political Reform and the American Experiment*. New York: Crowell.

Cutler, David, and Edward Glaeser. 1997. "Are Ghettos Good or Bad?" *Quarterly Journal of Economics* 112:827–42.

Dagger, Richard. 1981. "Metropolis, Memory, and Citizenship." *American Journal of Political Science* 25:715–37.

Dahl, Robert. 1961. *Who Governs?* New Haven: Yale University Press.

———. 1967. "The City in the Future of Democracy" *American Political Science Review* 61:953–70.

———. 1998. *On Democracy*. New Haven: Yale University Press.

Dahl, Robert, and Edward Tufte. 1973. *Size and Democracy*. Palo Alto: Stanford University Press.

Danielson, Michael. 1976. *The Politics of Exclusion*. New York: Columbia University Press.

Davis, Mike. 1991. *City of Quartz*. New York: Vintage Press.

Dewey, John. 1927. *The Public and Its Problems*. New York: H. Holt and Company.

Dionne, E. J. 1990. *Why Americans Hate Politics*. New York: Simon and Schuster.

———, ed. 1998. *Community Works: The Revival of Civil Society in America*. Washinton, DC: Brookings Institution Press.

Dobriner, William. 1958. *The Suburban Community*. New York: G. P. Putnam's Sons.

———. 1963. *Class in Suburbia*. Englewood Cliffs, NJ: Prentice-Hall.

Downs, Anthony. 1957. *An Economic Theory of Democracy*. New York: Harper and Row.

Duany, Andres, and Elizabeth Plater-Zyberk. 1991. *Towns and Town-Making Principles*. Cambridge: Harvard University Graduate School of Design; New York: Rizzoli.

Duncan, Greg J., and Jeanne Brooks-Gunn. 1997. *Consequences of Growing Up Poor*. New York: Russell Sage Foundation.

Duncombe, William, and John Yinger. 1997. "Why Is It So Hard to Help Central City Schools?" *Journal of Policy Analysis and Management* 16:85–113.

Eberly, Don E., ed. 1994. *Building a Community of Citizens*. New York: Commonwealth Foundation for Public Policy Alternatives.

Ehrenhalt, Alan. 1995. *The Lost City: Discovering the Forgotten Virtues of Community in the Chicago of the 1950s.* New York: Basic Books.

Eisinger, Peter. 1982. *Black Employment in City Government, 1973–1980.* Washington, DC: Joint Center for Political Studies.

Elazar, Daniel J. 1984. *American Federalism.* New York: Harper and Row.

Elkin, Stephen. 1987. *City and Regime in the American Republic.* Chicago: University of Chicago Press.

Erbring, Lutz, and Alice Young. 1979. "Individuals and Social Structure: Contextual Effects as Endogenous Feedback." *Sociological Methods and Research* 7:396–430.

Erie, Steven P. 1988. *Rainbow's End: Irish Americans and the Dilemmas of Urban Machine Politics, 1840–1985.* Berkeley and Los Angeles: University of California Press.

Farley, Reynolds. 1996. *The New American Reality: Who We Are, How We Got Here, Where We Are Going.* New York: Russell Sage Foundation.

Fava, Sylvia. 1975. "Beyond Suburbia." *Annals of the American Academy of Political and Social Science* 422:11–24.

Ferman, Barbara. 1996. *Challenging the Growth Machine: Neighborhood Politics in Chicago and Pittsburgh.* Lawrence: University Press of Kansas.

Finifter, Ada. 1970. "Dimensions of Political Alienation." *American Political Science Review* 64:389–410.

Fiorina, Morris. 1981. *Retrospective Voting in American National Elections.* New Haven: Yale University Press.

———. 1999. "Extreme Voices: A Dark Side of Civic Engagement." In Skocpol and Fiorina, *Civic Engagement in American Democracy.*

Fischer, Claude. 1976. "The City and Political Psychology." *American Political Science Review* 70:559–71.

———. 1982. *To Dwell among Friends: Personal Networks in Town and City.* Chicago: University of Chicago Press.

———. 1984. *The Urban Experience.* 2d ed. San Diego: Harcourt Brace Jovanovich.

———. 1996. "A Twentieth Year Assessment of the Subcultural Theory of Urbanism." *American Journal of Sociology* 101:543–77.

Fischer, Claude, and Robert Max Jackson. 1976. "Suburbs, Networks, and Attitudes." In *The Changing Face of the Suburbs,* edited by Barry Schwartz. Chicago: University of Chicago Press.

Fishman, Robert. 1987. *Bourgeois Utopias: The Rise and Fall of Suburbia.* New York: Basic Books.

Fitzpatrick, Kevin, and John Logan. 1985. "The Aging of the Suburbs, 1960–1980." *American Sociological Review* 50:134–68.

Flanagan, William G. 1993. *Contemporary Urban Sociology.* New York: Cambridge University Press.

Foley, Michael, and Bob Edwards. 1997. "Escape from Politics? Social Theory and the Social Capital Debate." *American Behavioral Scientist* 40:550–61.

Foster, Michael, and Frank Furstenberg. 1999. "The Most Disadvantaged Children: Trends over Time." *Social Service Review* 73:560–78.

Frantz, Douglas, and Cathy Collins. 1999. *Celebration U.S.A.: Living in Disney's Brave New Town.* New York: Henry Holt and Co.

Freedman, Jonathan. 1975. *Crowding and Behavior*. New York: Viking Press.

Frey, William. 1993. "People in Places: Demographic Trends in Urban America." In *Rediscovering Urban America*, edited by Jack Sommer and Donald Hicks. U.S. Department of Housing and Urban Development, Office of Policy Development and Research. Washington, DC: U.S. Government Printing Office.

———. 1994. "Minority Suburbanization and Continued 'White Flight' in U.S. Metropolitan Areas: Assessing Findings from the 1990 Census." *Research in Community Sociology* 4:15–42.

Frey, William, and Alden Speare, Jr. 1988. *Regional and Metropolitan Growth and Decline in the United States*. Census Monograph Series. New York: Russell Sage Foundation.

Frug, Gerald E. 1999. *City Making*. Princeton: Princeton University Press.

Gans, Herbert. 1964. "Urbanism and Suburbanism as Ways of Life: A Re-evaluation of Definitions." In *Human Behavior and Social Processes*, edited by Arnold M. Rose. Boston: Houghton Mifflin Co.

———. 1967. *The Levittowners: Ways of Life and Politics in a New Suburban Community*. New York: Pantheon Books.

Garreau, Joel. 1991. *Edge City: Life on the New Frontier*. New York: Doubleday.

Geoghegan, Thomas. 1998. *The Secret Lives of Citizens*. New York: Pantheon Books.

Gilens, Martin. 1999. *Why Americans Hate Welfare*. Chicago: University of Chicago Press.

Giles, Micheal, and Marilyn K. Dantico. 1982. "Political Participation and Neighborhood Social Context Revisted." *American Journal of Political Science* 26:144–50.

Giles, Micheal W., and Kaenan Hertz. 1994. "Racial Threat and Partisan Identification." *American Political Science Review* 88:317–26.

Gillette, Howard, Jr. 1986. "The City in American Culture." In *American Urbanism: A Historiographical Review*, edited by Howard Gillette, Jr., and Zane Miller. New York: Greenwood Press.

Glaser, James. 1994. "Back to the Black Belt: Racial Environments and White Racial Attitudes in the South." *Journal of Politics* 56:21–41.

Gottdiener, Mark. 1977. *Planned Sprawl: Private and Public Interests in Suburbia*. Beverly Hills: Sage Publications.

Green, Donald, and Ian Shapiro. 1994. *Pathologies of Rational Choice Theory*. New Haven: Yale University Press.

Greenstein, Fred. 1964. "Changing Patterns of Party Politics." *Annals of the American Academy of Political and Social Science* 353:1–13.

Greer, Scott. 1956. *Social Organization*. Garden City, NY: Doubleday.

Guest, Avery M. 1978. "Suburban Social Status: Persistence or Evolution?" *American Sociological Review* 43:251–64.

Gurin, Patricia, Arthur Miller, and Gerald Gurin. 1980. "Stratum Identification and Consciousness." *Social Psychology Quarterly* 43:30–47.

Guterbock, Thomas, and Bruce London. 1983. "Race, Political Orientation, and Participation: An Empirical Test of Four Competing Theories." *American Sociological Review* 48:439–53.

Haar, Charles. 1972. *The End of Innocence*. Glenview, IL: Scott, Foresman and Company.

Haeberle, Steven. 1985. *Planting the Grassroots: Structuring Citizen Participation.* New York: Praeger.

Hall, John. 1995. "In Search of Civil Society." In *Civil Society: Theory, History, Comparison,* edited by John Hall. Cambridge, MA: Polity Press.

Hamilton, Alexander, James Madison, and John Jay. 1982 [1789]. *The Federalist Papers.* New York: Bantam Books.

Hanushek, Eric A., and John E. Jackson. 1977. *Statistical Methods for Social Scientists.* San Diego: Academic Press.

Harrigan, John. 1993. *Political Change in the Metropolis.* 5th ed. New York: HarperCollins College Publishers.

Hauser, R. M. 1970. "Context and Consex." *American Journal of Sociology* 75:645–64.

Held, David. 1987. *Models of Democracy.* Stanford, CA: Stanford University Press.

Hill, Kim Quaile, and Jan Leighley. 1999. "Racial Diversity, Voter Turnout, and Mobilizing Institutions in the United States." *American Politics Quarterly* 27:275–95.

Hill, Richard Child. 1974. "Separate and Unequal: Government Inequality in the Metropolis." *American Political Science Review* 68:1557–74.

Hobbes, Thomas. 1973 [1651]. *Leviathan.* New York: Dutton.

Hoffman, Martin. 1981. "Is Altruism Part of Human Nature?" *Journal of Personality and Social Psychology* 40:121–37.

Holosko, Michael, and Marvin Feit. 1997. *Health and Poverty.* New York: Haworth Press.

Huckfeldt, R. Robert. 1979. "Political Participation and the Neighborhood Social Context." *American Journal of Political Science* 23:579–92.

———. 1984. *Politics in Context: Assimilation and Conflict in Urban Neighborhoods.* New York: Agathon Press.

Huckfeldt, Robert, and John Sprague. 1987. "Networks in Context: The Social Flow of Political Information." *American Political Science Review* 81:1197–1216.

———. 1995. *Citizens, Politics, and Social Communication: Information and Influence in an Election Campaign.* New York: Cambridge University Press.

Hunter, Floyd. 1953. *Community Power Structure: A Study of Decision Makers.* Chapel Hill: University of North Carolina Press.

Huntington, Samuel. 1983. *American Politics: The Promise of Disharmony.* Cambridge: Harvard University Press.

Jackman, Robert, and Robert Miller. 1996. "Renaissance of Political Culture?" *American Journal of Political Science* 40:697–716.

Jackson, Kenneth. 1985. *Crabgrass Frontier: The Suburbanization of the United States.* New York: Oxford University Press.

Jacobs, Jane. 1961. *The Death and Life of Great American Cities.* New York: Vintage Books.

Janoski, Thomas. 1998. *Citizenship and Civil Society.* New York: Cambridge University Press.

Janowitz, Morris. 1952. *The Community Press in an Urban Setting.* Glencoe, IL: Free Press.

Jones, Bryan, Saadia Greenberg, and Joseph Drew. 1980. *Service Delivery in the City: Citizen Demand and Bureaucratic Rules.* New York: Longman.

Jones, Kelvyn, and Craig Duncan. 1995. "Individuals and Their Ecologies: Analysing the Geography of Chronic Illness within a Multilevel Modelling Framework." *Health and Place* 1:27–40.

Judd, Dennis, and Todd Swanstrom. 1994. *City Politics: Private Power and Public Policy.* New York: HarperCollins College Publishers.

Judge, David, Gerry Stoker, and Harry Wolman. 1995. *Theories of Urban Politics.* London: Sage Publications.

Karnig, Albert, and Oliver Walter. 1983. "Decline in Municipal Voter Turnout: A Function of Changing Structure." *American Politics Quarterly* 11:491–505.

Kasarda, John D. 1980. "The Implications of Contemporary Distribution Trends for National Urban Policy." *Social Science Quarterly* 61:373–400.

Kasarda, John D., and Morris Janowitz. 1974. "Community Attachment in Mass Society." *American Sociological Review* 39:328–39.

Katz, Peter. 1994. *The New Urbanism.* New York: McGraw-Hill.

Katznelson, Ira. 1981. *City Trenches: Urban Politics and the Patterning of Class in the United States.* New York: Pantheon Books.

Keating, Michael. 1995. "Size, Efficiency and Democracy: Consolidation, Fragmentation and Public Choice." In Judge, Stoker, and Wolman, *Theories of Urban Politics.*

Key, V. O. 1984 [1949]. *Southern Politics in State and Nation.* New York: Knopf.

Kingston, Paul William. 1994. "Having a Stake in the System: The Socio-Political Ramifications of Business and Home Ownership." *Social Science Quarterly* 75:679–86.

Kirp, David, John Dwyer, and Larry Rosenthal. 1995. *Our Town: Race, Housing, and the Soul of Suburbia.* New Brunswick, NJ: Rutgers University Press.

Kling, Rob, Spencer Olin, and Mark Poster, eds. *Post-Suburban California: The Transformation of Orange County since World War II.* Berkeley and Los Angeles: University of California Press.

Kozol, Jonathan. 1991. *Savage Inequalities: Children in American Schools.* New York: Crown Publications.

Kunstler, James Howard. 1993. *The Geography of Nowhere: The Rise and Decline of America's Man-Made Landscape.* New York: Simon and Schuster.

Langdon, Phillip. 1994. *A Better Place to Live: Reshaping the American Suburb.* Amherst: University of Massachusetts Press.

Latane, Bibb, and John Darley. 1970. *The Unresponsive Bystander: Why Doesn't He Help?* Englewood Cliffs, NJ: Prentice-Hall.

Lau, Richard. 1989. "Individual and Contextual Influences on Group Identification." *Social Psychology Quarterly* 52:220–31.

Lee, Eugene. 1960. *The Politics of Non-Partisanship: A Study of California City Elections.* Berkeley and Los Angeles: University of California Press.

Leighley, Jan. 1990. "Social Interaction and Contextual Influences on Participation." *American Politics Quarterly* 18:459–75.

———. 1996. "Group Membership and the Mobilization of Political Participation." *Journal of Politics* 58:477–63.

Levine, Robert, Todd Martinez, and Gary Brase. 1994. "Helping in Thirty-Six U.S. Cities," *Journal of Personality and Social Psychology* 67:69–82.

Lewis, Paul. 1994. *Shaping Suburbia: How Political Institutions Organize Urban Development.* Pittsburgh: University of Pittsburgh Press.

Lien, Pei. 1997. *The Political Participation of Asian Americans: Voting Behavior in Southern California.* New York: Garland.

Locke, John. 1997. *Locke: Political Essays.* Edited by Mark Goldie. New York: Cambridge University Press.

Lofland, Lyn. 1973. *A World of Strangers: Order and Action in Urban Public Space.* New York: Basic Books.

Logan, John. 1981. "The Stratification of Metropolitan Suburbs, 1960–1970." *American Sociological Review* 46:175–86.

Logan, John, and Harvey Molotch. 1987. *Urban Fortunes: The Political Economy of Place.* Berkeley and Los Angeles: University of California Press.

Logan, John, and Mark Schneider. 1984. "Racial Segregation and Racial Change in American Suburbs, 1970–1980." *American Journal of Sociology* 89:874–88.

Mansbridge, Jane. 1983. *Beyond Adversarial Democracy.* Chicago: University of Chicago Press.

———. 1999. "On the Idea That Participation Makes Better Citizens." In *Citizen Competence and Democratic Institutions*, edited by Stephen Elkin and Karol Soltan. University Park: The Pennsylvania State University Press.

Martin, Walter. 1956. "The Structuring of Social Relationships Engendered by Suburban Residence." *American Sociological Review* 21:446–53.

Massey, Douglas, and Nancy Denton. 1988. "Suburbanization and Segregation in U.S. Metropolitan Areas." *American Journal of Sociology* 94:592–626.

———. 1993. *American Apartheid Segregation and the Making of the Underclass.* Cambridge: Harvard University Press.

Massey, Douglas, and Mitchell Eggers. 1993. "The Spatial Concentration of Affluence and Poverty during the 1970s." *Urban Affairs Quarterly* 29:299–315.

McAdam, Doug. 1989. "The Biographical Consequences of Activism." *American Sociological Review* 54:744–60.

Mills, C. Wright. 1956. *The Power Elite.* Oxford: Oxford University Press.

Mladenka, Kenneth. 1989. "Blacks and Hispanics in Urban Politics." *American Political Science Review* 83:165–91.

Monroe, Kristen Renwick. 1996. *The Heart of Altruism: Perceptions of a Common Humanity.* Princeton: Princeton University Press.

Muller, Peter O. 1981. *Contemporary Suburban America.* Englewood Cliffs, NJ: Prentice-Hall.

Mumford, Lewis. 1961. *The City in History: Its Origins and Transformations, and Its Prospects.* New York: Harcourt, Brace, & World.

Nie, Norman, Bingham Powell, and Ken Prewitt. 1969. "Social Structure and Political Participation: Developmental Relationships I." *American Political Science Review* 63:361–78.

Oliver, J. Eric, and Raymond E. Wolfinger. 1999. "Jury Aversion and Voter Turnout." *American Political Science Review* 93:61–77.

Olson, Mancur. 1965. *The Logic of Collective Action.* Cambridge: Harvard University Press.

Orfield, Gary, Susan Eaton, and Elaine Jones. 1997. *Dismantling Desegregation: The Quiet Reversal of Brown versus Board of Education.* New York: New Press.

Orren, Gary. 1997. "Fall from Grace: The Public's Loss of Faith in Government." In *Why People Don't Trust Government,* edited by Joseph Nye, Philip Zelikow, and David King. Cambridge: Harvard University Press.

Ostrom, Vincent, Robert Bish, and Elinor Ostrom. 1988. *Local Government in the United States.* San Francisco: Institute for Contemporary Studies.

Palen, J. John. 1995. *The Suburbs.* New York: McGraw-Hill.

Parenti, Michael. 1970. "Power and Pluralism: A View from the Bottom." *Journal of Politics* 32:501–30.

Parks, Roger B., and Ronald J. Oakerson. 1989. "Metropolitan Organization and Governance: A Local Political Economy Approach." *Urban Affairs Quarterly* 25:18–29.

Pateman, Carole. 1970. *Participation and Democratic Theory.* New York: Cambridge University Press.

Peterson, Paul. 1981. *City Limits.* Chicago: University of Chicago Press.

Phelan, Thomas, and Mark Schneider. 1996. "Race, Ethnicity, and Class in American Suburbs." *Urban Affairs Quarterly* 31:659–80.

Phillips, Kevin. 1975. *Electoral Reform and Voter Participation.* Washington, DC: American Enterprise Institute.

Pinderhughes, Diane. 1994. *Race and Ethnicity in Chicago Politics.* Urbana: University of Illinois Press.

Pitkin, Hanna F. 1967. *The Concept of Representation.* Berkeley and Los Angeles: University of California Press.

Piven, Francis Fox, and Richard Cloward. 1989. *Why Americans Don't Vote.* New York: Pantheon Books.

Plotkin, Sydney. 1987. *Keep Out: The Struggle for Land Use Control.* Berkeley and Los Angeles: University of California Press.

Polsby, Nelson W. 1963. *Community Power and Political Theory.* New Haven: Yale University Press.

Popenoe, David. 1985. *The Suburban Environment: Sweden and the United States.* Chicago: University of Chicago Press.

Pugliesi, Karen, and Scott Shook. 1998. "Gender, Ethnicity, and Network Characteristics: Variation in Social Support Resources." *Sex Roles* 38:215–38.

Putnam, Robert. 1966. "Political Attitudes and the Local Community." *American Political Science Review* 60:640–54.

———. 1993. *Making Democracy Work: Civic Traditions in Modern Italy.* Princeton: Princeton University Press.

———. 1995. "Tuning In, Tuning Out: The Strange Disappearance of Social Capital in America." *PS: Political Science and Politics* 28:664–83.

———. 2000. *Bowling Alone: The Collapse and Revival of American Community.* New York: Simon and Schuster.

Reisman, David, with Nathan Glazer and Revel Denney.. 1953. *The Lonely Crowd: A Study of the Changing American Character.* Garden City, NY: Doubleday.

Riker, William H., and Peter Ordeshook. 1968. "A Theory of the Calculus of Voting." *American Political Science Review* 62:26–42.

Rosenblum, Nancy. 1998. *Membership and Morals: The Personal Uses of Pluralism in the United States.* Princeton: Princeton University Press.

Rosenstone, Steven, and John Mark Hansen. 1994. *Mobilization, Participation, and Democracy in America.* New York: Macmillan Publishing Company.

Ross, Andrew. 1999. *The Celebration Chronicles: Life, Liberty, and the Pursuit of Property Values in Disney's New Town.* New York: Ballantine Books.

Rousseau, Jean-Jacques. 1988 [1761]. *The Social Contract.* Translated by G.D.H. Cole. Amherst, NY: Prometheus Books.

Rowe, Peter. 1997. *Civic Realism.* Cambridge: MIT Press.

Ruhil, Anivrudh, Mark Schneider, and Paul Teske. 1999. "Institutions and Reform: Reinventing Local Government." *Urban Affairs Review* 34:433–55.

Rusk, David. 1993. *Cities without Suburbs.* Washington, DC: Woodrow Wilson Center Press (Distributed by Johns Hopkins University Press).

Sandel, Michael. 1998. *Liberalism and the Limits of Justice.* 2d ed. New York: Cambridge University Press.

Scaff, Alvin. 1952. "The Effect of Commuting on Participation in Community Organizations." *American Sociological Review* 17:217–33.

Schattschneider, E. E. 1960. *The Semi-Sovereign People.* New York: Holt, Rinehart and Winston.

Schneider, Mark. 1987. "Income Homogeneity and the Size of Suburban Government." *Journal of Politics* 49:36–53.

———. 1989. *The Competitive City: The Political Economy of Suburbia.* Pittsburgh: University of Pittsburgh Press.

Schneider, Mark, and Thomas Phelan. 1993. "Black Suburbanization in the 1980s." *Demography* 30:269–79.

Schneider, William. 1992. "The Suburban Century Begins." *Atlantic Monthly,* July.

Schwartz, Nancy. 1988. *The Blue Guitar.* Chicago: University of Chicago Press.

Seeley, John R., Alexander Sim, and Elizabeth Loosley. 1956. *Crestwood Heights: The Culture of Suburban Life.* New York: Basic Books.

Seligman, Adam B. 1992. *The Idea of Civil Society.* Princeton: Princeton University Press.

Sennett, Richard. 1969. *Classic Essays on the Culture of Cities.* Englewood Cliffs, NJ: Prentice-Hall.

Shah, Dhavan. 1998. "Civic Engagement, Interpersonal Trust, and Television Use." *Political Psychology* 19:469–96.

Sharp, Elaine. 1984. "Citizen Demand Making in the Urban Context." *American Journal of Political Science* 28:655–70.

Sherif, Muzafer. 1966. *Group Conflict and Cooperation: Their Social Psychology.* London: Routledge and Kegan Paul.

Shihadeh, Edward, and Graham Ousey. 1996. "Metropolitan Expansion and Black Social Dislocation: The Link between Suburbanization and Center-City Crime." *Social Forces* 75:649–66.

Shingles, Richard D. 1981. "Black Consciousness and Political Participation: The Missing Link." *American Political Science Review* 75:76–94.

Shklar, Judith. 1991. *American Citizenship: The Quest for Inclusion.* Cambridge: Harvard University Press.

Sigelman, Carol K., Lee Sigelman, Barbara J. Walkosz, and Michael Nitz. 1995. "Black Candidates, White Voters: Understanding Racial Bias in Political Perceptions." *American Journal of Political Science* 39:243–65.

Simmel, Georg. 1969 [1905]. "Mental Life and the Metropolis." In Sennett, *Classic Essays on the Culture of Cities.*

Skocpol, Theda, and Morris Fiorina, eds. 1999. *Civic Engagement in American Democracy.* Washington, DC: Brookings Institution Press.

Skogan, Wesley. 1990. *Disorder and Decline: Crime and the Spiral of Decay in American Neighborhoods.* New York: Free Press.

Smith, Rogers. 1995. *Civic Virtues.* New Haven: Yale University Press.

Stahura, John. 1987. "Suburban Socioeconomic Status Change: A Comparison of Models, 1950–1980." *American Sociological Review* 52:268–77.

Staub, Ervin. 1975. *The Development of Prosocial Behavior in Children.* Morristown, NJ: General Learning Press.

Stephens, G. Ross, and Nelson Wikstrom. 2000. *Metropolitan Government and Governance.* New York: Oxford University Press.

Stone, Clarence. 1989. *Regime Politics: Governing Atlanta 1946–1988.* Lawrence: University Press of Kansas.

Suarez. Ray. 1999. *The Old Neighborhood: What We Lost in the Great Suburban Migration, 1966–1999.* New York: Free Press.

Swain, Carole. 1993. *Black Faces, Black Interests: The Representation of African Americans in Congress.* Cambridge: Harvard University Press.

Tajfel, Henri, and John Turner. 1979. "An Integrative Theory of Intergroup Conflict." In *The Social Psychology of Intergroup Relations,* edited by William Austin and Stephen Worchel. Monterey, CA: Brooks/Cole Publishing Company.

Takaki, Ronald. 1989. *Strangers from a Different Shore: A History of Asian Americans.* Boston: Little, Brown and Company.

Taylor, Charles. 1992. *Sources of the Self: The Making of Modern Identity.* Cambridge: Harvard University Press.

Taylor, Marylee. 1998. "Local Racial/Ethnic Proportions and White Attitudes: Numbers Count." *American Sociological Review* 63:512–35.

Teaford, John. 1979. *City and Suburb: The Political Fragmentation of Metropolitan America.* Baltimore: Johns Hopkins University Press.

Teixeiria, Ruy. 1992. *The Disappearing American Voter.* Washington, DC: Brookings Institution Press.

Terkildsen, Nayda. 1993. "When White Voters Evaluate Black Candidates." *American Journal of Political Science* 37:1032–53.

Tiebout, Charles. 1956. "A Pure Theory of Local Expenditures." *Journal of Political Economy* 64:416–24.

Tocqueville, Alexis de. 1969 [1835]. *Democracy in America.* Edited by J. P. Mayer. Translated by George Lawrence. New York: Harper and Row.

Tonnies, Ferdinand. 1988 [1898]. *Community and Society.* New Brunswick, NJ: Transaction Books.

Trivers, Robert. 1971. "The Evolution of Reciprocal Altruism." *Quarterly Review of Biology* 46:35–57.

Uhlaner, Carol. 1989. "Rational Turnout: The Neglected Role of Groups." *American Journal of Political Science* 33:390–422.

Uslaner, Eric M. 1998. "Social Capital, Television, and the 'Mean World': Trust, Optimism and Civic Participation." *Political Psychology* 19:441–67.

Verba, Sidney, and Norman Nie. 1972. *Participation in America.* Chicago: University of Chicago Press.

Verba, Sidney, Kay Schlozman, and Henry Brady. 1995. *Voice and Equality.* Cambridge: Harvard University Press.

Verba, Sidney, Kay Schlozman, Henry Brady, and Norman Nie. 1993. "Citizen Activity: Who Participates? What Do They Say?" *American Political Science Review* 87:303–18.

Waitzman, Norman, and Ken Smith. 1998. "Separate but Lethal: The Effects of Economic Segregation on Mortality in Metropolitan America." *Milbank Quarterly* 76:341–73.

Wald, Kenneth D., Lyman Kellstedt, and David Leege. 1993. "Church Involvement and Political Behavior." In *Rediscovering the Religious Factor in American Politics,* edited by David Leege and Lyman Kellstedt. New York: M. E. Sharpe.

Walzer, Michael. 1980. *Radical Principles: Reflections of an Unreconstructed Democrat.* New York: Basic Books.

———. 1995. "The Communitarian Critique of Liberalism." In *New Communitarian Thinking,* edited by Amitai Etzioni. Charlottesville: University Press of Virginia.

Warner, Sam Bass. 1962. *Streetcar Suburbs.* Cambridge: Harvard University Press.

Wattenberg, Martin. 1996. *The Decline of American Political Parties.* Cambridge: Harvard University Press.

Weber, Max. 1986 [1898]. *The City.* New York: Free Press.

Weiher, Gregory. 1991. *The Fractured Metropolis: Political Fragmentation and Metropolitan Segregation.* Albany: SUNY Press.

Welch, Susan, and Timothy Bledsoe. 1988. *Urban Reform and Its Consequences.* Chicago: University of Chicago Press.

West, Cornel. 1994. *Race Matters.* New York: Vintage Books.

Whyte, William, Jr. 1956. *The Organization Man.* New York: Simon and Schuster.

Williams, Oliver. 1980. "Life-Style Values and Political Decentralization in Metropolitan Areas." In *Urban Politics: Past, Present and Future,* edited by Harlan Hahn and Charles Levine. New York: Longman.

Wilson, Edward. 1975. *Sociobiology: The New Synthesis.* Cambridge: Harvard University Press.

Wilson, James Q. 1972. *Political Organizations.* New York: Basic Books.

Wilson, William Julius. 1987. *The Truly Disadvantaged.* Chicago: University of Chicago Press.

Wirt, Frederick, Benjamin Walter, Francine Rabinovitz, and Deborah Hensler. 1972. *On the City's Rim: Politics and Policy in Suburbia.* Lexington, MA: D. C. Heath and Company.

Wirth, Louis. 1969 [1939]. "A Cultural Theory of Urbanism." In Sennett, *Classic Essays on the Culture of Cities.*

Wolfe, Alan. 1999. "Littleton Takes the Blame." *New York Times,* May 2, A19.

Wolfinger, Raymond E. 1974. *The Politics of Progress.* Englewood Cliffs, NJ: Prentice-Hall.

Wolfinger, Raymond E., and John Osgood Field. 1966. "Political Ethos and the Structure of City Government." *American Political Science Review* 58:306–26.

Wolfinger, Raymond E., and Steven J. Rosenstone. 1980. *Who Votes.* New Haven: Yale University Press.

Wood, Robert H. 1959. *Suburbia: Its People and Their Politics.* Boston: Houghton Mifflin Company.

Wright, Gerald. 1977. "Contextual Models of Electoral Behavior: The Southern Wallace Vote. *American Political Science Review* 71:497–508.

Wuthnow, Robert. 1998. *Loose Connections: Joining Together America's Fragmented Communities.* Cambridge: Harvard University Press.

Zaller, John. 1992. *The Nature and Origin of Mass Opinion.* Cambridge and New York: Cambridge University Press.

Index

Page references followed by *f* indicate figured illustrations; *m* indicates maps; and *t* indicates tables.